THE GIANT BOOK OF WOODEN TOYS

BY PERCY W. BLANDFORD

TAB TAB BOOKS Inc.
BLUE RIDGE SUMMIT, PA. 17214

684
BLA

Other TAB books by the author:

No. 860 *The Woodworker's Bible*
No. 894 *Do-It-Yourselfer's Guide to Furniture Repair & Refinishing*
No. 937 *Modern Sailmaking*
No.1004 *The Upholsterer's Bible*
No.1044 *The Woodturner's Bible*
No.1114 *How to Make Early American & Colonial Furniture*
No.1179 *The Practical Handbook of Blacksmithing & Metalworking*
No.1188 *66 Children's Furniture Projects*
No.1237 *Practical Knots & Ropework*
No.1257 *The Master Handbook of Sheetmetalwork . . . with projects*
No.1365 *The Complete Handbook of Drafting*

FIRST EDITION

FIRST PRINTING

Copyright © 1982 by TAB BOOKS Inc.

Printed in the United States of America

Library of Congress Cataloging in Publication Data

Blandford, Percy W.
    The giant book of wooden toys.

    Includes index.
    1. Wooden toy making. I. Title.
TT174.5.W6B56   745.592   81-18382
ISBN 0-8306-0071-X   AACR2
ISBN 0-8306-1312-9 (pbk.)

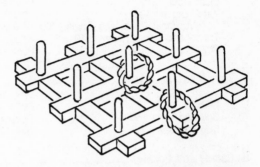

Contents

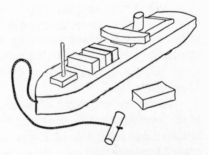

Introduction

Children generally have an insatiable demand for toys. In our product-oriented society a thriving industry supplies toys. Their advertising is geared to the adult market and is obviously designed to sell toys, preferably at the highest price. What the child may prefer is secondary to what an adult can be convinced is the right thing to buy at the moment. In other less affluent societies children still play with toys. The toys may not be sophisticated, but that does not mean the children get less satisfaction from them. This is not a plea for only having simple toys. There is a place for advanced and complicated designs, but it is not necessarily as big a place as manufacturers and their advertising agents would have us believe.

Parents enjoy buying toys for their children and seeing how the new playthings are received. Even greater enjoyment and satisfaction can be attained by making the toys yourself. If the child is old enough to understand that you made it, his or her appreciation and satisfaction will be even greater.

Another attraction of making toys is that each is an individual piece, not one of thousands from a mass production source. Size, design, and finish are under your control. You do not have to accept some average product that a remote designer has determined is good for every child. The toy you make is individually designed and produced to suit the needs of one person—your child.

At the outbreak of World War II, when the aircraft industry was under pressure to produce results rapidly, one famous designer was asked what he considered to be the requirements of the ideal material for building aircraft. He said the best material was wood. This also applies to individually made toys. There are other materials that have to be used, but for most toys wood is the best choice.

Wooden toymaking is possible, even if you claim no particular skill in woodworking. There are toys that require all the skill of an experienced craftsman, but many satisfactory toys can be made with only a few tools and minimum skill. If you choose what you will make, even if it means stretching your ability further than you thought possible, the satisfaction you will get from saying, "I made that," will only be exceeded by the child who says, "My Dad (or Mom) made that."

There are economic considerations regarding toymaking. Much toymaking can be done with wood salvaged from discarded furniture and other things. If you accumulate a stock of offcuts, broken furniture, and other oddments of wood, many toys can be made at no cost. Even if you have to buy the wood, the amount needed for most toys is quite small. The total cost is slight compared to buying toys that may not be as suitable or durable.

Wooden toymaking has possibilities as a business. You will almost certainly find that after you have made a few attractive toys, other parents will ask you to make similar toys for their children. You could suggest that they buy this book and make their own. If you take on the work, you may find that it grows into a spare time business. The growth may only be limited by what you are prepared to do. There is always a demand for individually made toys and other things. A product made by a craftsman will always have a demand. You may not consider yourself much of a craftsman, but your customers will. Your attitude should reflect this. You are not producing an inferior substitute for the mass-produced article. You are offering individual skill. Set your price accordingly.

In preparing this book I have included a variety of wooden toys. The skills needed range from basic to more advanced. There are some alternatives suggested, so there should be something in the book to suit every standard of woodworking ability.

The chapter on materials covers alternatives, but most toys are still best made of solid wood, although there are obvious places for plywood and manufactured boards. To avoid confusion, most things are described as made in one way with the specified materials. If other forms of manufactured woods are chosen, references to other projects will show what adaptions to techniques may be necessary.

For most toys there are materials lists. These include the main wooden parts. Small parts are not listed, as they can often be cut from offcuts and material that would otherwise be scrapped. In the lists widths and thicknesses are the finished planed sizes, although most could be smaller or larger without affecting results, providing allowance is made in the marking of joints. If you show a list to the man at the lumberyard, he may be able to suggest sizes that are economical. Lengths in the materials lists are for the most part slightly full to allow for trimming off ends that may have cracked or otherwise opened during storage. All sizes in the materials lists and on the drawings are in inches unless indicated otherwise.

Many toys may be made just as well by a woman as a man. Many of the toys can be made with little physical exertion, and a woman should be able to master the tool techniques as well as a man.

Chapter 1

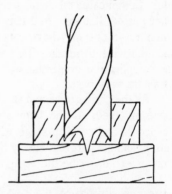

Planning Wooden Toys

Play is an important part of a child's education, as it is with the majority of young animals. Much play can be without the aid of apparatus. In the wild the play period does not last long; the animal is confronted with the problems of existence. A child is protected from those major problems for much longer. Play can become more complicated by the introduction of toys. Toys as a means of entertainment and enjoyment have their uses until a child is not far from adult age. In nearly all cases play can be regarded as educational, particularly with some of the more advanced equipment used by older children, but to the child it is still play.

Few animals can use even the most basic tools. A monkey or a bird may use a stone to break a nut, but that is about the limit of tool use without training by man. People, with their higher intelligence, have evolved tools and other equipment for doing many things that could not be done with bare hands. Toys are the child's introduction to using this inherent ability.

It is not easy to look at toys from the child's point of view. The most elaborate or complicated toy is not necessarily the one a child finds most attractive. It is certainly not the toy most heavily advertised that has the greatest appeal to a child. Much advertising is aimed at adults. It is often angled at presenting the most expensive product as the most attractive. The object of advertising is to sell, and the person with the money is usually an adult. Outdoing other adults in the amount of money spent on a present may become the aim, while consideration of what a child may like comes second.

Parents and others involved with children know that a child often selects the most basic toy as a favorite. The toy may be old, tattered, and possibly only fit to be thrown away, in the eyes of an adult. Complicated mechanical toys may have a novelty appeal for a brief period, but the child may return to some simple toy. The complicated one may have considerably greater value, monetary and otherwise, to an adult. This does not mean that there is no place for complication or mechanical ingenuity, but the young child's ideas are very basic.

As the child grows and reaches school age, toys may become more involved. At the later stage the equipment may become electronic and reach a stage where the child may understand it better than his parents, but by then most of us would not use the word toy to describe the equipment.

TOYS AND FURNITURE

Toys and furniture for children are related. This book is not about furniture. If you want to make furniture and children's toys, you will get help from my book *66 Children's Furniture Projects* (TAB Book No. 1188).

Children possess two qualities in abundance—imagination and energy. A toy is what a child wants it to be at the moment. To us it may be most unlike what he imagines, but to him it is just that. On another occasion it may be imagined to be something entirely different. The value of a toy to a child may be in its adaptability. A set of building blocks may be of much greater value in the eyes of a child than some one-purpose toy that costs a lot of money.

There is not always a clear dividing line between toys and furniture. An inverted table may be viewed as a raft. When the table is placed the right way up with a cloth over it, it becomes a den.

We must remember the child's physical energy. Toys should stand up to rough usage. The child may use the toy for purposes that were not intended. Has that possibility been considered? There should also be space to play in, and the furniture should stand up to rough handling.

WOOD AND METAL

The majority of toys throughout history have been made of wood. Wood can be easily worked. Its texture and quality make it safe in a child's hands and mouth. It is robust enough to stand up to most handling for some time.

Metal may have to be used for some toys, but for small children it may be heavy, sharp, and dangerous. Cloth is used for dolls' clothing and similar things, but some of it may suffer at the hands of a child. There are many attractions about plastics for toys, but these are the materials of mass production. They have little place in the making of individual toys except to complement wood and other materials—usually as handles and knobs.

WHY MAKE TOYS?

Parents get considerable satisfaction out of making things for their children. They may talk about educational advantages and other reasons, but part of their motive is to do something for their family. This is a good reason for making wooden toys. A child appreciates what is being done for him, particularly when meeting other children. "My dad made this," or "My granddad made this," are real exclamations of pride. If the toy being displayed is something the other child does not have, the sense of pride in the maker is tremendous.

The satisfaction of making toys can be great even if you have no children of your own, or they have passed the stage of playing with toys. It can come from using your hands and mind to produce something complete from the raw materials with which you started. It may not be anything very ambitious, but you made it. Most of us never get the opportunity of saying, "I made it," in our daily work. Not many people see a product right through. Most of us earn our living as part of a complex organization that may manufacture something, but what we do is only a small part of the process and often only remotely connected with the end product.

Many amateur craftsmen hesitate at trying to make furniture or other advanced wooden constructions. Toys are not as demanding. Some toys can be made with all of the woodworking qualities of advanced cabinetwork, but the majority can be very simply made. Joints can be of what you feel capable. Overall sizes of most toys are not critical. If what you make is slightly bigger or smaller than you planned, it usually does not matter.

CHOICE OF TOOLS

This is not a book about tool handling, except as applied to particular techniques. The number of tools needed for most toys is quite few. Obviously, a large tool kit is preferable to a small one. It is better to have a smaller number of good tools than a larger number of inferior ones, particularly those that are intended to cut. Sharp tools are important, and one or more *oilstones* should be included. Learn how to use them. The difference in the quality of work between a craftsman and a beginner is often due to the frequency of tool sharpening. Where the beginner tries to press on with tools that are getting blunter, the craftsman takes time to resharpen them.

Power tools are always useful but not essential, particularly if you buy wood that has already been planed to size and confine your toys to those of moderate sizes. In many ways handwork gives you better control as you are unlikely to go too far with a particular operation. One power tool that is particularly useful as a supplement to hand tools is an *electric drill*. It can be used for drilling with greater precision than some hand-operated drills, and it can take fittings for doing other work. Some of the accessories offered for use with drills are of doubtful value, so be selective when considering extras.

Consider the intended life of the toy you plan to make. Children grow up rapidly—sometimes more rapidly than we wish. Is a child likely to lose interest in a particular toy in a short time? How durable should a toy of brief interest be? How much work should be expended on it? A toy must be strong enough and safe enough for immediate use, but you have to decide if the large number of hours spent on achieving an advanced finish is justified if the toy can be cast aside after a short time. It is difficult to forecast whether a toy expected to be of short interest will be treasured for a long time or not. Some old toys that have survived have been works of art. One reason they have survived may be because children were not allowed to play with them. The toy may wind up in a museum, but it is unlikely to be allowed into a child's hands.

If there are several children of different ages, there is a case for making toys more durable so they can be passed on. A young child who already has to wear clothes that are passed on may not take kindly to toys that have already been used.

Chapter 2

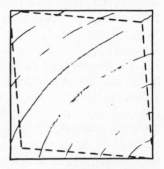

Materials

There are thousands of wood species, but those available at most lumberyards are few. Trees may be called by different names in different places, and the woods from some may be given names different from those of the trees. There are scientific names for woods, but these are not used commonly. With modern international transport, woods may come from distant parts of the world. At one time only local woods were used, and those available became well-known and their characteristics understood. In many places local woods are still available, but those that are imported may not always be the same. General names like oak and mahogany cover many subspecies and some that are not strictly related.

HARDWOODS AND SOFTWOODS

It is often best to let suppliers know what the wood is for and accept their recommendations for the species to be used. Wood used for furniture and toys is broadly divided into *hardwoods* and *softwoods*. These names are guides to relative hardness, although there are some hardwoods that are softer than some softwoods. The names are actually associated with the type of tree. Broadleaf trees produce hardwoods. Some of these are *oak, mahogany, ash, chestnut, maple, walnut,* and *teak*. The needleleaf trees produce softwoods like *cedar, fir, larch, pine, redwood*, and *spruce*.

Most softwoods are not as strong as hardwoods. They tend to be more open-grained, and some of them have frequent *knots*. Knots occur where a branch is connected to the tree. Forest trees have

5

fewer knots than those that grow isolated. In softwood lumber knots may be described as "live" or "dead". A dead knot has a dark outline and may fall out if it has not already done so. A live knot is closely linked to the surrounding wood and, for many purposes, can be ignored. The dead knot represents weakness, and that piece of wood may have a use in a hidden place of little importance. Otherwise, it has to be discarded, or the knot is cut out and the wood used for smaller parts.

Hardwoods tend to be heavier, more dense, and obviously harder than softwoods. Some woods like oak have noticeable open pockets in the grain, but most hardwoods have a close grain with little difference in coloring between the markings. These close-grained hardwoods are suitable for finer work where carving, detailed joints, or slim parts are required. The wood for young children's toys has to be chosen with the possibility of children putting the toys into their mouths. A few hardwoods are oily although not necessarily poisonous. *Teak* is the most obvious example. Fortunately, the lighter colored hardwoods are mostly free from impurities. Sycamore is an example. Some softwoods are very resinous and should be avoided for toys. Some woods, otherwise satisfactory, may have resin pockets which should be cut out.

Softwoods are not the choice for small toys. For large things, which may be wheeled about or used to carry a child, they have the advantage of being lighter as well as cheaper. Softwoods are usually easier to obtain. Wood is a natural product. The quality is not always consistent, even in one piece of wood. You may have to accept a piece of wood with a flaw, and in any woodworking you must expect to waste a small amount. It is usually possible to use up slightly inferior wood in a place where it does not affect the finished work.

Softwoods are often given a preliminary selection before being offered for sale at different prices. The quality of a lower grade with its knots, flaws, and rough grain may make it only suitable for unimportant outdoor carpentry. For toys it is worthwhile paying a little more for a better grade. If you are able to select what you want from stock, it may be possible to find wood in a lower grade with good parts where you want them.

SEASONING WOOD

When a tree grows, it increases its *girth* by the addition of annual rings outside those already formed. The lines shown by cutting through these rings make the grain in a board. Sap goes up and down the tree. When the tree is felled, there will be more moisture in the wood, due to the sap, than would be suitable for making furniture or toys. This has to be dried out to an acceptable level by *seasoning*. It does not have to be completely dry.

Traditional seasoning is by stacking the cut wood for years, so air can circulate, but there are modern methods of hastening the drying. Wood is a porous material, and it will take up and give out moisture according to the humidity in the atmosphere. A modern problem is central heating, which dries the atmosphere and takes away moisture from wood. Wood expands and contracts as well as warps and twists with considerable changes in moisture content. For anything to be made for keeping in central heating conditions, leave the wood in similar conditions for some time before working with it so it settles to a stable condition. This may not be of much consequence with small toys, but it is an important consideration if you are planning to make anything big. Softwoods are more susceptible to changes in moisture content than hardwoods.

The way that wood is cut from the log affects its tendency to shrink or warp. You can usually see which part of the section a particular piece comes from by examining its end. Not all boards are cut straight across. They may be cut radially to get special grain effects for furniture, but usually a log is roughly squared, then boards are cut straight across (Fig. 2-1A). The greater shrinkage is the direction of the annual rings. It is much less across them. A board cut radially may shrink slightly in thickness as it dries out (Fig. 2-1B). A board cut further from the center of the tree has curved lines, and this is more likely to warp if shrinkage along the lines occurs (Fig. 2-1C). If you look at the end of a board, imagine the annual rings trying to straighten. That will give you a picture of the possible direction of warp.

Seasoning takes place before lumber is offered for sale, so the risk of warping is slight. The wood may be cut to thinner sections, either at the lumberyard or by you after getting it home. It is still possible for distortion to occur. If possible, buy wood a few weeks before you use it. Store it in a similar atmosphere to that in which it will be when finished. If warping or twisting occurs, you can correct this as you prepare the wood for the toy you are making.

If wood merely gets smaller while keeping its shape, it does not matter, assuming you allow for the smaller size in making up the toy. A greater nuisance is if a piece of wood starts square, then shrinks to a diamond section (Fig. 2-1D) due to the grain being diagonal. This can happen to a round section that shrinks to an elliptical section (Fig. 2-1E).

7

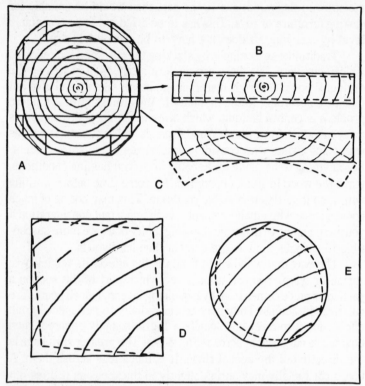

Fig. 2-1. Possible shrinkage and warping depends on the part of the tree from which the wood was cut. As wood dries, it loses bulk in the direction of the annual rings.

These are extreme examples to show what might occur. Wood that has been properly seasoned should not shrink or warp to any appreciable extent. If you know what can happen, you will be on your guard and take suitable precautions. Most hardwoods are less likely to shrink or warp than softwoods.

SUPPLY SOURCES

If you want to make just one toy, obviously you will get just enough wood. If you are thinking of making many toys and possibly doing other woodwork, you should build up a stock. When you buy wood for a particular project, get a little more. Besides having wood at hand when you suddenly decide to make something, the wood stored in your shop is continuing to season. You can expect it to be more stable and easier to work than wood just brought in from a lumber yard.

8

Consider other supply sources. Broken furniture may yield pieces of hardwood, about which there is no doubt about seasoning. For softwoods there are such things as *pallets* and packing cases. Some of the wood may only be used in rougher carpentry, but do not be misled by the rough sawed surface. It will often plane to a good finish. A plane stroke on an edge will show if it is worthwhile to clean off the surfaces. Packing cases are not always softwoods. If they have come from a tropical land, they are probably of hardwood, possibly a variety of mahogany.

Do not expect the impossible. Available wood can only be as big as the tree it comes from. Lengths will be more than you want, but in some woods you cannot get very wide boards because those trees do not have thick trunks. If wide boards are available, you may pay proportionately more for them than if you scheme your work to use narrower boards. Fortunately, plywood and other prepared boards have removed much of the need for very wide natural boards.

There are materials lists for most of the toys described. If you have to buy all the wood for a project, take a copy of the list to the lumberyard, so the supplier can select from his available stock to suit your needs. You can also go over his stock and find wood to match the list. Suppose you want 12 pieces 1 foot long in a particular section. If you ask for one piece 12 feet long, you will probably pay more than if you are able to take several short pieces that can be cut to what you want. You may get short extra lengths that would not be worth the supplier's time to cut off, and these can go into your stock.

Wood is converted into a large number of standard sections that suit the majority of uses. It is worthwhile checking what is available locally and arranging your work accordingly for economy. In most toys the sections of wood are not critical. It is possible to make a perfectly satisfactory toy with wood of a stock size.

If you order wood machine-planed, you may find that it is undersize as the quoted size is as sawed before planing. Machine planing can be expected to reduce the wood by 1/8 inch. If you buy wood that is 1 inch thick, it will actually be about 7/8 inch as planed. For most purposes this is acceptable, providing you allow for it in laying out the work. If you insist on the wood finishing 1 inch thick, you will have to pay more as the next stock size larger will have to be planed down. Where sizes are quoted in drawings and materials lists, sections can be considered nominal. Reduction due to planing will not matter. Stock sizes are more applicable to softwoods, and hardwoods are often kept in larger sections to be brought to ordered sizes as needed.

Wood is one of the more interesting materials available for your use. If you learn to appreciate and understand wood, you will get more enjoyment out of making toys.

PLYWOOD

The attraction of *plywood* is in its availability in large flawless sheets without visible joints. It does not expand and contract like natural wood. Plywood is all wood. It is made by joining thin wood veneers with glue, so the grain direction of each layer is across the adjoining ones. There is always an odd number of veneer layers, so the grains of the outside pieces are the same way. The thickness of a sheet of plywood depends on the number of veneer layers and how thick they are. A large number of thin veneers in a given thickness makes a stiffer board than a smaller number of thicker veneers. Veneers are shaved from a rotating log and can be any thickness.

The simplest form of plywood has three layers, and this may be referred to as *three-ply* (Fig. 2-2A). It may be up to ⅜ inch thick, depending on the thickness of veneer. Bigger sizes may have five or more veneers (Fig. 2-2B). If a piece of plywood has to keep its shape unsupported, and you have a choice of the number of veneers in its thickness, choose the greater number (Fig. 2-2C). If it is to be stiffened by framing in some way, it does not matter how many veneers there are.

The layers in a sheet of plywood are bonded together with glue. At one time it was a natural glue that was not waterproof, and dampness will cause veneers to separate. Nearly all modern plywood is bonded with *synthetic resin glue* which has a good resistance to moisture. Once set, nothing is likely to cause the glue to weaken. This is important in toys where loosened veneer might be picked away and sucked.

Many woods are used to make plywood. *Douglas fir* is common. It has a rather prominent coarse grain which makes finishing to a smooth surface difficult, but this may not be important in some toys. There are different grades of plywood available. These grades are mainly dependent on the quality of the outside veneers. For the small pieces needed for most toys, it is advisable to get the best grade. This will have good smooth surfaces, and there will be no gaps in the inner veneers.

If plywood is described as *exterior grade*, the glue used has a very high resistance to moisture. There may be different qualities, and there can be gaps between the edges of inner veneers. If the plywood is described as *marine grade*, the quality of veneer is uniformly high. The glue is waterproof.

Plywood made of any wood may be bought with a further thin veneer applied to one or both surfaces. This is a way of getting a match with solid wood adjoining or framing a plywood panel. For a painted toy this will not matter, but for a quality toy or model for an older child, matching may be important under a polished or varnished finish.

Plywood is made in thicknesses from about ⅛ inch to 1 inch and in several stock size panels. The largest panels commonly available are 4 feet by 8 feet, although larger sizes are made. There are many smaller size panels. A supplier will be willing to cut what you need, but you will have to pay for this work. You may find you are also paying for narrow pieces cut off, even if you do not get them. It is always more economical to scheme your requirements, so you can buy a standard panel and cut it to suit yourself. Plywood is always good stock. Offcuts from one toy will find uses in another.

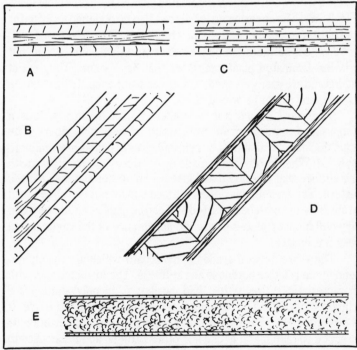

Fig. 2-2. Plywood is made of veneers glued together (A-C). Thicker wood may have a solid strip core (D). Particle board may be surfaced with veneer (E).

Although plywood is made up to about 1 inch thick, there are some alternatives in the thicker grades which are more economical. One type of blockboard or stripboard has a core made up of solid strips of wood sandwiched between veneers, which may be double or single thickness on each side (Fig. 2-2D), so the surface appearance is the same as plywood.

MANUFACTURED BOARDS

An alternative to plywood for some purposes is a thick manufactured board made of small shreds of wood embedded in resin called *particle board, chipboard,* or *flakeboard.* It is made in thicknesses from ½ inch upwards and is available in panels of similar size to plywood. Surfaces are smooth, but they are a drab gray/brown. Particle board can be worked with ordinary woodworking tools. In its uncovered form it is a constructional material and is not intended for face pieces, although it can be painted.

The particle board of more interest to us has its surfaces covered with wood veneers, laminated plastics, and other materials (Fig. 2-2E). The covering materials can also be obtained in strips for application to edges, so they match surfaces. Particle board with wood veneer surfaces can be treated as wood in a construction, but it is the laminated plastic surfaces that have value. They resist liquids and are easily cleaned. A child can paint or spill drinks on the surface, and it can be wiped clean.

Hardboard should not be confused with hardwood. It is a compressed material made from wood or vegetable fibers. The usual thickness available is ⅛ inch, and sizes of panels are similar to plywood. When hardboard is made by compression, it finishes with one surface that is smooth and glossy. The other side has a mesh pattern. The smooth, hard front surface should not be rubbed with an abrasive or scratched with tools. It can be used as an altenative to plywood in many places where the appearance of the reverse side does not matter.

There are several grades of hardboard which are mainly dependent on relative hardness and stiffness. The lowest grade, with characteristics little better than cardboard, is only suitable for unimportant parts. The harder grades are much more attractive. It is possible to buy hardboard with a regular pattern of perforations intended to take metal hooks and other fittings, and it has uses in some toys where holes are required. There are other forms with fluted and other patterned surfaces, but these have little use in toymaking.

Most makers of hardboard offer a grade which may be described as oil-tempered or something similar. Ordinary hardboard does not have much resistance to dampness. but the oil-tempered grade is one of the hardest. It has a good water resistance, although not as good as exterior or marine grades of plywood.

PLASTICS, METALS, AND CLOTHS

Glass should be avoided in toys because of the danger it presents if it is broken. There are several transparent plastics that can be used. Plexiglas acrylic plastic is a strong one that can be worked with woodworking tools. It can be drilled, and it is possible to bend it after heating. It is rather soft and easily scratched, but minor damage can be removed with metal polish or polishes made for the material.

Other plastics will be used most in knobs and handles. Plastics are less dangerous than metals. There are plastic hinges and other fittings that may be more bulky than metal, but they are better on toys. Sheet plastic does not have much use except as facings on particle board.

Not much metal will be used on wooden toys. Iron and steel should be avoided. *Aluminum* is a metal that can be made into safe toy parts, and it is easy to work. It is unlikely to corrode or become dangerous to a young user. Brass and copper can be used, particularly if metal parts have to be soldered. Aluminum is unsuitable for ordinary soldering. *Lead* is one of the heaviest common metals. It may have some use where a weight is needed, but then it should be embedded in wood and sealed. Exposed lead should not be included in a toy. It is possible to melt lead with an ordinary flame, so it can be poured into a mold to make a weight of a particular shape.

Some toys need cloth as dressing or upholstery. It is advisable to only use *synthetic cloths*. They are easily cleaned and are affected little by moisture. Fillings should also be synthetic or rubber foam, of the closed cell type, which will not absorb water. Where something leatherlike is needed, choose a fabric-backed plastic. All of these materials should be nonflammable.

Chapter 3

Hardware and Adhesives

Some toys are made from single pieces of wood, but where several pieces have to be joined they may be nailed, screwed, or glued. A combination of these methods might also be used. Modern glues are safe for use in things that children will play with, but glued joints may have to be supplemented by screws or nails. If the parts being joined can be fitted into each other so that glue alone is adequate, it is better than using metal fastenings—both for safety and for producing a craftsmanlike piece of work. Many toys are only expected to have a short life, so the making of comparatively complicated joints may not be justified.

Where nails can be used, it is usually possible to substitute screws. Screws are better. There are many places, though, where nails are the only fasteners needed. If two pieces of wood are to be joined in circumstances where a persistent child might lever them apart, nails alone are inadvisable because of their exposed points after separating. For the same reason, nails should be of sufficient length to provide a grip. This depends on circumstances and may be governed by experience, but remember that it is only the part of the nail in the lower part of the wood that is holding the parts together (Fig. 3-1A). That is where length is needed. As a guide, a 1½-inch nail ought to have about 1 inch of its length in the lower part, and a 1-inch nail may have ¾ inch there. If it is end grain in the lower part, more length of nail is needed to produce a grip. Compared with crosswise grain, about one-third more length would be justified (Fig. 3-1B).

Nail spacing requires experience. It is worthwhile to have nails closer near the end of a joint than in the center (Fig. 3-1C) to provide extra strength where the first leverage on the joint may come. Extra strength can also be obtained by driving nails alternate ways in *dovetail* fashion (Fig. 3-1D).

If two parts are to be joined at an angle, screws are preferable to nails as they have a better resistance to being levered apart (Fig. 3-1E). If there are more than two parts, nails might be satisfactory to give mutual support (Fig. 3-1F). Another consideration is the possibility of disassembling the parts later. If you are making a toy that may only last a child a short time, yet the wood is large enough to be used in something else later, screws can be withdrawn with minimum damage to the wood. Nails are often difficult to withdraw without splitting or otherwise damaging a fairly large area. In these circumstances glue would not be used. Forcing a properly glued joint apart will tear away surface grain.

NAILS

All general-purpose nails are made of mild steel, even if the

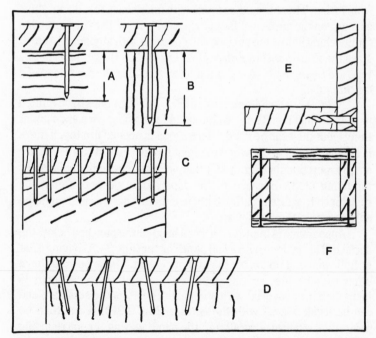

Fig. 3-1. Nailing strength comes from the penetration of the lower wood. Driving at alternate angles increases strength.

supplier calls them iron nails. *Zinc plating* may be used as protection against rust. Nails may be made of brass, copper, aluminum, and other metals, but for toys the steel nails will serve most purposes.

Ordinary nails may be collectively called *wire nails*. They are round, parallel, and have flat heads. Points may be round, but they are usually square (Fig. 3-2A). *Common* nails are slightly thicker than *box* nails of the same length. Nails are made in many lengths up to 6 inches. It is best to order nails by their lengths, but there is a system of penny size in which the figure refers to the number of nails to 1 pound. For instance, a two-penny nail is 1 inch long, and there are 840 to 1 pound. A tenpenny nail is 3 inches long, and there are 65 to 1 pound.

If you need a nail with a large head, as when nailing canvas to wood, you want a *shingle* or *roofing* nail (Fig. 3-2B). You can get more grip with a *barbed ring* nail (Fig. 3-2C). Others may have square twisted shanks to increase grip, and they are called *screw nails* (Fig. 3-2D).

The heads of ordinary nails appear prominently on the wood surface, but they have value in preventing the top piece of wood from lifting. There are other types with finer heads that do not show as much on the surface, although the grip is less. They are intended for punching below the surface and covering with stopping. In small sizes these are *panel* or *veneer* pins (Fig. 3-2E). Bigger nails of this type are *casing* nails. A variation on this head is the *brad* head of a *finishing* nail.

A *staple* is a double-ended nail (Fig. 3-2F). Staples have limited uses in toymaking. They are intended for holding wire and similar things, but they can be used where a loop is needed in a toy, if there is enough length in the wood to resist it being pulled out. *Tacks* are small tapered nails (Fig. 3-2G) that are mostly used in upholstery for fixing cloth. Because of the taper, they do not offer much resistance to a direct pull. Do not use them where a child might be able to strain them endwise.

Appearance is improved if a nail head can be punched below the surface. This is done with a nail punch or set (Fig. 3-3A) having a flat or hollowed end no longer than the nail head. These punches have other uses besides sinking nails. You can sink the head about ⅛ inch, then it is covered with stopping. The stopping sets hard and can be sanded level with the surface (Fig. 3-3B). It can then be painted or otherwise treated in the same way as the surrounding wood.

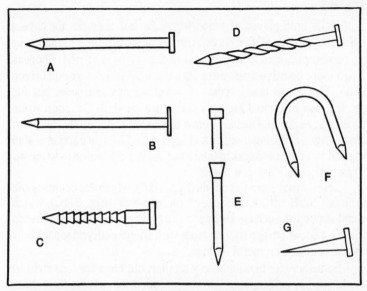

Fig. 3-2. A large variety of nails is available. Twists and rings increase grip. A double-ended nail is called a staple. A short tapered one is a tack.

If thin pieces of wood are to be nailed together, the nail will be too short to provide a grip if driven in the normal way. Instead, it can be taken right through and the end *clenched.* This is also the way to provide a *pivot* for two parts that have to move on each other. Many old *Victorian* toys that can be manipulated to provide action in a puppet or other figure have pivots made in this way.

The obvious way to clench is to merely bend over the end (Fig. 3-3C), but that leaves the point where it might scratch a youngster's hand. Instead, it is better to first bend the end over a spike or other piece of metal (Fig. 3-3D), then hammer it down to bury the point (Fig. 3-3E). The head is supported with an iron block or a heavy hammer. The greatest strength comes from burying the point diagonally to the grain, although it is easier to hammer it level along the grain.

For much nailing it is possible to merely hammer the nail through both thicknesses. If the wood seems liable to split or the nail is coming near an edge where the wood might break out, drill through the upper piece. Use a drill of the same diameter or slightly smaller than the nail. Do not drill the lower part, as that would reduce the grip of the nail. An undersize hole should be drilled partway in the lower wood only with very large nails.

SCREWS

Nails hold pieces of wood together, but they do not have a tightening action. With a screw, the top piece is pulled to the lower part under pressure from the head as the screw is turned. There is also a more positive grip, and a screw can be withdrawn and driven again. There are many types of wood screws available, but for general use in toymaking only a few are needed. Common wood screws have parallel shanks below the heads and then threads with sharp edges finishing in a point (Fig. 3-4A). The word *screw* is also applied to a threaded part to take a nut, so it is advisable to say *wood screw* if that is what you mean.

Screws may have flat heads (Fig. 3-4B), which are countersunk to finish flush with a surface, or round heads (Fig. 3-4C), which stand above the surface. Between the two are raised or oval heads (Fig. 3-4D), which are countersunk with slightly curved tops. Their use is in attaching metal fittings.

Some screws that look very similar, but have threads right to the head, are self-tapping screws intended for driving into sheet metal. They are hardened steel and will cut their way into metal. There are wood screws made in this way, but using self-tapping screws for woodwork is expensive.

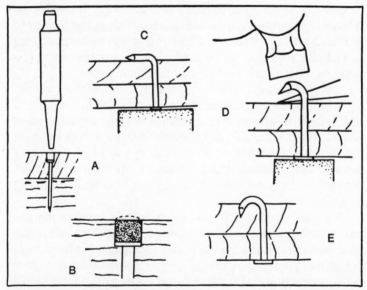

Fig. 3-3. Nails may be punched below the surface and covered with stopping (A,B). If a point projects, instead of turning it over flat (C), bend the end over a piece of metal and then bury the point (D,E).

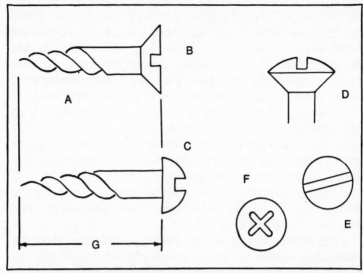

Fig. 3-4. Screw length is measured from the wood surface. There may be a slot or a star-shaped hollow for the screwdriver.

Common wood screws are made of mild steel, and these will serve most purposes in toymaking. Brass is also used, especially for its good resistance to corrosion. Stainless steel screws cost much more and are not usually necessary.

For most of the time that wood screws have been manufactured, screw heads have been slotted (Fig. 3-4E). There are screws with Phillips heads which have star-shaped sockets (Fig. 3-4F). They were developed for use with powered screwdrivers in quantity production, but they can be used instead of slotted heads for hand driving if special screwdrivers are available.

The quoted length of a screw is from the surface of the wood (Fig. 3-4G), so the overall length of a screw that stands above the surface is more than a flat head one. Lengths are from about ¼ inch upwards to sizes much bigger than those needed for toys. Thicknesses are by gauge size—the lower the number, the thinner the screws.

Your local hardware store will not stock the whole range of screw sizes. Larger screws are usually not available in even number gauges. Under ½ inch gauges will be 2 or 3, from ⅜ inch they will be 4 or 5, and over ¾ inch they will be 6, 8, or 10.

There is nothing to be gained by forcing a screw through the upper piece. It holds two pieces of wood together by squeezing the upper piece against the lower piece—compressing it between the

19

head and the pull of the thread in the lower piece—so there should be a clearance hole in the top piece. Make it just large enough for the screw to slide through (Fig. 3-5A). This hole should go right through the top piece. If that is very thin, you may have to continue it a short way into the lower piece if the plain neck of the screw will project below, particularly if you are using a very hard wood.

The size and depth of the hole in the lower piece depends on several things. A screw that will cut its own way into softwood may need a hole in hardwood. A small screw in softwood may be given a tap with a hammer, and it will then turn in with no other preparation. Other screws and other wood will need an undersize hole drilled to allow the threads to enter. Usually this tapping hole need not go the full depth in softwood (Fig. 3-5B), but in a harder wood a large screw will need a full depth hole.

The work done to the mouth of the upper hole depends on the wood and the screw. In some softwoods a flat head screw will pull itself in flush, but in hardwoods a *countersink bit* is needed to prepare the hole (Fig. 3-5C). It is best to try one screw first. If it does not pull in enough, withdraw it and countersink the hole.

Screw holes are best made with the small twist drills primarily intended for metal. For the smallest sizes it is sufficient to push in an awl.

If you want the narrow heads to be below the surface, do not just countersink excessively. That makes a wide tapered hole that will not hold stopping. Instead, counterbore the hole with a bit about the same size as the head, then drill the other holes in the usual way (Fig. 3-5D). Stopping may be used above the head, in the same way as dealing with a nail, or there can be a wooden plug glued over the screw.

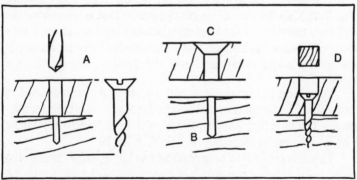

Fig. 3-5. All but the smallest screws need holes for drilling. Heads may be countersunk level or set below the surface.

Screw penetration and spacing should be similar to nails. Thicker screws should have a better grip than thin screws of the same length. An examination of other assemblies, not necessarily toys, will provide a guide.

BOLTS

Bolts are needed in toys that have parts moving over each other and that are of more substantial sizes than can be held by clenched nails. A bolt may have any of the wood screw types of heads, or it can be shaped to turn with a wrench. Although the name *bolt* is loosely applied to all these fastenings, it is only partly threaded (Fig. 3-6A). If the threads are taken to the head, it is more correctly called a metal-thread or *machine screw* (Fig. 3-6B). For toys there are some thinner bolts with flatter curved heads. They may be *stove bolts*. A convenient type for use with wood is a *carriage bolt*, which has a square neck under the head to pull into and grip the wood so the bolt will not turn (Fig. 3-6C).

Nuts are shaped to take a wrench and may be square or hexagonal. If parts have to move on each other, a single nut may work loose. This is prevented by using two nuts to form *locknuts* (Fig. 3-6D). It is insufficient to merely tighten the top one onto the lower one. There should be a wrench on each nut, they are turned against each other to jam them. There are also nuts that include something to provide friction and prevent accidental loosening, so a second nut is unnecessary. A nut can be locked with *epoxy adhesive*. You can also hammer over the end of the bolt to prevent the nut from coming off.

Wood rubbing on wood or the metal of a nut or bolt head pressing on wood will abrade away the wood surface. To reduce this, use washers whenever possible. A thin metal washer between parts will give smoother movement and reduce wear, while washers on each side will prevent the nut or bolt head from pulling in (Fig. 3-6E).

GLUES

At one time some of the common glues were made from fish, hooves, bones, and other undesirable things that could find their way into youngster's mouths, particularly as moisture would soften and melt these glues. In recent years nearly all glues have changed considerably, and they are now made with synthetic materials. Once set, in most cases there is nothing that will cause them to

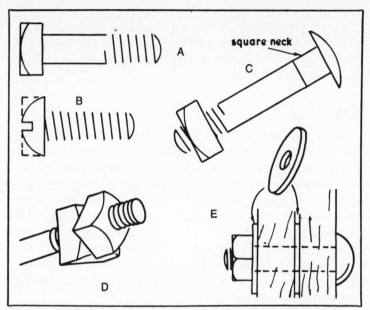

Fig. 3-6. A bolt is screwed partway (A). A screw is threaded to the head (B) The square neck of a coach bolt (C) grips the wood. A second nut will lock (D). Washers (E) reduce wear and friction.

soften. Any of the available glues that set solidly and permanently should be safe to use for toys. Read the instructions with a particular glue as satisfactory results may only be obtainable in the way suggested. Always check the description of a particular glue. For maximum strength and suitability for constructional work in wood, the glue should be described as suitable for wood and nothing else. If a glue is described as suitable for paper, cardboard, cloth, and other things besides wood, it is probably a general-purpose adhesive strong enough for fancy goods and things with very light use. It is no use for load-bearing wooden constructions.

Most glues supplied in one part depend on the evaporation of a solvent, which may be water, to make them set. Glued parts have to be held in contact until the glue has set, usually by light clamping. Warming the joint may speed setting, but do not heat excessively. This may damage some glue as well as distort the wood. Older craftsmen will remember the need for tight clamping with traditional glues, but modern glues are better with only just enough pressure to keep the surfaces in close contact. Excessive tightening may cause glue starvation by pressing most of the glue out of the joint.

For general work on toys there are several makes of white glue which are plastic-base and supplied usually in a semiflexible applicator bottle. These glues have good moisture resistance, but they will not stand up to really wet conditions. They should be suitable for most toys, except those intended for use outdoors or in water.

The strongest and most waterproof glues are in two parts, with the glue itself accompanied by a hardener that causes it to set. There are several trade names. It is not always obvious what form a particular glue is, but anything packed in two parts can be assumed to be strong and fully waterproof, or nearly so.

One two-part waterproof synthetic glue is *urea-formaldehyde*, often called *resin* glue. There is a resin of a thick consistency or a powder to mix with water to make a resin of thick consistency. With it is a hardener, which is a mild acid. In some of these glues the hardener is added to the glue just before it is applied. In another type the hardener is put on one surface and the glue on the other. Setting starts when they meet. Another type has a dry powder hardener mixed with the powder resin. Setting commences after water is added, and there is a limited time for use. Any excess mixture will harden in the pot.

Another two-part glue is *resorcinol.* It has a reddish color and is often used in plywood. It is not really a glue to choose for toys. The strongest and most waterproof glue is *epoxy.* It is more expensive and not necessary in toymaking, except it is the only wood glue that will also join most other materials, including metals to themselves or to wood.

The strength of most modern glues builds up progressively. The instructions may quote clamping times. After that clamps can be removed and work done on the assembly, but the glue may not gain its full strength for several days.

Some glues cause discoloration of the wood if they are in contact with metals. This may not matter with a painted toy, but the glues should not be mixed in metal containers or brushes used with metal bindings. For the glue areas likely to be covered in toys, the glue can be spread with a piece of wood. Screws or nails in contact with the glue may cause staining.

If you want to put *melamine* laminated plastic on wood to make a water-resistant hard working surface, it has to be attached with contact adhesive. This is unsuitable for wood to wood joints, but it is particularly suitable for one type of plastic. Usually both surfaces are coated and left to almost dry. The plastic sheet is then sprung to a curve and lowered from one end to the correct position, then pressed down. Once the surfaces have met, the parts cannot be repositioned. They have to be right the first time.

STOPPINGS

Materials used to fill cracks and holes in wood are collectively called *stoppings*. They are mostly puttylike pastes that can be squeezed from a tube or used with a knife from a can. Their purpose is to fill spaces. They do not provide strength like glue. Most will set quickly without expanding or contracting. It is normal to let them stand slightly above the surface and sand them level after they have hardened.

Stoppings colored to match the wood are available. Some are waterproof, but that will not be an important consideration for most toys. If the wood is to be stained, the chosen stopping should be one that will take stain and finish the same color as the wood. It should be of the final color and applied after staining. If the toy is to be painted, the color of the stopping does not matter.

There are flexible stoppings intended for use in boats and other situations where the wood may be expected to expand and contract. These stoppings never completely harden and will always be sufficiently flexible to allow for slight wood movements. Use the rigid stoppings for nearly all toys, but the flexible stoppings may have uses in toys that are to remain outdoors in wet weather.

Nearly all glues require the surfaces to be in close contact. They are not gap filling, so a poor open joint will not be successfully glued. If parts do not meet as they should, or there are holes or cracks to be filled where some strength is welcome, ordinary stopping will not do. The alternative is to mix sawdust with glue to a thick paste, which can be pressed into a space with a little excess left standing. Leave this to harden and sand level. Most untreated glues will craze if put into an open space—they set with minute cracks that weaken the glue considerably. By mixing in sawdust, the glue is given more small particles of wood to adhere to, and crazing is avoided.

Stopping should not be confused with fillers. Some woods have very open grain, so spaces in the grain pattern on a surface can be clearly seen. Fillers are used all over such a surface to close these small spaces and present a level surface for polishing or other finish. For a painted or varnished wood toy, there should be no need for a filler first. The finishing material will serve as its own filler.

Chapter 4

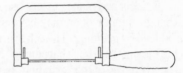

Tools and Techniques

Most toys can be made with few tools and little woodworking skill. Obviously there is an advantage in having a variety of tools and the skill to use them, but for the simpler things there is no need for a special shop. The work can be done on a strong table. This is not a book on more advanced woodworking techniques, but for anyone who wants to take up woodworking seriously see my book, *The Woodworker's Bible* (TAB Book No. 860). This chapter is more concerned with ideas that may help a beginner to produce wooden toys more efficiently and accurately.

SHARPENING

You will need some cutting tools, so you must also have the means of sharpening them. For general planing a good choice is a *Stanley* number 4 steel plane. If you buy wood machine-planed, this tool will do all of the hand planing you are likely to need. There will have to be one or two chisels; ½-inch and 1-inch bevel-edged ones are useful. A good knife also has uses. It may be a type with disposable blades or one with a permanent blade. Other useful cutting tools are those that work with a file action such as the *Surform*, with disposable blades, which may be flat or curved. They cannot be sharpened and are replaced when blunted.

Woodworking tools may have to be ground, and that requires a rotating grinding wheel. Grinding is a comparatively rare need, and you may get tools ground elsewhere. There is a more frequent need to hone them, and this is done on an oilstone. A useful size is about 2 inches by 8 inches by 1 inch, although you can manage with a smaller one. You need a coarse surface for the rapid removal of metal, as when you have to eliminate a notch caused by hitting a nail. That does not leave a very good edge, so there also has to be a fine surface for finishing. A convenient buy is a double-sided stone. Otherwise, you need two stones, although it is possible to use a medium one.

Use a thin oil. Thick oil prevents the grit in the stone cutting. Do not use a dry stone, as that rapidly wears away the surface. Light lubricating oil is suitable, or you can use kerosene.

Chisels and plane cutters usually have two bevels (Fig. 4-1A), although thinner ones may have single bevels. The long bevel is produced by grinding. The other is made by rubbing on the oilstone. This means that the "sharpening" bevel gets longer until there has to be a renewal of the "grinding" bevel to bring the sharpening bevel back to a reasonable narrow size. If there is only one bevel on a thinner blade, all of the sharpening can be done on the oilstone unless the edge gets uneven or damaged.

Hold the tool so the sharpening bevel is flat on the stone (Fig. 4-1B), with one hand on the handle to provide control and the fingers of the other hand spread just above the cutting edge to provide pressure. Keep the same angle as you rub the tool over the stone. To keep wear on the stone even, move the tool about (Fig. 4-1C). Continue until you appear to have rubbed a thin edge. Wipe off the oil and stroke a finger towards the edge on the other side. If the edge is sharp, there should be a burr or *wire edge* there (Fig. 4-1D). This is a particle of steel rubbed from the tool but still clinging to the edge. Put the blade flat on the stone and rub it with a circular motion (Fig. 4-1E) to remove the wire edge. To make sure the wire edge has gone, slice the tool diagonally across a piece of scrap wood. If you have been using a coarse stone, go through this complete sequence on it, wipe the blade clean, and then repeat the actions on a finer stone. You will not have to do this for long, as all you are doing is removing the marks made by the coarse stone.

A knife edge is restored in a similar way, but sharpening has to be done from both sides. Use one hand to control and the other to provide pressure. Tilt the blade on the stone so the edge is in contact, and rub one side until there appears to be a good bevel to the edge. Turn the blade over, and do the same on the other side. Wipe the steel. If the two bevels meet, there will be a wire edge on the side that was uppermost. If there is not, continue sharpening on both sides, then remove the wire edge by slicing across scrap wood.

It is often possible to see bluntness. Hold the tool edge upwards with a light in front of you. A blunt edge will shine white, as it reflects light. This check is useful with a curved knife edge, as it will show parts needing further attention.

SAWING AND PLANING

A *vise* is useful for holding wood being worked on, but another useful tool to make is a *bench hook*. It is just a flat piece of wood with strips nailed or screwed across (Fig. 4-2A). You can hook it over the edge of a bench or table and push wood against it, particularly for sawing (Fig. 4-2B). A *backsaw* about 10 inches long will make most cuts in small toys.

It is also possible to hold smaller pieces of wood against the bench hook for planing. For longer pieces you need a *bench stop*, which can be a piece of wood nailed temporarily to the bench top (Fig. 4-2C). Use two hands on the plane and stand so you are pushing it, not swinging it across in front of you.

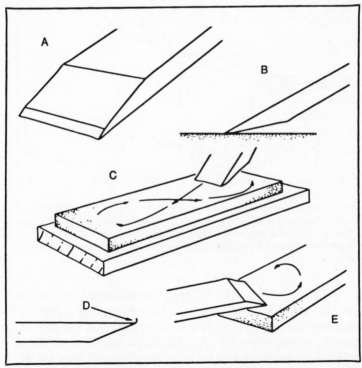

Fig. 4-1. Chisels have two bevels, and the smaller one is whetted on a stone (A-C). A wire edge (D) is removed by rubbing flat (E).

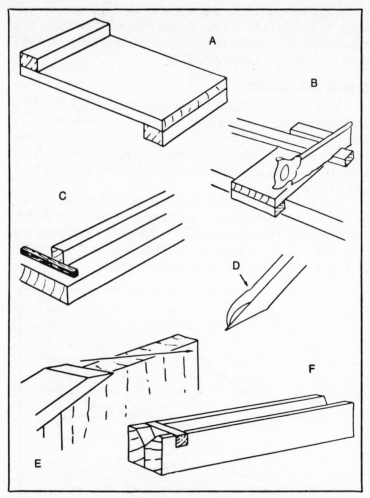

Fig. 4-2. A bench hook helps in sawing (A,B). Strips are planed against a stop (C). Set the cap iron or chip breaker close to the edge in a plane (D). A slicing cut gives a better finish (E). A trough holds squares when corners have to be planed off (F).

The plane blade—often called an *iron* although it is made of steel—has a cap iron or chip breaker over it (Fig. 4-2D). Adjust that fairly close to the edge, certainly no more than 1/16 inch from it. Adjust the cutting edge so it only projects just enough to cut. If you try to take off too much with each cut, the plane will jump and the surface will be poor. If the surface tears up, turn the wood around and plane the other way.

There is not much difficulty in using a chisel, but consider safety. Never cut toward your body or hand. Have the wood held down in a vise or with a clamp. Use two hands on the chisel. One hand is for control, while the other hand directs and is ready to restrict if the cut begins to go too far.

If you are *paring* with a chisel, move it sideways and forward to get a slicing action. This is particularly important if you are cutting across the grain (Fig. 4-2E).

There are many toys that include round rods. You may use prepared dowel rods, but in some circumstances it is simpler and just as satisfactory to use octagonal pieces made by planing the corners off square strips. A *trough* is needed to hold the pieces while planing. It can be simply made by planing angles off two strips. Nail or screw them together and make a notch for a stop to fit in (Fig. 4-2F). Otherwise, make it shallow to go on top of the bench against the bench top.

DRILLING

Small holes for screws and similar things can be made with metalworking twist drills, but they leave ragged edges. For holes over about ¼ inch, use proper woodworking drills, either the type for use in an electric drill or those intended for a hand brace.

If a hole is to be drilled right through, always have a piece of scrap wood tightly against the far side to prevent grain from breaking out (Fig. 4-3A). Even better, only drill until the point breaks through, then drill back from the other side (Fig. 4-3B). The second method is more easily applied when using a brace and bit.

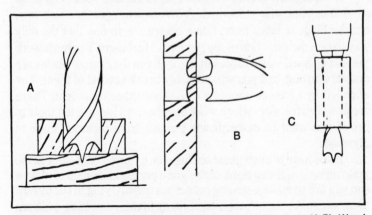

Fig. 4-3. Drill into waste wood or reverse the drill for a clean hole (A,B). Wood sleeved on a drill acts as a depth stop (C).

There are many places where a series of holes ought to be at the same depth. If you use an electric drill in a stand, there should be a depth control. For hand use there are depth stops available to attach to the bit. A simple stop is a piece of drilled wood on the bit (Fig. 4-3C).

To sharpen a woodworking drill bit, use a fine small file. If it is a bit with a rotating spur to cut the outline of the hole, only sharpen on its inside, or you will alter the size of the hole and may cause the chip-removing blade to go outside the spur.

CURVES

Many toys have shaped outlines. An electric *jigsaw* is a useful tool, but there are handsaws that will do the same work. A *coping saw* (Fig. 4-4A) has a disposable blade about ⅛ inch wide, and it will follow curves in softwood up to about ⅝ inch thick. There are two ways of using the saw. You can either cut on the push or the pull strokes.

To cut when pushing, the wood is held upright in a vise (Fig. 4-4B). The blade is put into the frame so the teeth point away from the handle. Both hands grip the handle. Use most of the length of the blade and keep it moving, particularly when turning corners. Cutting toward the handle gives better control over fine details. Notch the end of a piece of wood to act as a sawing board (Fig. 4-4C). Have the teeth pointing towards the handle. Sit so you can hold the handle with one hand and steady the wood with the other (Fig. 4-4D). For an internal cut, drill a hole in the waste part and thread the blade through (Fig. 4-4E).

A coping saw leaves a rather ragged surface which has to be sanded or otherwise smoothed. A *fretsaw* works in the same way, but the blade is much finer. Some blades are so fine that the only way to test the direction of the teeth is to feel them. For most work there is no need to use blades that fine. Even the coarser blades are not very strong, and you will probably break several of them. The edge left by a fretsaw should not need any other treatment. There are powered fretsaws which work accurately. They are the tools to use if you want to make jigsaw puzzles from pictures stuck to plywood.

If you have to use a plane or chisel on a curved edge, look at the grain direction. If you think of the grain parts as a bundle of straws and you are to make a sloping cut across them, trying to cut toward them will make the straws bend. Slicing in their direction will pare them off. Make cuts with the grain whether the curve is *concave*

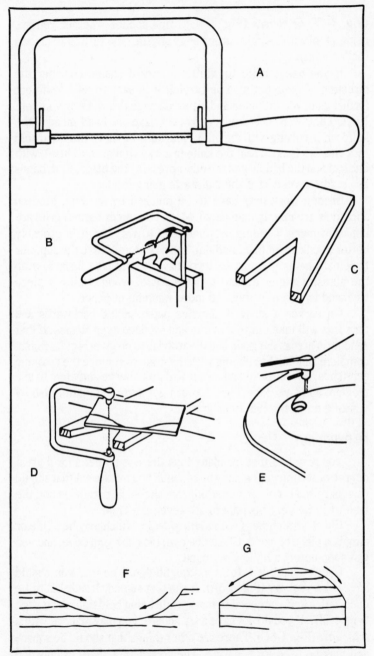

Fig. 4-4. A coping saw is the hand tool to use for curves (A-E). Smooth curves in the direction of the grain (F, G).

(Fig. 4-4F) or *convex* (Fig. 4-4G). This applies whether you are using a tool with a single cutting edge or a file type such as a Surform tool or a *rasp*.

If you use a knife to whittle a curved shape, consider the direction of grain but also be careful. It is easy to let a knife out further than you intended and either damage the work or yourself. Never cut toward your body, and never have one hand ahead of the knife while cutting with the other. It is better to have the wood held by a vise or clamp. Treat the knife in a way similar to a chisel, with one hand on the handle and the other pressing the blade. Both hands are ready to restrict if the cut starts going too far.

Shaped work may have to be finished by sanding. Modern abrasives are mostly manufactured, and the older natural grits are not used much. Grading systems tend to vary, so it is probably better to talk about fine, medium, and coarse and leave the supplier to select what is appropriate. If you have to sand a flat surface, wrap the abrasive paper around a flat block of wood. Using a piece freehand is less effective and more wasteful of paper.

On curves a strip of abrasive paper pulled backwards and forwards will take out tool marks and produce even shapes. If that sanding is across the grain and the wood is to be given a clear finish, complete sanding by rubbing with the grain to remove the crossing scratches. For most toy finishes it will probably be sufficient to use medium abrasive paper, but you can get a very smooth finish by working down through finer grades.

MARKING OUT

You may feel that for many toys there is no need for a great degree of accuracy. That may be so, but if you make a cut that should be square and is not, or something that should be parallel is not, the faults will be very obvious to all—even the child.

Check straightness with a *straightedge*, which may be a rule or simply a piece of wood. Close one eye, look along an edge, and you can soon detect a hollow or round.

Check squareness from a straightedge. The tool you should have is a *try square* (Fig. 4-5A). It can test an end already cut or be used with a knife or pencil to mark while being held tight to an edge (Fig. 4-5B). If you do not have a try square, you may manage with a *set square* (Fig. 4-5C). There are other things that should be square and may be used for squaring. The corner of a sheet of plywood should be true, and you can make a set square from that. Even the corner of a magazine page should be true and can be used for checking. You will not get very far in woodworking without a try square, though.

If parts have to match, mark them out together as far as possible. Suppose there have to be four matching legs. Put the pieces of wood together and mark across them all (Fig. 4-5D). Where there have to be saw cuts, you will get a cleaner edge by severing the grain fibers with a knife. If all the marks are for is to locate a hole, then use a pencil. Be careful not to put knife scratches across a face that will be exposed in the finished work.

If you have to make lines parallel to an edge, the expert's tool is a *marking gauge*, but that is not an easy device for a beginner to handle. If you have to mark the same distance many times from an edge, it helps to notch a scrap of wood and use it with a pencil (Fig.

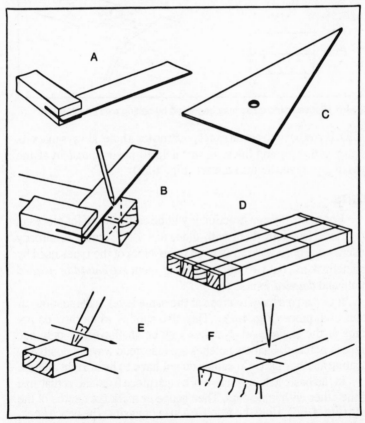

Fig. 4-5. Lines are squared across wood with a try or set square (A-D). Lines parallel with an edge may be drawn with a notched piece of wood (E). Mark drill positions with a spike (F).

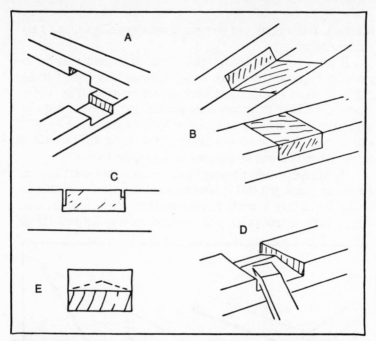

Fig. 4-6. Pieces which cross may be halved by cutting away each piece.

4-5E). If you have to get an exact position for a hole, always mark its center with crossing lines. It will help to push an *awl* in at the crossing to give the drill a start (Fig. 4-5F).

JOINTS

For much toy construction it will be sufficient to let pieces of wood overlap. Join them with glue, nails, or screws as already described. There will rarely need to be joints of the types used by cabinetmakers, but two worth knowing about are *halved* or *notched* joints and *doweled* joints.

If two strips have to cross at the same level, half must be cut from each piece (Fig. 4-6A). This also applies when they do not come at the same level. Notches may be shallower, or only one piece is notched. Shallow notches are also good ways of positively locating another part. Crossings do not have to be at right angles.

In the basic halving joint, mark each piece from the actual size of the other with knife cuts. Then gauge or mark the depths of the cuts (Fig. 4-6B). Hold the wood in a vise or against the bench hook, and saw on the waste sides of the lines (Fig. 4-6C). If you saw on the lines, the notches will finish too wide.

34

Remove the waste with a chisel, but first cut from each side, sloping upwards to the center (Fig. 4-6D), before paring straight across (Fig. 4-6E). Check flatness across; it is better to be slightly hollow than rounded at the center.

Dowels have taken the place of traditional mortise and tenon joints and other constructions particularly in industry, where they are more suited to quantity production. In making individual things, dowels are easier to use and produce satisfactory results. Dowel rods may be bought in many diameters and in long lengths. This makes them suitable for other things besides joints. It is worthwhile to build up a stock of dowel rods in many sizes. It is also possible to get short dowels already prepared for making joints, but for most toys it is better to cut your own from rods.

Joints are usually made with at least two dowels (Fig. 4-7A). A single dowel might allow for twisting. If there are more, the parts are definitely located in relation to each other. That means you have to get them right, or one part may not be exactly in the correct position, and you can't do much about it. Accurate marking out and drilling are important.

There are doweling jigs that are useful for anyone making a large number of joints in furniture, but for toymaking you can rely on marking out. In the joint shown, square the end of one piece, but

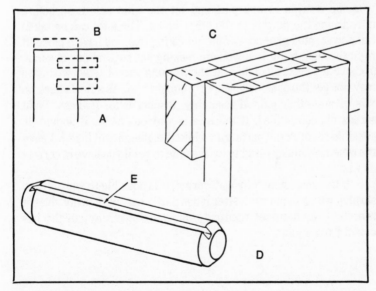

Fig. 4-7. Dowels make good joints, but they need careful marking out. A groove in a dowel lets out air.

there can be a little extra left on the other piece to clean off later (Fig. 4-7B). Gauge or mark lines on both pieces the same distance from the front surface. Put them together and square across the dowel positions (Fig. 4-7C).

Dowel diameters are usually slightly more than half the thickness of the wood, but you have to choose sizes to suit available dowel rods. The distance the dowels go in is not critical, but somewhere between two and four times the diameter will do. It is important to get the holes drilled squarely with the surfaces. If you have an electric drill mounted in a stand, that should take care of squareness. Otherwise, have the wood in a vise. As you drill, look over to see that the drill is held squarely in that direction. Have an assistant looking in a direction at right angles to your view, so he can check that the drill is true. It does not matter if the holes are deeper than the dowel is to go, as that will allow some air space and prevent the bursting tendency that may be present if the entering dowel compressed air and glue.

Cut the dowels to length. Use a chisel to pare the ends slightly (Fig. 4-7D). Use a saw lengthwise to make a shallow groove (Fig. 4-7E). This allows air and surplus glue to escape as the dowel is driven in.

Make a joint completely in one operation. It is unsatisfactory to glue the dowels in one part and let the glue set there before introducing the dowels to the other holes. The joint can be taken tight so surplus glue oozes out, indicating that you have a close fit right through. If the item you are making has several dowel joints, prepare and make all of them at one working period. Otherwise, you may not get the assembly properly squared up. As a final check on this or any other jointed assembly, inspect it for flatness. Sight across opposite sides. If there is an obvious twist, it should be possible to force the parts true while the glue is still liquid. Leave the assembly under weights for the glue to set if you have to correct a twist.

If the glue is not fully waterproof, it is possible to wipe off any surplus with a damp cloth after it has partly set. With many glues it is better to let them set, then use a chisel to chip off any glue that has oozed from a joint.

Chapter 5

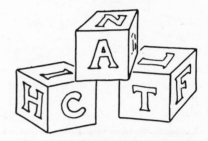

Simple Toys

It may seem easy to provide a child with plenty of wood blocks for building homes, walls, forts, and other structures, and for use as loads in trucks and boats. There are a few points to consider, though (Fig. 5-1).

BUILDING BLOCKS

The blocks should be made of a close-grained hardwood that is unlikely to splinter in use. Corners should be rounded. For most purposes the faces of the blocks should be squared properly, although there may be used for triangular and other shapes. Make sure that blocks for a young child are not too small. The child must be able to handle them, but he or she cannot deal effectively with things that are tiny. Many things a child handles will find their way to his or her mouth. For older children this is not such a problem, and a boy or girl at the stage of playing with models may prefer plenty of smaller bricks so walls, roads, and buildings more nearly in proportion to the models can be assembled.

It may seem like a good idea to provide a miscellaneous collection of blocks of many shapes and sizes, so the child can build whatever suits his or her fancy. He or she will actually do better with some standard size pieces. The child will build something more satisfying with perhaps 20 blocks all the same size than he or she can with 20 which are all different. There can be some blocks in odd sizes which have been created by using up offcuts of wood from

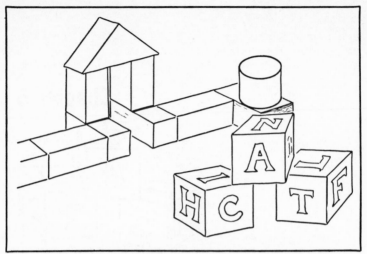
Fig. 5-1. Building blocks make many things and are early learning aids.

other projects. The basis of a collection of building blocks should be pieces that conform to standard sizes.

Adopt a unit and let all the dimensions be multiples of that unit. It will then be possible to put the blocks together systematically. For some blocks it may be best to halve the unit one way, but most blocks should be multiples of whole units. For the youngest child attempting his or her first building with blocks, it is best to keep to cubes. With the dimensions the same all ways, it does not matter how blocks are put together. Other blocks are better if they are 1 by 1 by 2 units or 1 by 2 by 3 units (Fig. 5-2A).

Prepare strips to the section you want (Fig. 5-2B). If you have a table saw—even a small one—the blocks can be carefully squared to size using a slide and the fence (Fig. 5-2C). If you have to cut by hand, carefully square around the wood with a pencil and a try square (Fig. 5-2D). In both cases allow a little extra for the thickness of the saw cut, particularly if you are making cubes. Otherwise, a block turned on end may not match one the right way. Use a fine backsaw for hand cutting. Watch the lines on two surfaces as you cut (Fig. 5-2E).

It is difficult to plane end grain satisfactorily, although it can be done with a sharp finely set plane while the wood is held with the minimum amount extending above the jaws of a vise. It is safer to rely on sanding. With a powered belt sander, the sawed ends can be quickly smoothed (Fig. 5-2F). For hand leveling, have a sheet of fairly coarse abrasive paper on a flat surface and rub the wood in

38

circles on it (Fig. 5-2G). Follow with a finer abrasive on the end grain and the other surfaces. Use folded abrasive paper in your hand to round the edges and corners slightly.

Triangular blocks are most used if their apexes are right angles (Fig. 5-2H). Let the thickness be one or more units. Have an exact

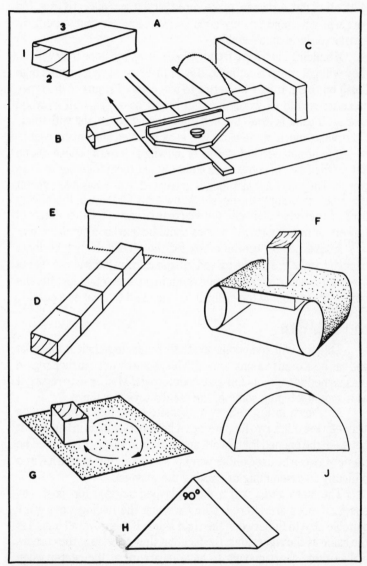

Fig. 5-2. Cut building blocks carefully and sand them smooth. Include a few special shapes.

number of units along the short sides of the base. Avoid triangles with little height and rather acute and sharp angles at each end of the base; they might harm a child. Semicircular blocks can also be included (Fig. 5-2J). Round rod in unit thickness may be in any lengths from one unit upwards, so pillars and chimneys can be made. With all of these shapes, make sure that flat surfaces are true. If a part will not stand or only does so at a slope, it cannot perform satisfactorily in an assembly.

If building blocks are frequently used, as you hope they will be, they will get rough treatment. It is of little use trying to put a high finish on them. It may be better to use colored stains of the types sometimes sold as wood dyes, in bright colors as well as wood shades. If paint is used, the end grain should be treated with filler. Otherwise, much of the paint will soak in, even after many coats.

It is possible to buy decals of individual letters. These can be put on the faces of cubes, so a child can put them together to form words. They may not last long if untreated. It is advisable to paint the cubes, then apply the decals. Allow a day for them to thoroughly harden, then give them one or two coats of varnish. Other decals of flowers or nursery rhyme scenes could be used in a similar way.

A final project can be a box for the blocks. It may be large enough to take the blocks tossed in haphazardly. For a simple set of standard sizes, you can arrange them in a pattern that just fits the box, while not being too difficult for the child to treat as a puzzle.

DOLL'S PLAYPEN

This toy will keep dolls and their things together. It folds flat and can be stored in a small space. The young owner can then regard it as something like its full-size counterpart. Mother may regard it as a way of keeping some of the child's toys together.

As shown in Fig. 5-3, two opposite sides fold inwards to go between the other two for packing. A bottom that folds in half will fit between the opened framework and keep it in shape (Fig. 5-4). The framework can be used either way up, so a young girl should have no difficulty in assembling or packing the playpen.

The sizes given will make a playpen suitable for most purposes. If sizes are altered, take care that the folding sides are a suitable size to fit between the rigid sides. If their overall length is the same as the rigid sides, the fact that they overlap at the corners makes them short enough to have clearance at the center when folded. Making all four sides the same simplifies setting out and construction.

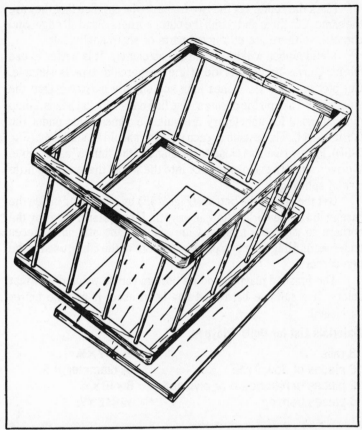

Fig. 5-3. A doll's playpen keeps toys together and may be folded flat.

Mark out all the top and bottom rails as if they were all to be rigid (Fig. 5-5A). The half sides can be cut across the middle later (Fig. 5-5B). Cut the rails to length and drill for the dowel rods (Fig. 5-5C). If possible, use a depth gauge on the drill to get all the holes the same depth. Check the size of the hole against the dowel rod by drilling scrap wood first. The joint should be a push fit. It is better to reduce the ends of the rods slightly to fit a smaller hole than to have the joint loose. Glue alone will not fill spaces and form a rigid construction. Cut all the rods at the same time and to the same lengths.

Assemble all four sides. Glue the dowels in place. Check squareness and be sure the overall depths are the same. If one framework is assembled satisfactorily, the others can be checked by assembling over it. Let the glue set before continuing.

Mark the centers of the two frames to be cut. See that they are the same. Cut them and round the outer corners. Sand all edges and corners, so there are no ragged parts or sharp angles left.

Metal hinges will be too large and clumsy. It is better to use fabric. Canvas-backed plastic of the leathercloth type is suitable. Cut pieces about 1½ inches long and slightly narrower than the wood rails. Take off the corners. Use fine nails with flat heads. Gimp pins intended for upholstery are suitable. Smear glue under the fabric as well. Three nails in each position should be sufficient (Fig. 5-5D). Put two nails as close to the angle of the "hinge" as possible. If driven slightly diagonally back into the wood, there will be little risk of splitting.

Get the size of the bottom (Fig. 5-5E) by measuring inside the assembled framework. Allow an easy fit. If necessary, cut away the corners to clear the hinges. Glue and nail the stiffening pieces underneath. Hinge the two parts with more of the fabric used at the pen corners.

The finished playpen and its bottom can be painted in bright colors. If a suitable hardwood has been used, it may be better varnished.

Materials List for Dolls' Playpen

8 rails	¾×17×¾
16 pieces of dowel rod	⅜ diameter × 9
2 pieces of hardboard or plywood	8×16×⅛
6 pieces framing	½×16×½

Fig. 5-4. The doll's playpen and its base are partly folded. When opened, the base fits into the playpen and locks it in shape.

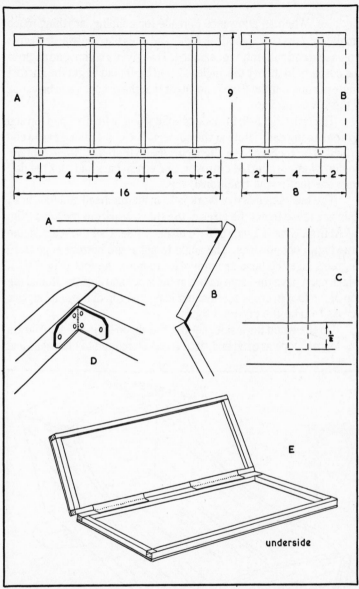

Fig. 5-5. The playpen is made with strips and dowel rods. The sides and bottom are hinged with pieces of cloth.

DOLL'S ROCKING CRIB

This model crib is based on a pioneer design. The example is about 24 inches long, but sizes can be easily adapted to suit a doll of any size. When an allowance is made for bedding, anything much smaller ceases to be practical. Sides and ends flare outwards to give a pleasing and authentic appearance. This gives a compound angle at the corners. In theory the angles should be set out to get the correct angle of cuts, but the flare is so slight that the grooves can be cut as if there was no flare.

The crib (Fig. 5-6) is made of solid wood, with plywood top and bottom, using dado joints at the corners. A close-grained hardwood is best. The rockers have slight curves, so there is little fear of the young owner turning the crib over. She can sit back and rock her doll with one foot in the traditional way.

The best sequence of work is to make the head and foot first, then use these to get the sizes of the sides. Mark out the head (Fig. 5-7A) first. Give it 1 inch of flare on each side. Use the scale on the drawing to obtain sizes. The angle to plane the bottom edge is 15 degrees. Use the head as a template to mark the foot (Fig. 5-7B), which must have the same angles at the sides and bottom. Round the top of the foot in cross section, but leave the top of the head square across to take the plywood top.

On the wood for a side, set out the shape (Fig. 5-8A). Allow a 15-degree slope at each end, with grooves marked to take head and

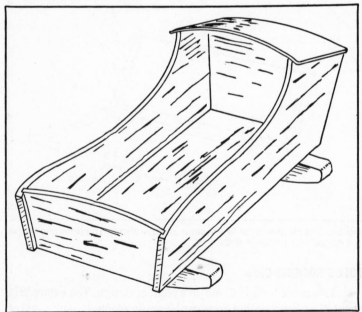

Fig. 5-6. A doll's rocking crib follows a traditional design.

44

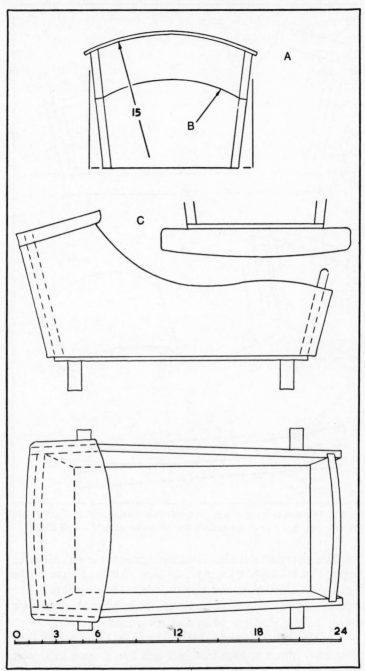

Fig. 5-7. The crib has flared sides and matching ends.

45

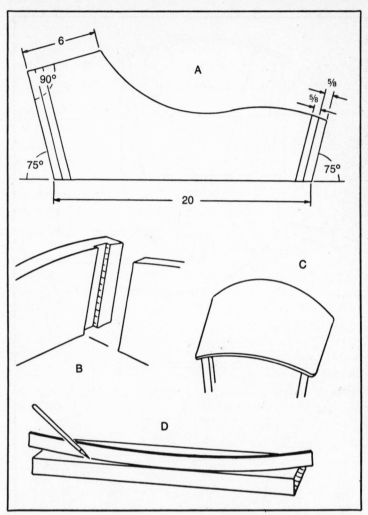

Fig. 5-8. The size of the crib side controls other measurements. Corners are notched, and the curve of the rockers can be drawn around a bent strip.

foot. The upper part at the head is at 90 degrees to the end. Allow for the part that will support the top, then draw a freehand curve for the shaped edge. Cut this out and mark the other side as a pair to it. The slope of an end's side can be used to set an adjustable bevel for testing the bottom edges when they are planed.

Cut the shallow trenches for the dado joints (Fig. 5-8B). Drill for screws—three at each foot joint and five at each head joint should suit most woods. To get a good hold in end grain, use

1½-inch by 6- or 8-gauge screws. Assemble the four parts with glue and screws. Let the glue set before continuing.

Plane the lower edges to fit the plywood bottom. Glue and nail that on. While doing this, check squareness of the assembly when viewed from above. Round the edges that will be exposed to a child's hands.

The top is a piece of plywood sprung to a curve (Fig. 5-8C). Round the front edge, both in plan view and in cross section, but leave the other edges slightly oversize to be trimmed after fitting. That will give you something to press on. Allow for correction if you get the plywood located slightly out of true. It is possible to bend and nail flexible plywood, but small screws will pull and hold the plywood to a curve better. Use glue as well. Trim and round the other edges when the top is securely in place.

The rockers (Fig. 5-7C) have flat tops, but get the curve for the bottoms by springing a lath and drawing with a pencil around it (Fig. 5-8D). Cut the curve on one rocker. Sight around it to see that it follows a smooth shape, then use it to mark the other rocker. Round the ends and all exposed edges. Attach the rockers a short distance in from the ends by screwing through the bottom from inside.

Traditional cribs of this type were given a natural finish or left bare, probably because the pioneers did not have paint to spare. The paint they had contained lead, which could be dangerous to a child. This toy crib may be finished in bright colors, although it looks best with a light color on inner surfaces and any color that appeals to you on outer surfaces.

Materials List for Doll's Rocking Crib

2 sides	9×24×⅝
1 head	10×12×⅝
1 foot	6½×11×⅝
1 bottom	10×20×¼ plywood
1 top	7×15×1¼ plywood
2 rockers	2×14×1

DOLL'S CRIB

This is one of the simplest cribs (Fig. 5-9). All of the parts can be plywood. If suitable pieces of solid wood can be obtained, the finished crib will look better. Construction will be slightly simpler.

Set out the shape of the head (Fig. 5-10A). The heart-shaped cutout is not just decoration. It is intended to admit two fingers for lifting the crib. Mark out the foot from the head, but cut it down to size (Fig. 5-10B). The curved tops of the cutouts can be drilled. The shapes are completed with a jigsaw or a coping saw (Fig. 5-10C). See that head and foot match. Mark on them where the sides will come.

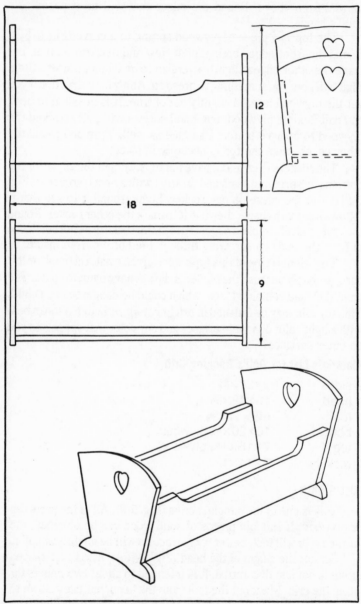

Fig. 5-9. This crib stands on feet and has lifting holes at the ends.

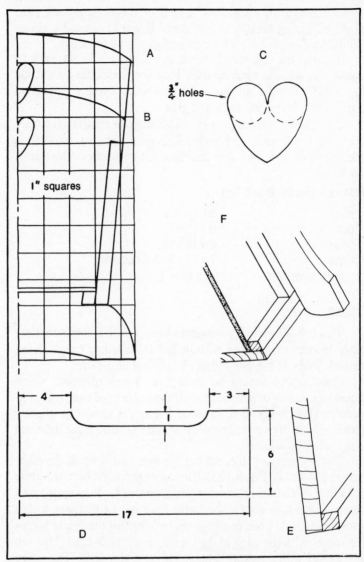

A

B

1" squares

C

¾" holes →

F

D

|← 4 →| |← 3 →|

1

6

|←———— 17 ————→|

E

Fig. 5-10. The crib ends match, and the bottom rests on strips inside.

Make the sides (Fig. 5-10D). Top edges do not have to be cut out, but that improves appearance and accessibility. Cut the ends of the sides squarely, so they butt against the head and foot closely. On all four parts, round the exposed edges where the child's hands may come. Put strips to support the bottom inside the lower edges of the sides (Fig. 5-10E), but do not put strips across the ends yet. Drill for screws through the ends. Four 2-inch by 6 screws at each joint should be strong enough in end grain. If you have used a close-grained hardwood, 1½-inch screws might be long enough.

See that the crib stands level. Put strips across the ends to support the bottom, keeping their tops level with the side strips (Fig. 5-10F). Cut the bottom to size and fasten it to the supporting strips with a few small nails and glue.

Give the wood a final inspection for sharp or rough edges, then finish the whole crib with paint. The head and foot could be a different color from the sides, and there can be decals on the ends if you wish.

Materials List for Doll's Crib

1 head	9×12×½
1 foot	9×10×½
2 sides	6×18×½
1 bottom	7×18×½ hardboard
3 bottom supports	½×18×½

ROCKER

This toy allows two youngsters to rock with a seesaw action, either indoors or out, but with little risk of falling out or being harmed. Stops at the ends limit the amount of rocking.

Construction should be mainly of ½-inch plywood, which should be exterior or marine grade if the toy is to be used regularly outdoors (Fig. 5-11). If solid wood is used, it should be slightly thicker. Using plywood allows the whole toy to be quite light and easily lifted by an adult.

The key part is a side. Set out one side first, with all the other parts marked on it (Fig. 5-12A). The curve should be part of a circle that will give a better action than using a curve made by springing a batten, which may not be the same. Improvise a compass with a piece of wood and a nail or awl as center. See that the center is on a line square with the edge of the rocker side (Fig. 5-12B). This can be checked with an experimental swing to the ends. The curve should cut both ends at the same distance from an edge. If it does not, manipulate the wood so it does before drawing the curve. The stops (Fig. 5-12C) need not project much, but they should all be the same and to smooth curves. Cut the two sides together and mark the second one as a pair to the first. Round all edges in cross section.

When making the crosswise members, check them against each other to see that they are all the same length. Shape the tops of the seat backs, but otherwise all edges are straight. Round the edges that are away from supports.

For the best finish, round all exposed edges of battens (Fig. 5-12D). Glue and nail or screw the battens in position on the sides. Then fit the footrest, seats, and seat backs. Check squareness

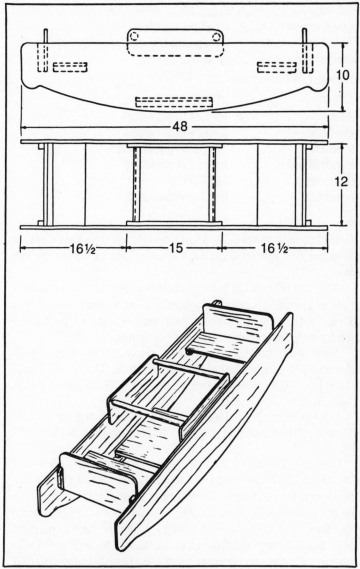

Fig. 5-11. A rocker gives pleasure to two young children.

across. Have the assembly upside down and see that it will rest squarely. When you sight across the curves, make sure they match. If there is any twist, correct it before the glue has started to set.

Mark the handrail side pieces and make them with all exposed edges rounded (Fig. 5-12E). It may be possible to fit the handrails into holes that do not go right through (Fig. 5-12F). It may be better to take the rods through (Fig. 5-12G), either with the ends level or allowed to project slightly and be rounded.

Rubber could be stuck around the curved edge. Finish the rocker by painting in bright colors.

Materials List for Rocker

2 sides	10×48×½ plywood
2 seats	6×12×½ plywood
2 seat backs	6×12×½ plywood
1 footrest	12×12×½ plywood
2 handrail sides	4×15×½ plywood
battens from	¾×72×¾
2 handrails	¾×13×round rod

FORT

If a boy has toy soldiers, a fort provides a place to use them. It may serve as a medieval castle, a frontier fort, or a modern barracks.

This fort (Fig. 5-13) is large enough to provide a central area for use as a parade ground or an assembly place for vehicles or horse troops. There are towers where sentries can stand on duty and a ramp for vehicles or horses to enter or leave.

Most of the construction is ¼-inch plywood frame around with strips about ⅝-inch square glued and nailed on. This gives a light and strong construction. The overall sizes (Fig. 5-14) can be varied to suit available materials.

Start by making the floor (Fig. 5-15A). This is framed around, but leave off the piece that will join on the ramp (Fig. 5-15B) until later.

The castellations on the top edges around the sides are based on widths of 1 inch and depths of ¾ inch. For the sake of appearance, they should be cut evenly. It will help in marking out if a card template is made (Fig. 5-16A). The back and front match the length of the floor, and the ends overlap them. Make the back to go right across, but cut down the front to make the entrance (Fig. 5-15C). Both ends are the same except for the extension on the one that supports the top of the ramp (Fig. 5-15D). Glue and nail the back, front, and ends to the floor. Put short framing pieces in the corners below the floor.

Make up the inside pieces for the towers (Fig. 5-16B) and assemble them to the main parts. Framing strips should be high

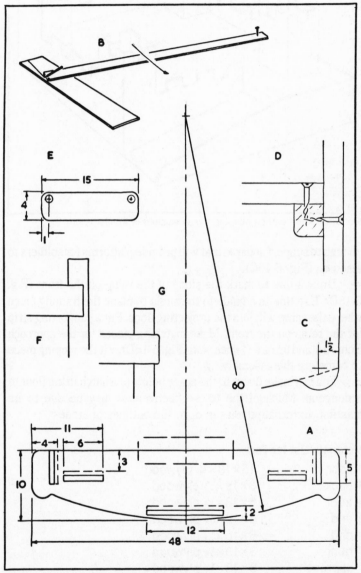

Fig. 5-12. Constructional details of the rocker. A strip of wood serves as a long compass.

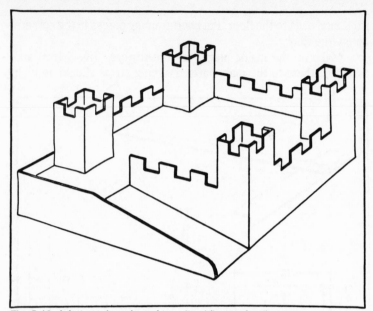

Fig. 5-13. A fort can be adapted to suit soldiers or frontiersmen.

enough to support squares that will provide platforms for soldiers to stand on (Fig. 5-16C).

Draw a line to mark the slope of the ramp on the front (Fig. 5-15E). Use this as a guide to the angle to plane the framing piece where the ramp will join the projecting floor. Put a supporting strip for the ramp on the front. Make matching pieces for the approach front to stand up as a ¾-inch wall (Fig. 5-16D). Fit the sloping piece to complete the assembly.

You can make doors to the space below or a hatch in the floor to a dungeon. Much of the toy's effectiveness may be due to its painting. Externally, you can draw the outlines of stones.

Materials List for Fort

1 floor	15×18×¼ plywood
1 back	6×18×¼ plywood
1 front	6×18×¼ plywood
1 end	6×12×¼ plywood
1 end	6×15×¼ plywood
1 ramp	3×13×¼ plywood
1 approach	3×18×¼ plywood
framing from	2 pieces 80×⅝ square

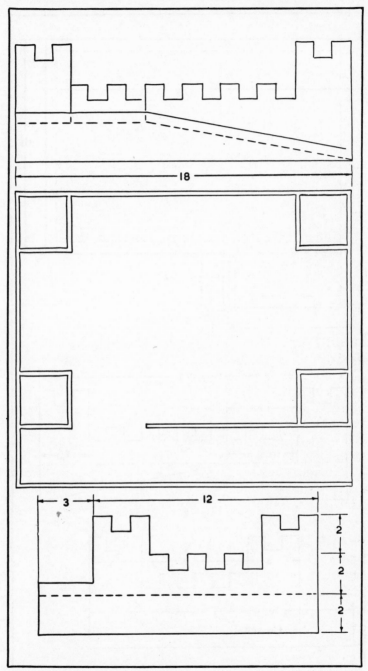

Fig. 5-14. Suggested sizes for the fort.

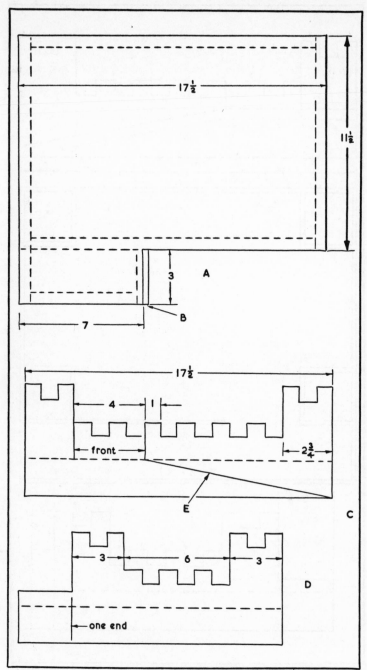

Fig. 5-15. Cut plywood panels for parts of the fort.

GEOMETRIC TOY

This is an educational toy (Fig. 5-17) for the youngest child who is just learning to reason and sort things out. There are three each of four shapes which can be put over pegs, either sorted into

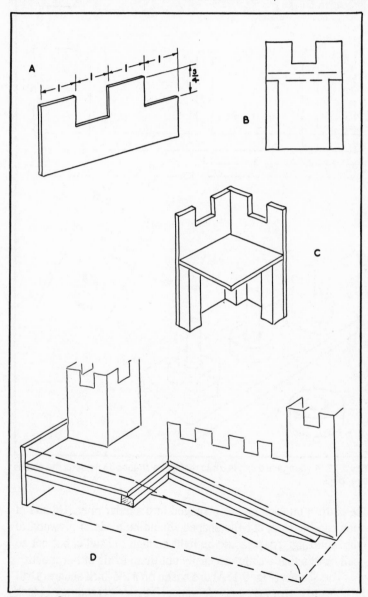

Fig. 5-16. Corner towers and the ramp are made over stiffening strips.

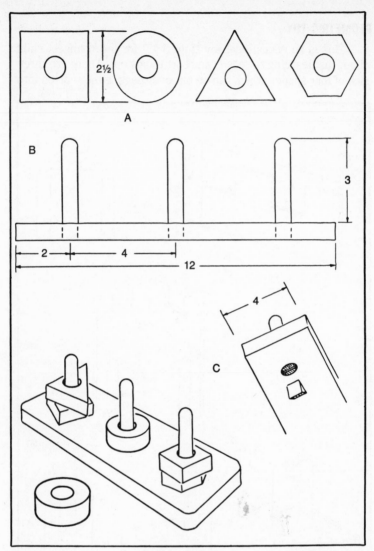

Fig. 5-17. A young child can learn to recognize shapes as he sorts the pieces over pegs.

one pattern on each peg or arranged into similar piles. Offcuts of wood can be used, but the shapes should be made of plywood to avoid splitting. They should be light enough to handle, but not so small or thin that a child can easily put them in his or her mouth.

The shapes (Fig. 5-17A) are based on a 2½-inch square. Drill the holes to give a very easy clearance. If the dowel rods are ½ inch in diameter, the holes could be ¾ inch. Round all edges and take the sharpness off the angular corners.

Round the tops of the dowels (Fig. 5-17B) and the corners of the base. Drill squarely so the rods stand upright. If the sizes are altered, the distances between the pegs should be enough for two squares to clear each other when set diagonally. It may be sufficient to glue the dowels into holes that are a good fit, but for security glue wedges into saw cuts (Fig. 5-17C).

Finish with bright colors. Use a different color for each shape and another color for the stand.

Materials List for Geometric Toy

1 base	4×12×⅝
3 pegs	½×4 round rod
Shapes from ½ plywood	

JIGSAW PUZZLES

Jigsaw puzzles were first called "dissected puzzles" when they became popular in the eighteenth century. They were intended as teaching aids, particularly for history and geography, with historical scenes or maps appearing as the parts were assembled. They developed into adult puzzles cut in mahogany or other quality wood. They were kept in wooden boxes. Modern puzzles are intended more as tests of skill in assembling large numbers of parts, and those commercially available are usually pressed out of card. Jigsaw puzzles made in the old-fashioned way with the picture stuck to plywood are fine whether the result is an educational scene or just a picture that appeals to the child.

For a beginner's jigsaw puzzle, keep the parts large and comparatively few. If you are using ¼-inch plywood, no part should be much less than 2 inches across (Fig. 5-18A). The overall size will depend on the picture, but 10 inches square is reasonable. That divides into 25 parts. If that seems too many for a child, make the cuts further apart—2½-inch spacing makes 16 parts.

Plane the edges after gluing on the picture. Use a fairly fine fretsaw and do not force it too hard. In that way edges will be left smooth enough not to need any further treatment. You can probably cut across freehand. There is no need for precision, but you have to keep the general spacing fairly even. It may help to put paint guidelines across with a soft pencil (Fig. 5-18C).

A young child may have difficulty in deciding on overall sizes. You can make a frame in which to assemble the puzzle (Fig. 5-18D).

If you obtain several pictures of the same size, one frame can be used for all of them.

PUPPET THEATER

If a child has glove puppets, he wants a place to display them in a performance. The child needs a stage, preferably one large enough for a second child to sit with him or her and use more puppets. Parents obviously do not want anything bulky that will be in the way when out of use. This arrangement (Fig. 5-19) will fold flat, but it opens to hide the operator(s) and only show the performers.

The height will have to suit the child. A stage just above table height can be arranged by making the total height 48 inches—the standard width of a sheet of plywood or hardboard.

Cut the panels for the front and both sides. Cut the stage opening, but leave trimming it exactly to size until after framing. Edges can be brought level with the strips. Frame them all round with strips glued and nailed on. It will help the theater to stand on uneven ground if feet are added (Fig. 5-19A). Put a strip across the bottom of the opening to form a stage (Fig. 5-19B).

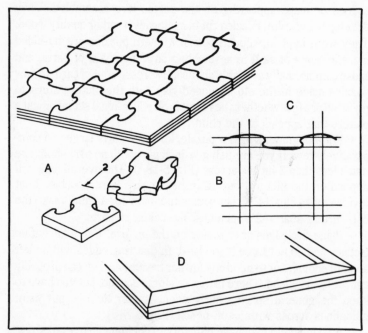

Fig. 5-18. A jigsaw should be cut with interlocking parts using a fretsaw. A frame helps to keep the parts together.

It will probably be best if the child sits on a stool low enough for his or her head to come below stage level. There can be ledges to take a loose board as a seat or something to lean against (Fig. 5-19D).

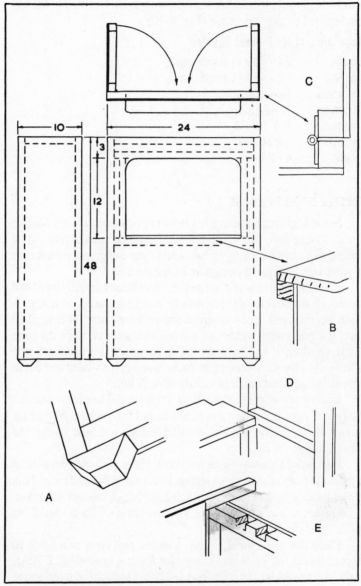

Fig. 5-19. A puppet theater is simply made to fold flat.

This toy can be decorated by painting. The opening might be made into an impressive *proscenium* with canopy and pillars painted around it. Curtains can be hung to draw across. Scenery may be hung from rods across the top, so the puppets perform in front of it. Cloth or paper scenery or strips of wood will be kept by the operator and changed while the curtains are drawn across. Notches in the top framing will locate the strips (Fig. 5-19E).

Materials List for Puppet Theater

1 front	24×48×⅛ hardboard
2 sides	10×48×⅛ hardboard
6 frames	⅞×48×⅞
4 frames	⅞×24×⅞
4 frames	⅞×10×⅞
1 stage	3×24×⅝
1 seat	4×24×⅝

TRESTLE ROCKING HORSE

Some traditional rocking horses were produced in very lifelike forms. Youngsters may have got just as much satisfaction out of using a more basic rocking horse, while their imagination took care of what was lacking in design and appearance.

An elaborately carved horse may have been carefully used and preserved for several generations in a stately European home. A much simpler and more easily made rocking horse is described here. If it gets rough treatment and does not survive more than one or two children, it will have served its purpose. This rocking horse is basically a trestle mounted on rockers and given a head and tail to provide some semblance of reality (Fig. 5-20).

If sizes are altered, maintain a good spread to the rockers so the risk of tipping sideways is minimal. Let the rockers project far enough ahead and behind so normal use does not tend to roll the horse too far.

Figure 5-21 shows suggested sizes. Make a full-size drawing of at least the body with the legs and rockers in side and end view. This allows for checking of sizes and angles. Although the legs are raked in both directions, you can use squared strips with no need for special section angles.

Plane the wood for the body. Use the end view as a guide to angles. Bevel the ends and cut a slot for the head (Fig. 5-22A). Taper the pieces for the legs (Fig. 5-22B). They can be overlong at this stage. Check that they are all the same.

Make the two rockers (Fig.5-22C). Test the accuracy of the curves by turning one on the other. Plane the lower edges parallel with the floor, but round the edges to reduce any tendency to mark carpets.

Mark where the legs will come on the body and rockers. Keep the bottoms of the legs a short distance above the curved edges. The tops of the legs can overlap the top surface of the body and be trimmed after assembly. Join these parts with glue and screws.

The plywood top can be left parallel, but it is better to hollow it slightly where the child's legs will come (Fig. 5-22D). Cut a slot for the head to match that on the body. Round the corners and the edges. A smoothly sanded outline looks good and makes for comfort. Attach the top to the body with glue and nails or screws.

A step is shown across the rockers (Fig. 5-22E). This may also serve as a footrest if the child's legs are long enough, but another footrest is shown on the front legs (Fig. 5-22F). This will have to be positioned to suit the child and may have to be moved after he has grown. The step is worth having even if the child's legs are short. It

Fig. 5-20. A simple rocking horse will always give pleasure.

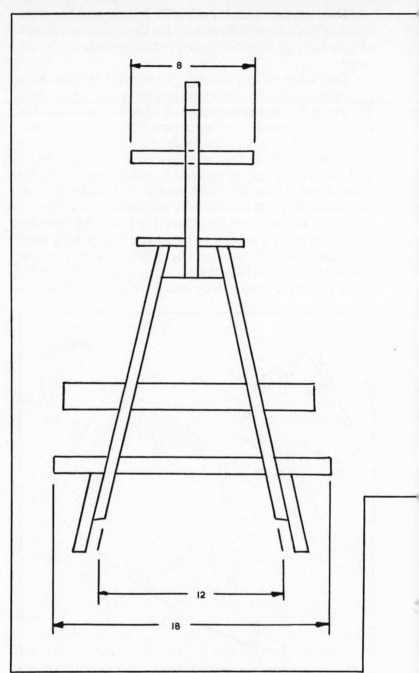

Fig. 5-21. The rocking horse is based on a trestle construction.

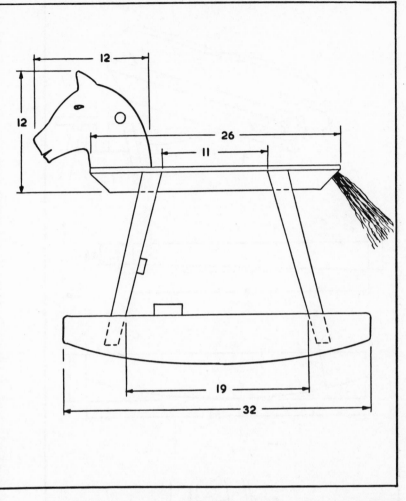

is a help when climbing on the horse. Round the ends of both pieces and round the parts where feet will come. The exposed angles of the horse's legs may also be rounded between parts that are attached to them.

The head gives character to the horse and can be given just a token shape, but it is better to cut it with a recognizable outline. Then use paint to make it more lifelike. A possible outline is shown on a grid of squares (Fig. 5-23). If two pieces of plywood are used to make up the thickness, cut one piece to shape. Glue it to the other piece before cutting that to match. Leave the part that fits into the slot with square edges, but round all other edges.

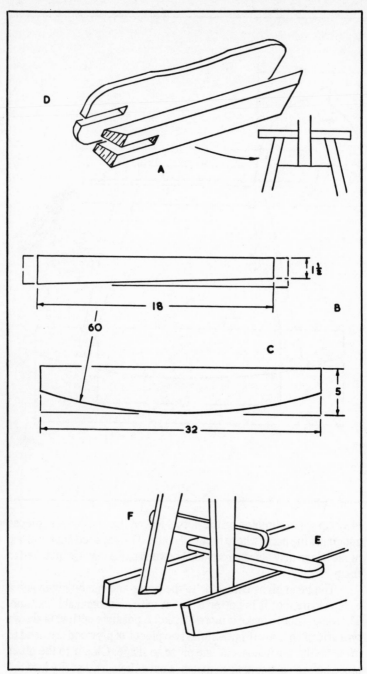

Fig. 5-22. Constructional details of the rocking horse.

The handle is a piece of dowel or other round rod. Round its ends. Be careful when drilling the head for the handle to get it true. If the handle does not fit squarely, any error will be very obvious.

Glue the handle in the head and the head into the body. A tail may be made from a piece of rope about ½ inch diameter. Bind one end for a short distance with adhesive tape. Drill a hole to take this rope in the end of the body, then glue the rope in. Fray the rope by carefully separating the parts down to the finest fibers.

Choose horse colors of brown, black, or white. A *piebald* arrangement of two of these colors can be attractive. The rockers can be the same color or green or black to represent the ground. An

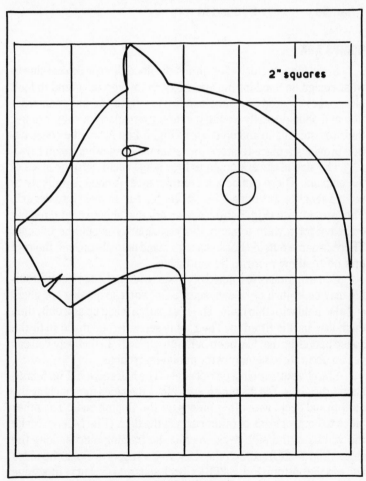

Fig. 5-23. A suitable shape for the horse's head.

eye painted in the right places helps the effect. A mane can be made with more frayed rope, or it can be indicated with black paint.

Materials List for Trestle Rocking Horse

1 body	4×27×2
1 top	7×27×½ plywood
2 rockers	5×33×¾
4 legs	2×20×¾
1 step	19×3×¾
1 footrest	17×1½×¾
1 head	12×12×1 plywood
or two	12×12×½ plywood
1 handle	1×9 rounded rod

NOAH'S ARK

In the biblical story of Noah and the flood there is no real clue to what design he used for his ark. Modern toy versions tend to look like houses erected on a simple hull. This makes for easy construction and should satisfy young owners, particularly if they can put their toy animals in and on the ark (Fig. 5-24). A boxlike construction provides a place to store these animals and other small toys.

The size of the ark ought to bear some relation to the sizes of the animals. There can be a lot of tolerance. A child is unlikely to bother about proportions if he can get his toy animals into the ark. The sizes shown (Fig. 5-25) make an ark that should not be too big or heavy for a child to carry, but its capacity should be enough. There is some outside deck space to stand animals on, and the roof lifts off to allow more to be put inside.

Construction is of framed plywood to keep the toy light. Framing may be ½-inch or ⅝-inch square softwood strips that are glued and also held with thin nails. The boat part is made up as a unit, then the house part is fitted in. The roof is separate and made to fit the house part after that has been built into the hull. In that way you can get an accurate assembly with minimum trouble.

Start by setting out a pair of sides. The half section (Fig. 5-25A) shows the sizes. Put framing pieces along the sides for attaching the bottom and deck, with other pieces for the sloping ends. The other piece to control sizes of other parts is the deck (Fig. 5-26A). Make the widths of the side decks to suit the framing pieces along the sides (Fig. 5-25B). Attach the deck to its supports along the sides and add the bottom (Fig. 5-26B). Check squareness, but at this stage the bottom may overlap the sides slightly. Both the bottom and the

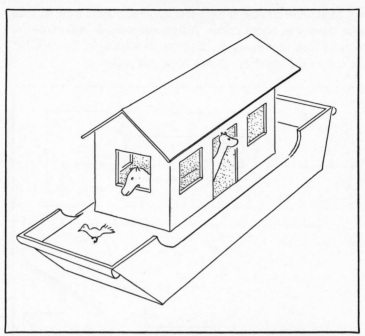

Fig. 5-24. A Noah's ark is a traditional toy that will also store toy animals.

deck can have some excess length left to trim to the slopes of the ends. Put strips across to support the house ends (Fig. 5-25C) at the same time as you add the bottom. Trim the ends of the assembly and add the sloping ends of the hull. The top edges of the ends can be left as they are, but rounded pieces outside improve appearance and provide something to grip when lifting (Fig. 5-26C).

Make the house ends to fit in the hole through the deck. Give the top slopes of about 30 degrees. Cut window openings of any shape you prefer, but keep their top edges low enough to miss the roof ends that will fit inside (Fig. 5-26D).

Make the house sides to fit tightly between the house ends. Cut openings. A door on one side only, with windows beside it and more windows at the other side, should be satisfactory. Fit these parts in place with stiffening pieces in the corners (Fig. 5-25D).

Make two roof ends of solid wood to fit between the house and framing and with slopes to match (Fig. 5-26E). Notch these to take a ridge piece planed to the slopes. Make the two sides of the roof to overhang about ½ inch all around. Join them to the roof ends and ridge piece (Fig. 5-26F). Arrange the fit so a child can lift off the roof. Be sure it is not so loose as to shake off when the ark is moved.

Make sure all sharpness is sanded off edges and corners, then paint the toy in bright colors. A light color inside will allow the contents to be seen easily. A light brown is suitable for the deck, but the rest of the wood can be any color you prefer.

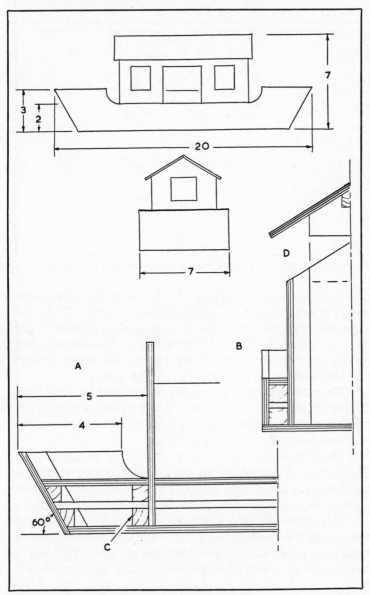

Fig. 5-25. Suitable sizes for a simply constructed ark.

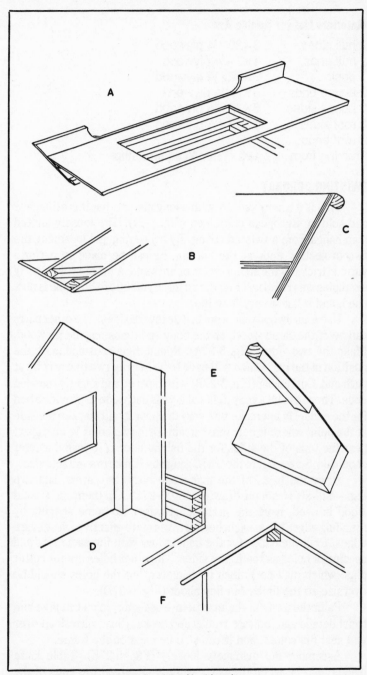

Fig. 5-26. Constructional details of the Noah's ark.

Materials List for Noah's Ark

2 hull sides	3×20×¼ plywood
2 hull ends	4×7×¼ plywood
1 deck	7×20×¼ plywood
2 house ends	6×7×¼ plywood
2 house sides	6×10×¼ plywood
2 roof sides	4×12×¼ plywood
2 roof ends	2×4×½
Framing from	120×½ or ⅝ square strip

TWISTING ACROBAT

This is a traditional toy with a long history, but it is still made and sold by European craftsmen (Fig. 5-27). The loosely jointed man hangs from a twisted string. By squeezing and loosening the two projecting ends at the bottom, he can be made to perform various tricks as the string twists or untwists. A problem with early examples was rapid wear on the string. Synthetic fishing line is now used, and it has a very long life.

Use a hardwood that is not brittle for the sides. The other parts can be of the same wood, or the body and limbs may be plywood. Make the two sides (Fig. 5-27A). Round their ends and mark the position of the bar, which will have to be held by two thin screws at each end. Cut the bar (Fig. 5-27B) with tapered and slightly rounded ends. There can be a very light cut across each side to provide a bed for the ends. Do not make this very deep, or it will weaken the side at the point where it gets most strain. Drill two holes ¼ inch apart near the tops of the sides for the fishing line; 1/16-inch diameter should do. Screw it into the bar; 2 gauge by ¾ inch is a suitable size.

Draw the parts of the man—one body, two arms, and two legs—full-size from the drawing (Fig. 5-27C). Cut them out. If solid wood is used, have the grain lengthwise. Do some shaping by rounding edges if you wish, but the toy is quite effective with square edges. Drill the hands for the fishing line with the same size and spacing of holes as the frame sides. The other holes are for cotter pins, which may be ⅛ inch in diameter, but the holes should be oversize so the limbs can flop about (Fig. 5-27D).

Paint the parts of the man before assembly. You can give him facial details and indicate trunks and socks. Clear varnish all over will seal the colors, and it can also be used on the frame.

Assemble the man very loosely (Fig. 5-27E). Table knife blades held between the parts while you spread the ends of the cotter pins should give a satisfactory amount of play.

The fishing line you need is *monofilament*. It is a single piece and not several strands twisted together. The line is graded in pounds. The choice is not critical, but about 30-pound grade will do. Pass the line straight through without twists and temporarily tie the

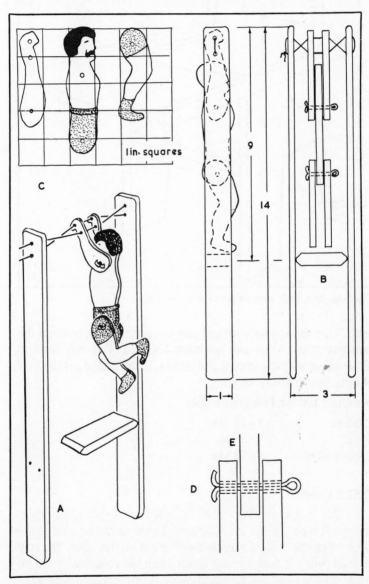

Fig. 5-27. This easy to make acrobat performs when the bottoms of the sides are squeezed.

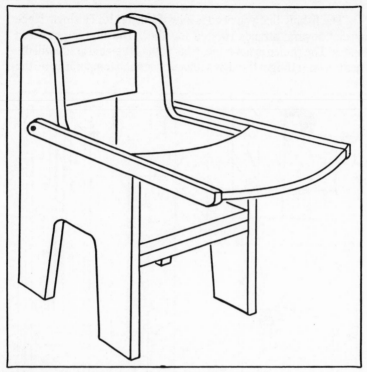

Fig. 5-28. This chair allows a girl to feed her doll.

ends. Turn the acrobat over and over to twist the line. Squeeze the bottoms of the sides and see what happens. You may have to experiment with the amount and tension of the line to get the best results before finally knotting.

Materials List for Twisting Acrobat

2 sides	1×14×⅜
1 bar	1×3×⅝
a body from	1×12×⅜

DOLL'S CHAIR

This is a chair (Fig. 5-28) intended for a doll which a girl nurses. It is not for use in a dollhouse. The chair can be used on the floor when the child is playing there or put on the table. The tray swings over the back to hang down when not required. It can be made of solid wood, but ½-inch plywood is better able to stand up to use without risk of cracking.

Mark out a side (Fig. 5-30A) to sizes from the general drawing (Fig. 5-29A). Mark on the positions of the seat and the back. Use this as a guide for marking the other side and the other parts. Cut the

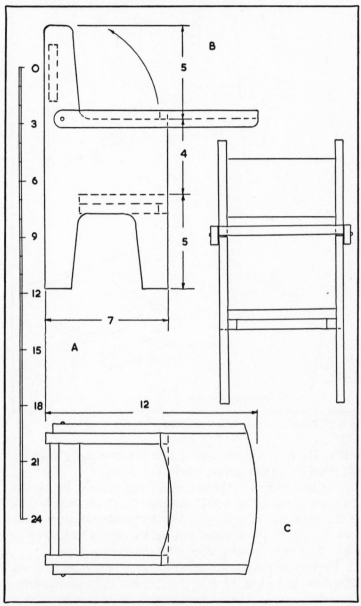

Fig. 5-29. Suitable sizes for a doll's chair.

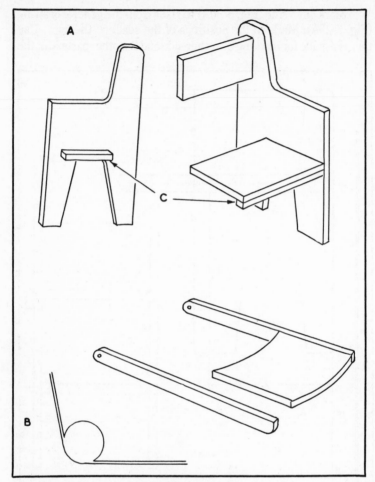

Fig. 5-30. Constructional details of the doll's chair.

outline. The curves in the internal cuts can be made by drilling a hole about 1 inch and cutting into it (Fig. 5-30B).

Thicken the front of the seat with a strip under it. Put similar strips on each side (Fig. 5-30C) to support it. Check that the back and the seat are the same length. Assemble by screwing through the sides, but drill for the threaded part and the neck of each screw to reduce the risk of splitting when driving into edge grain.

The tray swings on two arms,and it must be pivoted so it will swing over the back of the chair (Fig. 5-29B). Make the two arms and cut the tray to fit between them, slightly longer than the width of the chair so the arms will swing freely. Curve the tray edges (Fig.

5-29C). The rear edges of the tray should rest on the chair arms. Fit the tray between its strip with thin washers in the joints and under the screwheads.

If the parts are then found to function properly, remove the tray and round all exposed edges before painting. The sides of the chair can be decorated with decals.

Materials List for Doll's Chair

2 sides	7×14×½ plywood
1 seat	7×7×½ plywood
1 back	3×7×½ plywood
1 tray	6×7×½ plywood
2 tray sides	½×12×1

SAILBOAT

Many toy sailboats may float, but they do little else. The owner becomes frustrated with the boat being incapable of going anywhere except broadside to the wind, and then falling flat on the water in the slightest gust. No very small craft can sail very efficiently because the wind and the water are still full-scale, and their effect on the little model is more like the effect of a hurricane on a full-size boat. A little sailboat may sail reasonably well on such sheltered water as a swimming pool or a pond when the wind is only a gentle breeze.

This boat (Fig. 5-31) is 12 inches long with other sizes in proportion. It does not have a rudder but is steered by adjusting the main sail with its "sheet", which is the controlling string. The foresail works automatically. There are no shrouds or other *mast stays*. They are unnecessary on a model of this size, but they can be added. The mast and sails can be lifted out and folded for storage or transport.

Hull

A woodworker unused to the compound curves of a boat hull may wonder how to set about shaping it. In this case there are two thicknesses, and their outlines provide a guide to shaping.

The half drawings (Fig. 5-32) are on a grid of squares. Copy the two hull drawings full-size. Use stiff paper or hardboard, so the outlines can be cut and used as templates turned over on the centerlines.

The top piece (Fig. 5-32A) also has a hole cut out of its center. Use the same outline to cut the deck, except that it has a hatch cut in it (Fig. 5-32B). This should be marine plywood if possible, but other plywood bonded with waterproof glue is suitable. Mark out the lower piece (Fig. 5-32C) in the same way. Cut to the outline.

There has to be a slot for the keel cut in the bottom piece, and that is more easily done before the parts are joined. The keel is cut

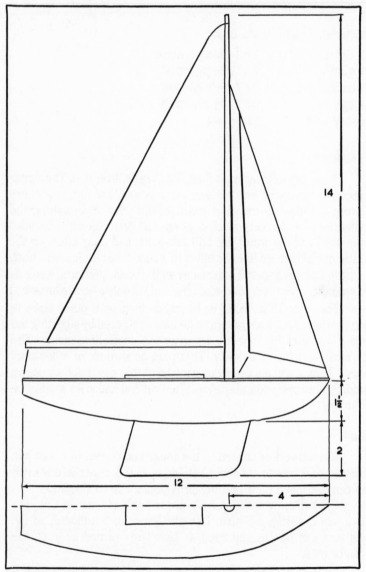

Fig. 5-31. This boat will really sail.

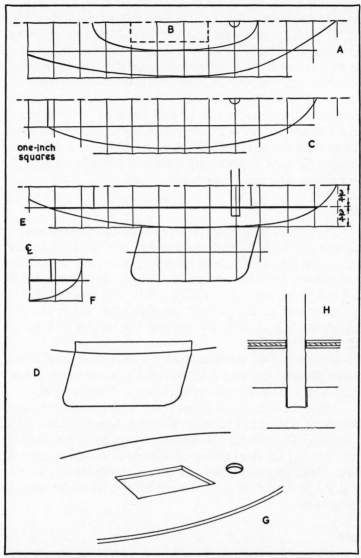

Fig. 5-32. The boat hull is made of two pieces glued and shaped with a plywood deck on top.

from ⅛-inch sheet metal. It can be brass. If steel is used, painting will protect it from rust. Cut the slot about ⅜ inch deep with a narrow chisel and a knife, so the keel will press in (Fig. 5-32D).

Glue the two hull parts together. Be careful to get them symmetrical on each other. Use waterproof glue. When the glue has set, trim the blocks so they have the correct shape in side view (Fig. 5-32E). At the center of the boat, get the hull into a smooth curve crosswise (Fig. 5-32F). Trim the stern to a similar but smaller curve. You now have the hull the right shape when viewed from the side or the end. Round off the other parts to the same shape on each side, using the joint between the two blocks as a guide to how far to go. Remove large pieces with a chisel, but closer work is better done with a *spokeshave* or a Surform tool. If your final curves come just into the outline of the joint, there cannot be much difference between the sides. At this stage you can leave the hull surface rough for finishing after other constructional work.

Mast

The mast is made from a piece of ⅜-inch dowel rod. Check its size and drill to make a push fit in the deck (Fig. 5-32G). Glue the deck to the hull. There can be some small brass nails around the edges as well. Drill through the mast hole in the deck to go about ⅜ inch into the bottom of the hull (Fig. 5-32H). Make sure the drill is upright in both directions. Trim the deck edges to the hull and smooth the hull all over. Fit the keel into its slot with epoxy adhesive.

The hatch cover can be cut from a solid piece of wood or two pieces glued together (Fig. 5-33A). Make it a push fit in the opening in the deck, so it can be removed to stow cargo or empty out water.

Leave the bottom few inches of the mast parallel, but taper from there to about half thickness at the top. Remove plane marks by sanding. The main boom is another piece of dowel rod about ¼ inch thick. In a full-size boat it is joined to the mast with a universal joint called a *gooseneck*. Here you can use two linked screw eyes (Fig. 5-33B). Lever one open, then close it with pliers after linking to the other.

Sails

The sails will remain attached to the mast for most of the boat's life, so there is no need to fit them as you would on a full-size boat. Several materials can be used. Light synthetic woven cloth is difficult to sew into satisfactory shapes. Cotton is better. It should be fairly closely woven, but in this small boat it does not matter much about the weave. Turn in and sew the edges to the sizes shown (Fig. 5-33C). There has to be an attachment at each corner. You can sew around little holes, like miniature buttonholes, or there can be *eyelets* or *grommets* squeezed in. The smallest size intended for leatherwork is suitable. Make the sleeve of the main sail to slide easily over the mast.

Slide the main sail over the mast and attach the lower corner with thread around the screw eye or through a hole in the wood (Fig. 5-33D). Do the same near the top of the mast (Fig. 5-33E) with a

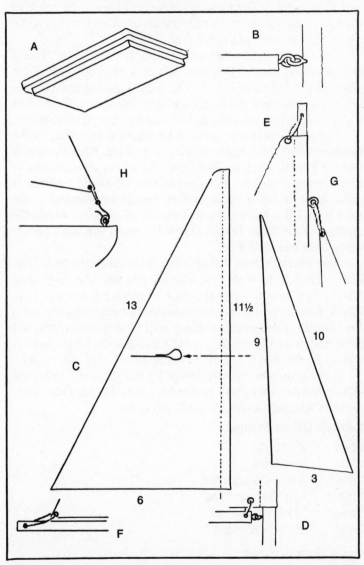

Fig. 5-33. A hatch (A) seals the hull. Mast and boom join with screw eyes (B). The sails join to the spars with thread.

moderate tension, but do not stretch enough to crease the cloth. At the end of the boom, use thread through a hole there (Fig. 5-33F). In use you may want to adjust this attachment, so have the hole in the boom a little way further out than the end of the sail foot. Tie the thread in a way that can be easily altered.

At the top of the foresail, use a thread to a screw eye into the mast (Fig. 5-33G). The forward corner will have to be released when you want to remove the sailing gear, so either knot to a screw eye or make a wire hook there (Fig. 5-33H).

The aft corner of the foresail has a "sheet" to a "horse". This is an arrangement where a line from the sail is attached to a ring that slides on a rod across the deck (Fig. 5-34A). As the boat changes direction in relation to the wind, the ring travels across. The amount of slack in the line will have to be found by experimentation.

The main sheet will have to be adjusted according to the direction the boat is to sail in relation to the wind. When the boat is to sail before the wind, the boom has to be let out almost square to the centerline of the boat. If it is to sail across the wind, the boom is hauled in a little, but not as far as 45 degrees to the centerline. If the boom is hauled in further, the boat should sail slightly towards the direction of the wind. Do not expect too much windward performance from this little boat.

Knot the main sheet through a hole in the end of the boom (Fig. 5-34B). Lead it down through a screw eye near the stern (Fig. 5-34C), then forward along the deck to another screw eye (Fig. 5-34D). It can be knotted here and adjusted by reknotting, but a little sheet metal runner, similar to those used on some tent ropes, will allow quicker adjustment (Fig. 5-34E). Bending the runner helps it to grip. A little flag at the top of the mast is a decorative touch.

If you have used a good hardwood for the hull, it will look great with several coats of varnish, preferably a marine grade. Otherwise, paint the hull and varnish the deck and spars.

Materials List for Sailboat

1 hull	4×12×¾
1 hull	4×11×¾
1 deck	4×12×⅛ plywood
1 mast	⅜×16×round rod
1 boom	¼×8×round rod
1 keel	2½×5×⅛ metal

DOLL'S BUNK BED UNIT

The sizes of this unit are intended to suit dolls about 15 inches

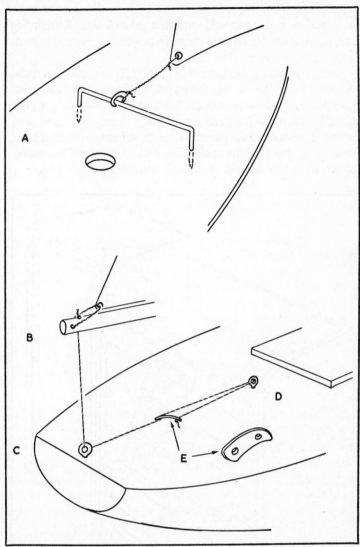

Fig. 5-34. The foresail is controlled by a sliding ring (A). The mainsail has an adjustable sheet (B, C, and D).

tall. The unit will accommodate two dolls. There is a large clothes closet at one end where dresses can be hung, as well as storage under the bottom bunk for other things. The whole unit should be stood against the wall in a girl's bedroom (Figs. 5-35 and 5-36).

Construction is of ⅜-inch plywood. Hardboard is used for the bottom of the bunks and as an alternative to plywood for the back.

The parts are glued and held with thin nails or pins. Reinforcing some of the joints inside with strips strengthens them and in most places serves other purposes, too.

Start by making the back (Fig. 5-37A). If you mark on it the positions of other parts, that shows you the layout and their sizes. Make the two closet sides and the bunk end (Fig. 5-37B). The ends extend ¾ inch to the floor and are cut away so they will stand firm. The top of the bunk end is curved down at the front to the bunk side. Cut down the fronts of the bunks (Fig. 5-37C) and round the edges. Cut pieces for the bottom of the unit and the bunk bottoms.

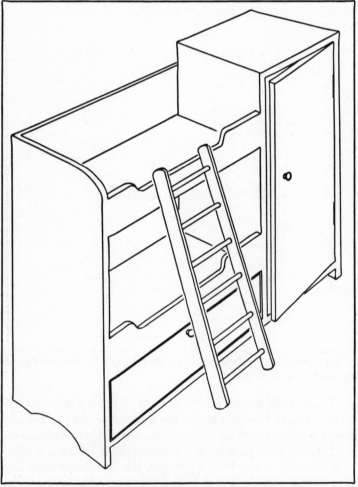

Fig. 5-35. The dolls' bunk bed also has a clothes closet and underbed storage.

84

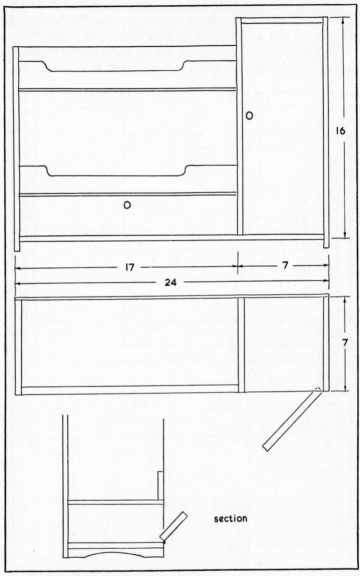

Fig. 5-36. The bunks suit dolls of average size.

Put 1-inch wide strips with a piece of ¼-inch dowel rod between as a clothes rail inside the top of the closet (Fig. 5-38A). Cut back the strips at the front so they will act as doorstops. Do the same at both ends below the bottom bunk to act as stops for that door (Fig. 5-37D).

Use the back as a pattern when assembling parts, but do not nail it on until all the other joints have been made. The hardboard bunk bottoms will need supporting along their backs (Fig. 5-38B).

With the assembly completed, cut the doors to fit. Use small hinges if possible (Fig. 5-37E), preferably within the joints, but

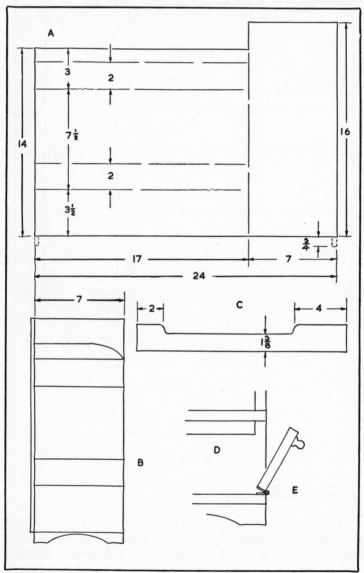

Fig. 5-37. Lay out sizes on the back, ends, and fronts.

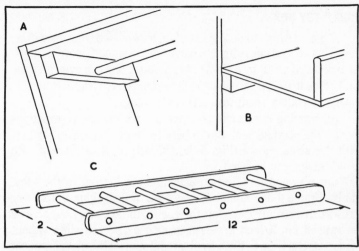

Fig. 5-38. Stiffening also supports a clothes rail and bunk bottom. Make a ladder with dowel rod.

wider hinges can be put on the surface. Alternatively, use strips of cloth as hinges. You need handles for opening, but if you cannot get small knobs, strips of wood may be used. To keep the doors closed, provide friction at the meeting surfaces. A short length of rubber or cloth in the opening should be sufficient.

For an authentic appearance there should be a ladder to the top bunk, but it need not have any attachment as it will not actually be climbed. A suitable one can be made with ¼-inch dowel rod and some light strips (Fig. 5-38C).

Paint everything in bright colors, but the inside will be clearer if they are lightly colored. Add decals if you wish.

Materials List for Bunk Bed Units

1 back	16×24×⅛ hardwood
1 bunk bottom	7×17×⅛ hardwood
2 closet ends	7×17×⅜ plywood
1 bunk end	7×15×⅜ plywood
2 bunk fronts	2×17×⅜ plywood
1 closet top	7×7×⅜ plywood
1 base	7×24×⅜ plywood
1 closet door	7×16×⅜ plywood
1 bunk door	3×17×⅜ plywood
stiffeners from	2 pieces 1×34×½
2 ladder sides	⅝×13×3/16
6 rungs	¼×2×round rod

MOBILE TOY BOX

A box in which to put toys is often improvised from something else. This special one is light to handle, has a smooth interior, and it can be moved about by a child or his mother. She can even give the child a ride in it. It is strong enough to stand up to rough use and big enough to collect small toys and other things.

All framing is outside, so there are no obvious obstructions inside. The arrangement allows bars to be put across as handles. With the sizes shown (Fig. 5-39), ¼-inch plywood framed with ¾-inch strips can be used.

Cut plywood for the two ends and the bottom to the same widths. Frame these outside (Fig. 5-40A) by using glue and nails or screws driven from inside. Join the ends to the bottom. Long screws can be used, but ⅜-inch dowels make neat and secure joints without exposed metal (Fig. 5-40B). Drill through and let the dowels project until the glue has set. Trim them level.

Glue and nail plywood sides to the ends and the bottom. Add stiffening strips to the top edges with nails driven from inside, but at the corners use dowels (Fig. 5-40C). When the corners are rounded, the dowel ends will shape with them. Make the handles from similar square strips, but round towards the center by taking off sharpness (Fig. 5-40D). Attach the handle ends with dowels in a similar way to the top corners.

There have to be some pads under the bottom corners to take the casters (Fig. 5-40E). Size will have to suit the caster plates, but 3 inches square should be adequate.

Round off all angles, but at the corners make fairly large curves. If you have used attractive wood and the finish is with varnish, the dowel ends make a decorative feature. Otherwise, paint all over and decorate with decals if you wish.

Materials List for Mobile Toy Box

3	panels	18×18×¼ plywood
2	panels	18×20×¼ plywood
16	frame strips	¾×20×¾
4	pads	3×3×½

ACROBAT

This toy goes back at least to *Victorian* days. The figure might be human (Fig. 5-41), although monkeys and other animals were also used. There is a long stick and a shorter one held against it.

When the shorter stick is moved up and down, the acrobat performs tricks on the top of his pole.

There can be some plywood used in the figure in a modern version, but oddments of hardwood will probably be stronger. Strength is mainly required lengthwise. The two sticks are square with straight grain, as any tendency to warp might affect movement.

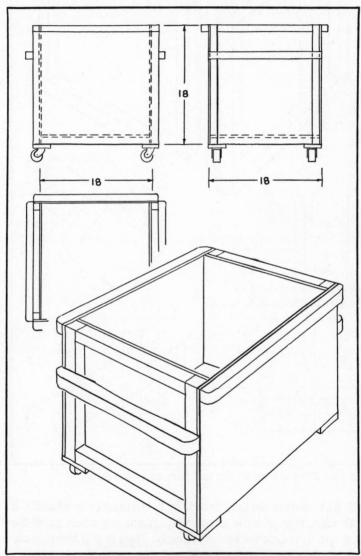

Fig. 5-39. A box on casters makes a mobile storage place for toys.

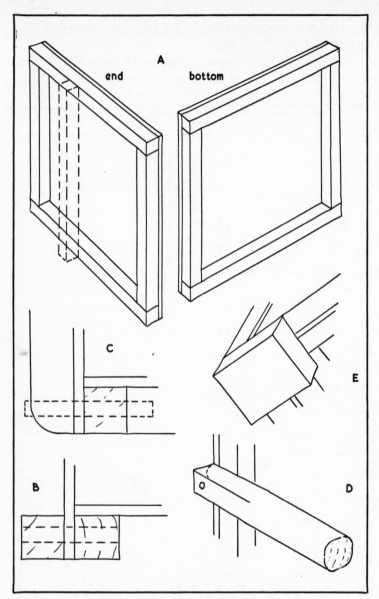

Fig. 5-40. The box is assembled from framed plywood panels.

The case around the sticks (Fig. 5-41A) serves as a handle. If both sticks start with the same section, plane just a shaving off the long one to reduce its section slightly. Then it will move easily through the case (Fig. 5-41B). Round all corners of the case.

Make the body (Fig. 5-41C) the same thickness as the short stick. It can be left in outline form, or you can whittle it to a more lifelike shape by taking off the sharp angles.

The arms and legs (Figs. 5-41D and 5-41E) will look better if fairly thin. Round on the outer surfaces only if you want to improve their shapes.

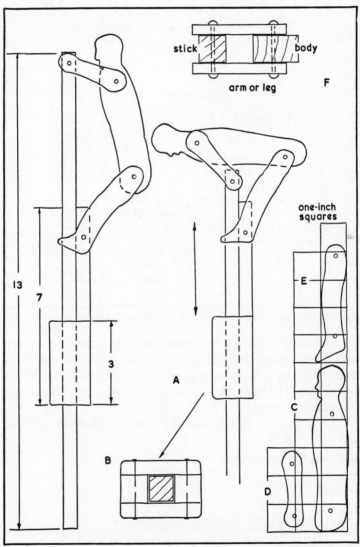

Fig. 5-41. When the slide is moved up and down, the acrobat performs on the top of his pole.

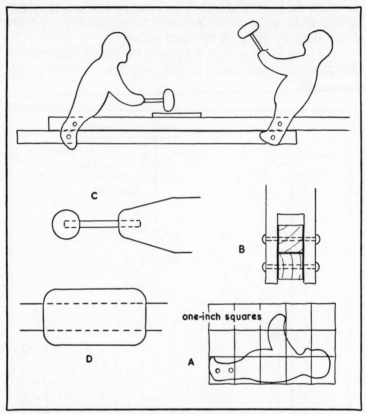

Fig. 5-42. Moving the sticks causes the men to wield their hammers.

The simplest pivots are cotter pins. Neater joints are made with rivets, which can be lengths of ⅛-inch copper or aluminum wire lightly hammered on opposite sides (Fig. 5-41F). Do not overtighten. The parts must move very easily to be effective and workable by a child.

Paint the parts of the figure if you wish. The sticks and case may be left plain.

Materials List for Acrobat

1 stick	½×13×½
1 stick	½×7×½
1 body	1×6×½
arms and legs from	1½×14×3/16

HAMMERING MEN

Like the acrobat, this is a toy that goes back to Victorian days and uses sticks with a sliding action to produce movement in the figures. The example (Fig. 5-42) is shown with two men wielding hammers on an anvil, but some traditional types have animals. One common one had a bear at one side and his trainer at the other.

The two figures are solid blocks (Fig. 5-42A). Their legs have to be made from the full thickness to fit over the two sticks (Fig. 5-42B), but the other parts can be whittled to more lifelike shapes. The action can put quite a strain on the arms, and they should not be reduced too much.

The hammers can be metal. They are easier to make with short pieces of ½-inch dowel rod as heads and ⅛-inch wire handles (Fig. 5-42C).

The sticks may be longer than shown. It is a good idea to have them too long until you are quite satisfied with the action, then trim and round the ends to a length that suits you.

Pivots may be cotter pins taken right through, or you can lightly rivet pieces of copper or aluminum wire. With this thickness, wood nails can be used in drilled holes. Choose a length that will just go through, then file the points level.

The pivot points may be 8 inches apart. Locate the points with the figures upright. If you are uncertain about the action, put thin nails loosely in the pivot and try the movement. When you have the figures permanently pivoted, put a piece of plywood on the top stick as an anvil (Fig. 5-42D). If you substitute metal there, the noise may be more satisfying to the young user. Paint the figures if you wish, but the other parts may be left plain.

Materials List for Hammering Men

2 sticks	½×13×½
2 men	3×5×1

Chapter 6

Wheeled Toys

The freighter is a pull-along toy, and it is not intended to float. As designed, it will tend to turn over if put in water, although that can be prevented if a strip of lead is nailed along the center of the bottom as *ballast*. This boat is best used as a dry land toy. It is given a cargo of four blocks which can be loaded and unloaded. This toy can be made from offcuts of wood. The sizes can be adjusted, but as drawn (Figs. 6-1 and 6-2) the hull is made from a block of 2-inch by 4-inch wood. Other sizes are proportional. You can use softwood, but the hull will be stronger if made of hardwood. As much of the wood is cut away, the total weight will not be very much. Some weight in the toy helps to keep it running smoothly.

FREIGHTER

Mark out the wood for the hull (Fig. 6-3A). Hollowing should be done before the outline is shaped, as the squared wood is easier to hold when in a vise or clamped to a bench. The bulk of the waste in the recesses is most easily removed with a powered router. That will work away most of the waste in stages and, if carefully done, only corners will need to be trimmed with a chisel to finish the shapes.

Alternatively, drill many holes into the waste parts and remove the waste by chiseling. Be careful not to drill too deeply. If the drill is used in a drill press, its stop will limit the depth. Otherwise, have a depth stop on the drill. Drill across for the roller axles. These may be steel or brass rods about 3/16-in. diameter. Also, drill for the towing string. A ½-inch hole upwards will take the knot, and another small hole diagonally into it passes the string (Fig. 6-3B).

Shape the outline. The curve to the bow should be the same each side, or any error will be obvious. Curve the stern evenly and slope up underneath.

The deck house is a simple block of wood (Fig. 6-3C) beveled at one end and with a notch to take the bridge at the other end. Make the bridge (Fig. 6-3D) to match the width of the hull and fit into the notch. The funnel is a piece of round rod (Fig. 6-3E). Drill at a slight angle so it slopes aft, but to keep modern lines cut the top parallel with the deck. Glue these parts together and to the hull. A few nails will help to keep the parts correctly located and supplement the glue, but punch the heads below the surface and cover with stopping.

The mast block is a simple piece. A tall mast might look effective, but there is the risk of it being broken. Keep it fairly short (Fig. 6-3F) and round its top. Attach this assembly to the foredeck.

Plane a piece of wood of sufficient length to the width and thickness of the cargo blocks, then cut them to length and round their corners. The blocks should be easy to fit into the "hold," so the young owner is not frustrated by trying to force them in.

The rollers are pieces of 2-inch diameter rod. If a lathe is available, they can be turned and drilled accurately on it. Otherwise,

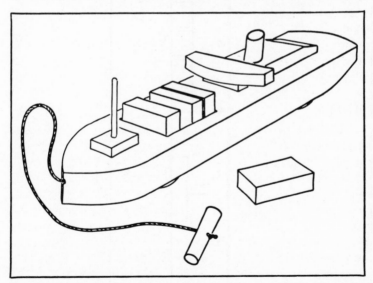

Fig. 6-1. This freighter is towed on wheels, and its cargo of blocks can be removed.

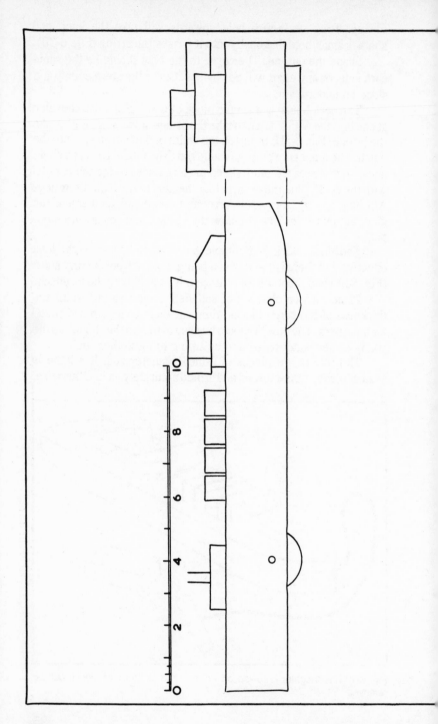

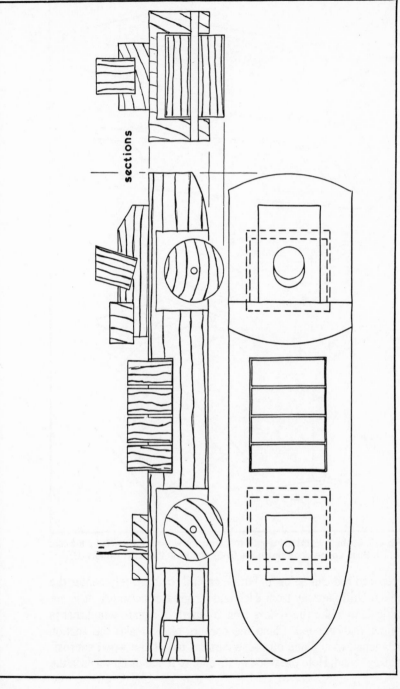

sections

Fig. 6-2. Suggested sizes for the freighter.

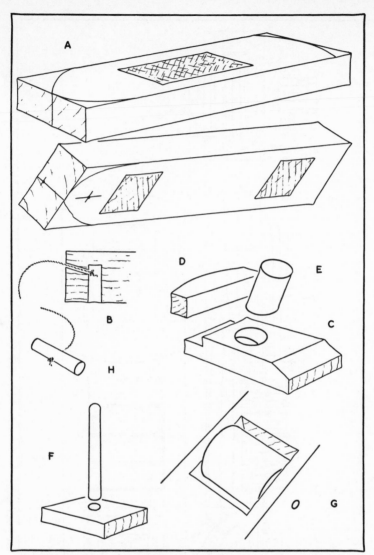

Fig. 6-3. Cut hollows in the freighter for cargo and wheels and a hole for the cord (A, B). Build up the deck structures (D-F) and let in the roller wheels (G).

prepared rod can be used, but be careful to accurately center the holes. Drill partway from each end for greater accuracy. It is not difficult to make the rollers from a length of square wood that is longer than needed. Plane the corners off to make the section octagonal, then plane off those corners to get the wood approximately round. Hole the wood by its end, so it stands upwards in the vise. Round it by pulling a strip of abrasive paper backwards and forwards around it.

The rollers should fit easily into their recesses and turn easily on their axles. Make a trial assembly. If this is successful, cut the axles exactly to length with smooth ends. Fasten them into the holes in the hull with epoxy glue (Fig. 6-3G).

Paint all parts brightly. The deck and upper parts can be a lighter color than the lower part of the hull, while the cargo blocks can each be a different color.

It will help the user if the towing string is taken through a short piece of dowel rod to form a grip (Fig. 6-3H). Have a large knot inside the hole in the hull, so the string will not pull out.

Materials List for Freighter

1 hull	2×16×4
1 deck house	2×4×1
1 bridge	1¼×3×¾
4 cargo blocks	1½×2½×¾
1 mast block	1½×2×½
1 funnel	1×2×rounded
1 mast	⅜×4×rounded
2 rollers	2×3×rounded

WAGON

A box on wheels is a basic toy for any youngster. If the wagon has a handle so it can be pulled along, it can be loaded with toys. The child can pretend that a big transport operation is underway. Dolls can be taken for rides. Sand and stones may be moved about.

Many sizes are possible. A larger wagon may have more uses outdoors. If it is made large enough that a child may ride on it, the wheels and their supports have to be stronger than if it is a lighter and smaller toy for use indoors as well. The sizes shown (Fig. 6-4) are suitable for a young child and can be increased. The wagon will be just as satisfactory if the sides are ½ inch deeper or shallower. Use hardwood. The grain of many softwoods will not stand up to wrenching and splitting strains.

The parts are overlapped and either nailed or screwed. If nails are used, punch them below the surface and cover with stopping. Screws are preferable, as they hold better in end grain. For most of the assembly, flat head screws 1 inch by 6 gauge will be suitable. Drill for all screws to minimize the risk of splitting.

Make the box first. It is shown with the ends attached first to the bottom (Fig. 6-5A). Then the sides are added (Fig. 6-5B). If all of the parts are carefully squared, there should be no difficulty in assembly. Round the top edges slightly before assembly.

The axle and wheel assemblies depend on the chosen wheels. Plastic wheels may be bought. Metal wheels with rubber tires are suitable, particularly if the wagon will be used over carpets. All of these wheels have fairly small central holes, and they can be arranged to run on stout round head screws (Fig. 6-5C). Arrange for

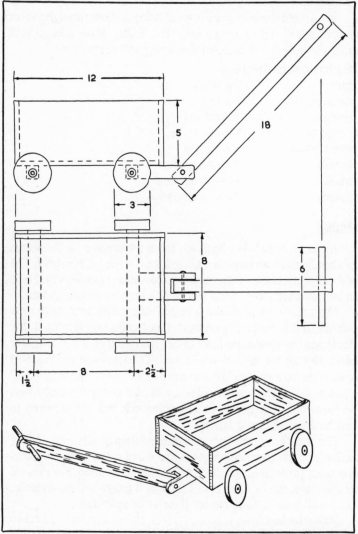

Fig. 6-4. A wagon that can be pulled may be small enough for use indoors.

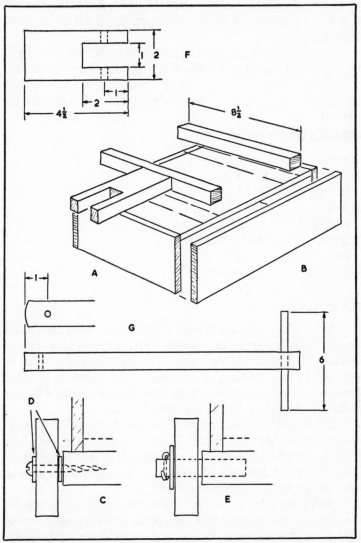

Fig. 6-5. The wagon is a box with framing underneath and a swinging handle. Wheels may go on screws or stub axles.

a washer to be under the screwhead and another between the wheel and the end of the wood axle (Fig. 6-5D).

You can make wooden wheels. It is possible to saw and sand discs. If a lathe is available, production of truly circular wheels is easy. With a lathe the outer surfaces can be turned to stimulate a wheel and tire effect. Whichever way the wooden wheels are made, they revolve with less risk of wobble if they are given axles thicker than screws. A piece of ⅜-inch or ½-inch dowel rod can be used (Fig. 6-5E).

Let the wooden axles project a little each side of the box. Drill for screws or dowel rods. Allow enough dowel rod to project through the wheel, so there can be a washer and a hole drilled through for a split pin. Screw the wooden pieces in place from inside the box.

Materials List for Wagon

2 sides	5×12×⅜
2 ends	5×8×⅜
1 bottom	8×12×⅜
2 axles	1×9×1
1 handle	1×18×1
1 grip	½×6×round rod
1 link	1×5×2
4 wheels	3 diameter

PUSH TRUCK

Some children prefer to push wheeled toys rather than pull a wagon. Girls may prefer to have their dolls seated in front of them instead of following in a box behind. This push truck (Fig. 6-6A) is constructed in a generally similar way to the wagon. It is wider because a child pushing needs more stability, particularly if the toy is being used to help him or her learn to walk.

The box can be made in the same way as the wagon's box, but it is shown with a plywood bottom. There is a taper to the front (Fig. 6-6B). Cut the two sides to match each other first, then nail or screw them to the back and front. Round all the top edges. Use glue and nails or screws to attach the plywood.

Make the axles and wheel assemblies in the same way as described for the wagon. Allow the wooden axles to project ¼ inch each side. Attach them to the box with screws from inside. Make sure the axles are parallel and square across the bottom; otherwise, the youngster will have difficulty in pushing the truck straight.

The handle shown (Fig. 6-6C) is at a height that should suit most young children. The handle is drawn at 60 degrees to the floor, but the exact angle is not critical. Do not slope the handle too far back, or it may be liable to tilt the truck backwards unintentionally.

The part of the handle that is held is a piece of round rod. Check what diameter a particular child finds most comfortable to grip. If a lathe is available, shoulder the ends of the rod to fit into holes in the sides (Fig. 6-6D). Otherwise, cut the ends to length. Use two nails or screws into each end (Fig. 6-6E). Bevel the bottom ends of the handle sides. Round the tops and all edges before screwing to the box sides. Thoroughly sand all parts and finish the wood with paint.

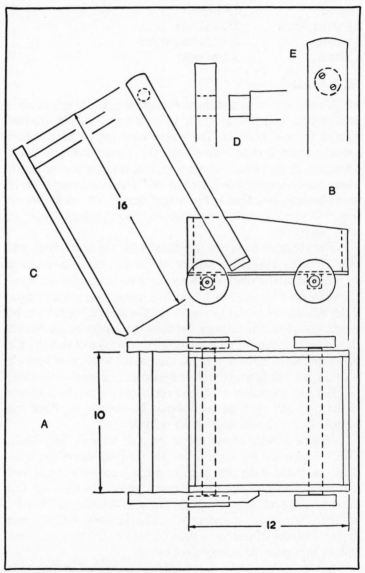

Fig. 6-6. A push truck will carry toys.

103

Materials List for Push Truck

2 sides	4×12×⅜
1 end back	4×10×⅜
1 front	3×10×⅜
1 bottom	10×12×¼ plywood
2 axles	1×11×1
2 handle sides	1½×17×¾
1 handle	⅞×12×round rod
4 wheels	3 diameter

YARD WAGON

If a wagon is to be made large enough for a child to ride in while another youngster pulls it, it has to be of a size and construction suitable for use outdoors. The wagon must not be heavier than necessary, and it must have wheels that revolve with minimum resistance. It must also be steerable, so the child pulling can take it where he wishes without having to skid wheels sideways. There must obviously be a limit to the weight carried. The wagon shown (Fig. 6-7) should carry a seven-year-old child. A bigger child or an adult can pull it.

Sizes of other parts are governed by the available wheels and axles. Wooden wheels are unsuitable. The dimensions given allow for metal or plastic wheels with rubber tires, having overall diameters of about 6 inches, with a ⅜-inch diameter steel rod as an axle. If the axle cannot be cut to length and the assemblies have to be bought complete, the distance between the insides of the wheels should be 15 inches or a little more. For the sake of stability the wheel spread should be at least the same as the width of the wagon's body. Do not make a wagon with wheels inside the width of the base.

Because the wagon will be used outdoors and may be left there in the rain, any plywood used should be waterproof. Paint and varnish should also be suitable for outdoor use.

Make a drawing of one end of the body full-size (Fig. 6-8A). This will give you the angle to cut and the positions of the slats. Mark the widths of the slats from the actual pieces of wood. It does not matter if they are slightly different from the size specified. Cut the ends and bevel the bottom edge. From the drawing mark the slat positions and cut away the edges ⅛ inch for them (Fig. 6-8B). Round the tops and take off sharpness at the corners. Attach the ends to the bottom with glue and screws from below.

Get the lengths of the slats from this assembly. Cut their ends parallel with the wagon ends, but round the edges before putting

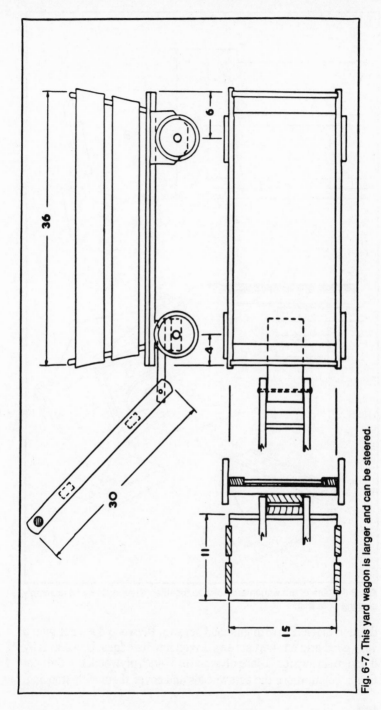

Fig. 6-7. This yard wagon is larger and can be steered.

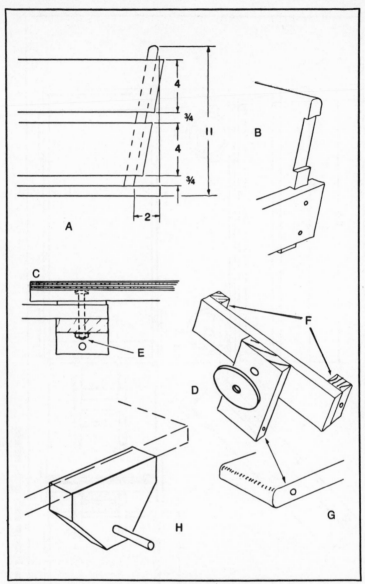

Fig. 6-8. Parts of the wagon are notched together. Steering is by an assembly pivoting on a bolt.

them in place. Fit with glue and screws. Plywood does not give a very good grip on short screws driven into its edges. Use 2-inch by 8-gauge screws for ¾-inch plywood to ¾-inch plywood. For the best finish, counterbore the screwheads and cover them with stopping.

Check squareness and be sure that opposite sides measure the same during assembly.

The method of pivoting the front axle determines the construction of the underframing. It is possible to get turntables intended for revolving chairs or such things as radio stands. Not all are strong enough if they are only intended for table use. If a suitable one can be obtained of not more than 5 inches in diameter, it will make a neat and satisfactory pivot. The alternative is to use a bolt which has a shallow head and a square neck to pull into the wood. The bolt may go right through the wagon bottom, but it is better let into the bottom stiffener (Fig. 6-8C).

It is unsatisfactory to let the moving parts rub directly on each other, so allow for a large washer. A piece of sheet metal can be cut. A piece of ¼-inch plywood will have a reasonable life. In either case make the diameter the same as the width of the link wood (Fig. 6-8D). The bolt goes through and is secured with a washer and nut, then the end of the bolt is hammered over to prevent the nut working loose (Fig. 6-8E). Use grease or candle fat on each side of the washer in the final assembly.

Cut the front axle piece to size. Make blocks to go across the ends to take the axle rod (Fig. 6-8F). The thickness of these blocks has to be enough to allow the axle to clear the end of the pivot bolt, if that is used. If there is a turntable, the steel axle can be higher.

The link is a parallel piece. It is glued and screwed to the front axle strip and projects forward. Drill for a ¼-inch rod that will form the handle pivot. Keep this far enough back from the end, so there is sufficient wood left to prevent the end grain breaking out (Fig. 6-8G). Drill for the bolt if that is to be used or fit the turntable temporarily. Try the assembly in position.

Check the distance the axle rod comes from the bottom of the body. The rear axle has to be at the same distance. Make the rear axle supports accordingly (Fig. 6-8H). Join them with glue and screw through the bottom. Check the fit of the axle through the two blocks. Allow for washers to keep the wheels away from the blocks.

The handle assembly can be given some rough use by a child when there is a comparatively heavy load and the wheels are on rough ground, so make it strongly. The sides (Fig. 6-9A) have two spacers as well as the handle rod. For the strongest construction they should be tenoned (Fig. 6-9B). They can be cut squarely, and then screws can be used. The width between the sides should allow an easy fit on the link. Drill that end to suit the pivot rod, but keep the hole far enough back to reduce the risk of splitting.

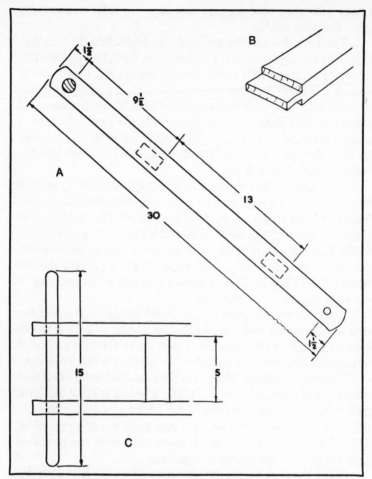

Fig. 6-9. A double handle on the wagon provides strength.

Round the ends of the rod used for the handle (Fig. 6-9C) and fit it through its holes with glue and thin nails driven edgewise. After all of the wooden parts have been painted, attach the handle with a piece of steel rod. The rod should be long enough to allow for washers on each side and for the rod ends to be lightly hammered over to prevent the washers coming off.

The whole wagon can be varnished, but it will be more appealing if it is painted brightly. If an attractive hardwood has been used for the slats and the handle, however, they might be varnished while the other parts are painted. In any case a two-color scheme seems appropriate. Decals may be added to the ends, but they are not

Materials List for Yard Wagon

1 bottom	15×36×¾ plywood
2 ends	11×15×¾ plywood
4 slats	4×36×¾
1 bottom stiffener	5×36×1
1 link	5×12×1
1 front axle	4×15×1
2 rear axle supports	6×7×1½
2 handle sides	2×30×1
1 handle	¾ or 1×15×round rod

waterproof. Apply two coats of varnish over them for protection.

CONSTRUCTIONAL TRUCKS AND TRAINS

A pull-along toy that can be assembled in several ways has obvious attractions. Parts can be made into trucks of various types or put together as a train with a diesel locomotive and assorted freight cars. The parts can be made into a snake or other animal that wobbles as it is pulled along the floor.

The toy described here is shown with parts that will assemble into trucks and trains. The shapes are basic, and much depends on the painting schemes used to indicate what the parts are. Great detail would not be appropriate for this toy (Fig. 6-10).

The sizes shown will make a fairly substantial toy that should stand up to rough treatment. Sizes can be modified up or down, but making the parts too small might lead to trouble. Small section wood can be broken or chewed and small wheels might be too easy for the youngster to remove or put in his or her mouth. The parts shown as 2½ inches square should not be reduced to less than 1½ inches, and other parts are made in proportion. Increasing sizes will make a rather heavy toy, but that might suit a well-developed child.

Use a close-grained hardwood so the risk of splintering is reduced, but choose a wood that is not heavy as well as hard. Select wheels at the same time as the wood. They can be turned if you have a lathe, but if bought they might be plastic or rubber instead of wood. Choose a diameter that will clear the bodies of parts. If you have to accept slightly larger wheels, you may have to use thicker wood for the linking pieces.

The materials list gives the sizes of wood for individual parts, but a set may consist of a locomotive with two passenger cars, one flattop car, one open freight car, and one closed car. There can be several truck and van bodies. If all of these parts were assembled at

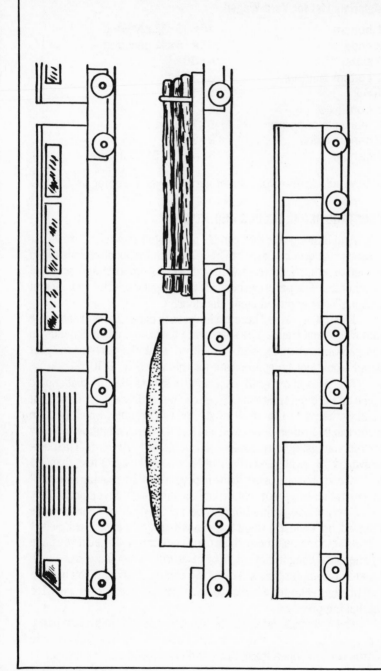

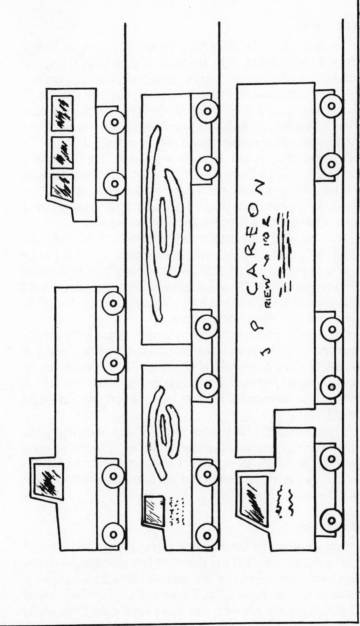

Fig. 6-10. With linking wheeled blocks it is possible to assemble a variety of vehicles like those used on the road and railroad.

the same time, a child might use at least 10 linking pieces. It is best to limit the assemblies by only providing four or five linking pieces, so the child only puts together one set of parts at a time.

Linking Pieces

The basic parts that all other parts should fit are the *linking pieces*, and these should all be the same (Fig. 6-11A). It helps to make a jig to get the hole spacings the same in all parts. This can be a piece of plywood the size of the linking piece, with two small holes at the correct spacing (Fig. 6-11B). If the holes are no more than 1/16-inch diameter, the drill used to make them can also be used to mark through, either to just make a dent or actually drill into the wood. At that size it will serve as a guide for the center of a woodworking drill bit. Use a piece of plywood and put stops at each side to get the line of holes central in the wood marked, whether it is 2 inches or 2½ inches wide (Fig. 6-11C). Check the actual widths of the wood being used and center the hole line to suit.

Mark out all the linking pieces you intend to produce on one long piece. Locate the holes with the template and drill for the dowel rod pegs (Fig. 6-11D). A drill press will help you get the holes drilled perpendicularly. If you drill by hand, get an assistant to sight the direction of the drill so you hold it squarely. Round the tops of the pegs and glue them into the base.

Position the wheels in line with the pegs. Arrange the heights of their centers so the wheels come far enough below the top edge of the base to clear anything added above. Most wheels can be mounted on wood screws with washers on each side (Fig. 6-11E). If the wheels are intended to be mounted on a rod axle, drill right through for it.

Where two parts have to pivot on the linking piece, their ends must have enough clearance to allow for turning without interfering with each other. Cut ends squarely. Use a compass set for half the width to draw the curved amount that will be trimmed off to provide turning clearance (Fig. 6-11F).

Passenger Car

A *passenger car* for the train assembly is a simple thing to start with (Fig. 6-12A). Use the jig to mark for holes at each end—double at each position as the end car in a train will have the linking piece underneath its end (Fig. 6-12B). Besides shaping the ends, round the top to represent the roof. Any other details are indicated by painting (Fig. 6-12C). The holes can be enlarged to allow the pegs to be fitted easily by work with a round file, and the pegs can be eased by sanding around them.

Flatcar

A *flatcar* (Fig. 6-12D) is thin enough to drill right through. Except for shaping the ends, there is no special work. You can put

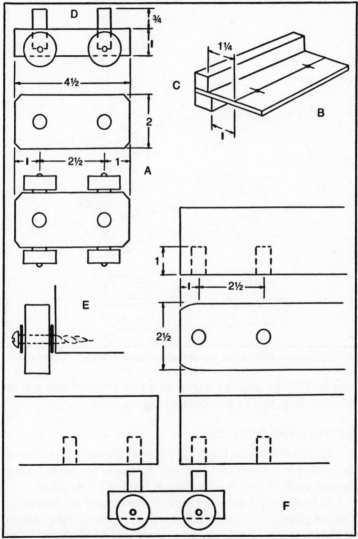

Fig. 6-11. The parts of the constructional truck toy are linked with dowels engaging with holes.

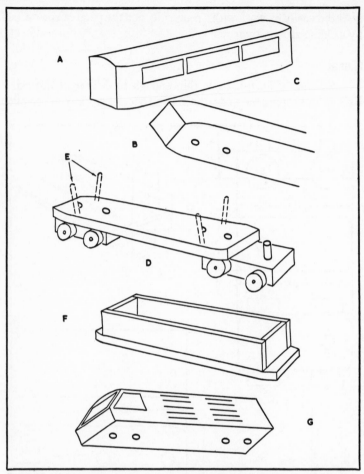

Fig. 6-12. Wagons and coaches can be painted blocks, flatbeds, or boxed trucks.

some small pegs near the edges, so a load of round rods can be lashed on (Fig. 6-12E) to represent logs or pipes.

Open and Closed Freight Cars

An *open freight car* (Fig. 6-12F) is a development of the flatcar and is merely a box nailed together. Keep the box ends a short distance back, so only the base needs shaping for clearance.

A closed freight car is the same as a passenger car, except for different painting. A diesel locomotive can be very similar, except for sloping the front and painting it to indicate windows and other parts (Fig. 6-12G).

Trucks

The simplest road truck can have a front shaped like a diesel locomotive. A better shape can be made with two cuts (Fig. 6-13A). A plain van is just a parallel block. Drill below to allow the linking pieces to go fully under to make an eight-wheel vehicle. A trailer might be made like the rail passenger car and coupled with the linking piece (Fig. 6-13B).

A child may prefer to have an open truck, so he or she can load it with wood blocks or other things. A solid block might be cut down behind the cab, but it is easier to start with a base like a flat rail car, then make a box over the rear part (Fig. 6-13C). A trailer to attach to it can be the same as a rail freight car, and the same thing might serve a dual purpose.

Semitrailer

A semitrailer makes an interesting assembly. The towing part is made like a short truck or van, but of a size to fit over one link piece (Fig. 6-13D). The towed part also travels on one link piece, or may be extended to two, but it projects forward (Fig. 6-13E). Cut away the two parts so they will lap on each other while still remaining level—about half the depth of each piece should be satisfactory (Fig. 6-13F). Put a peg in one piece to make sure there is enough clearance for both parts to turn without fouling each other (Fig. 6-13G).

Snake Assembly

If an assembly is to be made like a snake or other creature, construction is much the same as a train (Fig. 6-14A). It is possible to give the parts some shape with a band saw or jigsaw. The forward part must have some semblance of a head, while the last piece tapers as a tail (Fig. 6-14B). Cross sections may be rounded (Fig. 6-14C). The effect is heightened by suitable painting.

Painting is important for the other assemblies. Seal the wood first and give all parts a coat of primer to form a base for the colors. The link pieces should not attract attention. They might be gray or black. Other parts making up a train can be in colors to match the local line or painted brightly to appeal to the young owner. Windows can be simulated with aluminum-colored paint. Sides can be emblazoned with names of a genuine trucking company or something made up to include the owner's name. Good paint has a reasonable resistance to rough use and abrasion, but clear varnish over the paint will brighten and protect it.

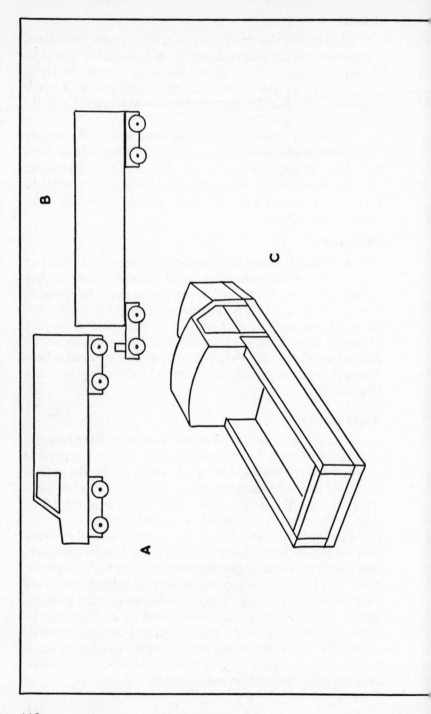

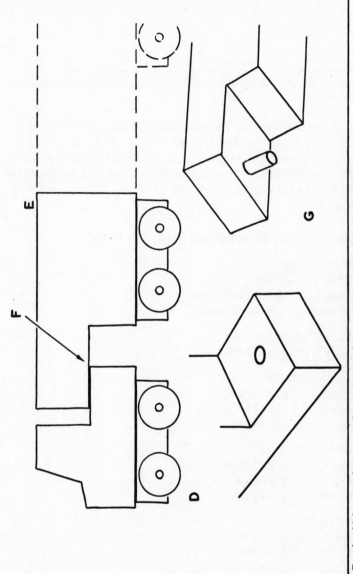

Fig. 6-13. Road vehicles may be mounted over the blocks, or trailers can be linked with them.

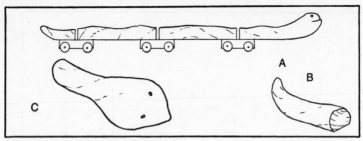

Fig. 6-14. Instead of making wagons, there can be parts linked to form a snake or other animal.

Some children may be quite happy pushing a locomotive or truck and pushing, as they imagine themselves to be driving it. Others may prefer to pull with a string. To allow for that, put a screw eye in the end of one linking piece. This will not interfere with its use for linking, and it can be turned inwards when not required.

Materials List for Constructional Trucks and Trains

Linking Piece
1 base	2×5×1
2 pegs	½×1½ round rod
4 wheels	½×1½ diameter

Loco or Passenger Car
1 body	2½×12×2½

Open Freight Car
1 base	2½×12×¾
2 sides	1½×12×½
2 ends	1½×2×½

Truck
1 base	2½×12×¾
1 cab	2½×4×4
3 backs	1½×9×½

Semitrailer
1 cab	2½×6×4
1 trailer	2½×9×4
or	2½×15×4

Flatcar
1 body	2½×12×¾

TRACTOR AND TIPPER TRAILER

This is a toy to push or pull along. The tractor can be used alone, or a trailer may be hooked on. The front tractor wheel axle can be turned, so the toy may follow a curve when pushed. The trailer described has a tipping body, so it can be loaded with blocks or sand. The user can tip them after a delivery. Other trailers can be made, so the tractor may tow a variety of loads. Sides might be hinged for unloading from the side. There can be a flat top for awkward loads or removable parts to allow for carrying straw or logs.

Construction is fairly basic with no fine detail that can be broken or cause accidents (Figs. 6-15 and 6-16). Some detail can be painted on, but general painting in bright colors is simpler and more acceptable.

Sizes are dependent on the wheels. If a lathe is available, they may be turned to size to suit what you want. If wheels are bought, they are not always to exact measurements. Other parts may have to be altered. The large rear tractor wheels settle the height from the floor, as they turn on screws driven into the center of the thickness of the base piece. The depth of the front axle has to be

Fig. 6-15. A tractor and trailer will appeal to a child familiar with country life.

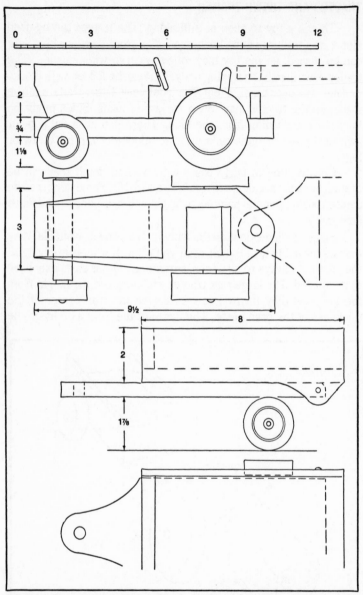

Fig. 6-16. The tractor profile is basic. Its trailer hooks on to a peg and can be made to tip.

made to allow those smaller wheels to lift the base parallel with the floor. The trailer base goes above the tractor base, so that wheel axle piece has to be of a suitable depth to lift it level.

120

Make the tractor base (Fig. 6-17A) and mark on it the positions of the other parts. It looks best with the front slightly rounded. At the rear use the center for the peg with a compass to draw the shape before drilling a ⅜-inch hole. Keep the parts where the large wheels come parallel and flat, but taper and round the other edges.

The engine can have as much shape as you like to put into it. If the child is familiar with a particular make of tractor, the shape can be modeled on that. In the example (Fig. 6-17B) the top is rounded

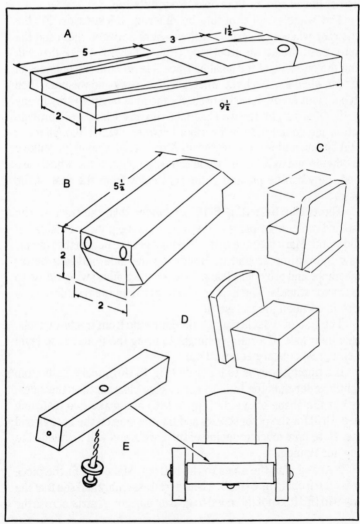

Fig. 6-17. Constructional details of the tractor.

slightly, and the front has a curve similar to the front of the base. It is undercut, and two round upholstery nails represent lamps. At the other end there can be a part cut away below a sloping instrument panel. A small wheel free to pivot on a screw will provide the user with a steering wheel to twiddle.

The seat can be cut from a solid block (Fig. 6-17C), but it may be easier to use a piece of plywood for the back (Fig. 6-17D). In either case round the top, so there is nothing rough to scratch a hand. Glue and screw these parts through the base. Also, glue a piece of dowel rod into the hole. Round its top.

The wheels will probably be different thicknesses. Fit the large rear wheels on screws with washers between them and the tractor base. Make the front axle (Fig. 6-17E) of a size that will bring the outsides of the smaller wheels level with the outsides of the rear wheels. Attach the wheels with screws and washers, then drive a pivot screw into the base. As the axle ought to stay in any position it is put, let the wood surface rub on each other to provide friction and do not include a washer between them, although there could be one under the screwhead. After a trial assembly, remove the wheels and axle so the wood can be painted. If the wheels are wood, they can be painted a different color from the rest of the tractor.

The trailer base (Fig. 6-18A) is wider than the tractor. The base and most other parts of the trailer can be plywood instead of solid wood. Mark the hole that will hook over the peg on the tractor. Draw the outline around it. Hollowing the sides gives a better appearance and provides clearance when the trailer swings close to the tractor wheels. The hole can be larger than the tractor peg, as there is no need for a close fit.

The tractor wheels may be similar to the front tractor wheels. Make their axle of a suitable height to bring the trailer base level when the wheels are screwed on.

If a tipping body is to be made (Fig. 6-18B), make its bottom slightly wider than the trailer base to give clearance for the sides. Lay out the shape on a side (Fig. 6-18C) and make two matching sides. Drill for the pivot screws and try one side on the bottom and base. Note how much rounding of the base's end will be needed to allow for tipping.

Nail and glue the sides to the bottom. Make and fit the piece across the front (Fig. 6-18D). Make a trial assembly and see that the body will tip. It is not intended to go past upright. A strut across the front may swing on a screw and support the body at a moderate angle (Fig. 6-18E).

If other trailers are made, do not have much behind the line of the wheels. Otherwise, there is a risk of tipping unintentionally. If a trailer is to be very long, it will be better four wheels

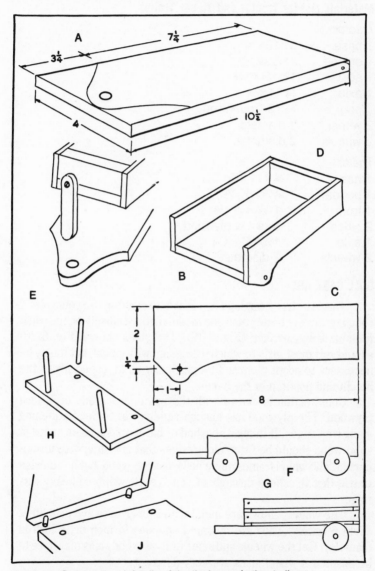

Fig. 6-18. Constructional details of the tipping and other trailers.

(Fig. 6-18F). An alternative to a plain box trailer is to make one with solid ends and one or two rails along the sides (Fig. 6-18G). Holes around the edge of a flatbed trailer would allow pegs to hold logs (Fig. 6-18H) or sides with dowels to lift off (Fig. 6-18J).

Materials List for Tractor and Tipper Trailer

Tractor

1 base	3×10×¾
1 engine	2×6×2
1 seat	1¾×2×1¾
1 axle	¾×4×¾
1 peg	⅜×2×round rod
2 wheels	3 diameter
2 wheels	2 diameter

Trailer

1 base	4×11×½
1 bottom	4⅛×8×½
1 front	1½×4½×½
2 sides	3×8×¼ plywood
1 axle	1½×4½×¾
2 wheels	2 diameter

DOLL CARRIAGE

This is a strong carriage that is able to stand up to a youngster's rough treatment better than one modeled more closely on the usual full-size baby carriage (Fig. 6-19). The sizes shown (Fig. 6-20) should suit most girls to which the design will appeal, but it may be necessary to adapt them to fit a particular child, especially in the height and position of the handle.

Construction is shown with the main parts made of ⅜-inch plywood. The plywood has enough rigidity not to need stiffening along free edges. If thinner plywood or hardboard is used, strips of solid wood should be fitted along edges that are otherwise unsupported. The wheel frames might be ½-inch plywood, but it is unwise to use that thickness throughout. The result will be a heavy carriage.

The wheels shown are metal with rubber tires and diameters about 6 inches. They are mounted on axles ⅜ inch or ½ inch in diameter. Get the wheels and axles first, as wood sizes may have to be adapted if wheel sizes are very different.

Start by marking out the two sides (Fig. 6-22A). Fit ½-inch square strips at the ends above where the bottom will come (Fig.

6-21A). Allow for the wheel frames overlapping by 1 inch (Fig. 6-21B). Use glue and thin nails for assembly. Cut hollows in the top edges and round the corners (Fig. 6-21C). Make sure the opposite sides are properly paired and that their shapes match. Mark on the positions of the handles at 45 degrees to horizontal (Fig. 6-22B).

Mark out the wheel frames (Fig. 6-22C). See that their lengths match the carriage sides. it will help to get the shapes right if you make a template of half a frame, then use it to mark the parts each side of a centerline. Cut the outlines, clean off any raggedness, and round and sand the edges. Note that the hollow in the curve of the ends is needed to give clearance to the hood when it is lowered.

Cut the pieces for the ends and the bottom to the same width between the sides. The ends of the bottom and the top edges of the end pieces can be trimmed after assembly.

Glue and nail the ends between the sides. Put stiffening pieces across the bottom edges of the ends, planed to the angle of the bottom, and then put the bottom plywood in (Fig. 6-21D). Add the wheel frames inside the carriage sides close under the bottom (Fig. 6-21E). Use glue in all meeting parts. Nail down through the bottom into the edges of the wheel frames before the glue hardens. Check that the whole assembly is square. Stand it level, under weights if necessary, until the glue has set.

The handle sides (Fig. 6-22D) are simple strips with rounded ends. Drill for the round rod deep enough for the joints to be glued and screwed from outside (Fig. 6-22E). Make sure that the distance

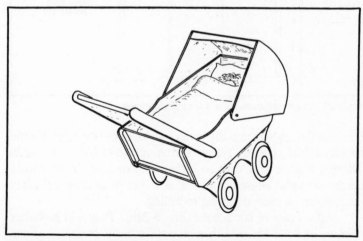

Fig. 6-19. A sturdy all-wood baby carriage will satisfy a young girl just as well as one made more like a full-size one.

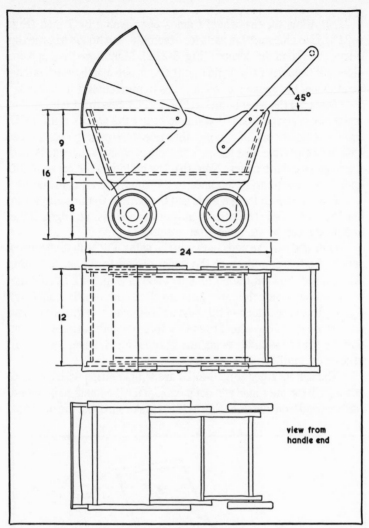

Fig. 6-20. Suggested sizes for a doll's baby carriage.

between the sides match the overall width of the carriage. Fit the handles to the sides by screwing from inside or bolting through. These are joints that may be better without glue. If the handle height has to be altered as the child grows or another girl takes over, it can be done easily be redrilling.

Make a pair of hood sides (Fig. 6-22F). They will be better pivoting on bolts and nuts than on wood screws, so drill the hood sides and carriage sides for ¼-inch bolts. Mark on a side first where

126

the hood will come and mount it temporarily on the carriage side. Swing it to see that the finished hood will clear the corners and go low enough at the wheel frame.

The bottom hood frame piece is straight and nailed between the sides (Fig. 6-21F). The top piece can have its lower edge slightly hollowed and rounded in section (Fig. 6-21G). Make a temporary strut to go between the bolt holes while the hardboard is

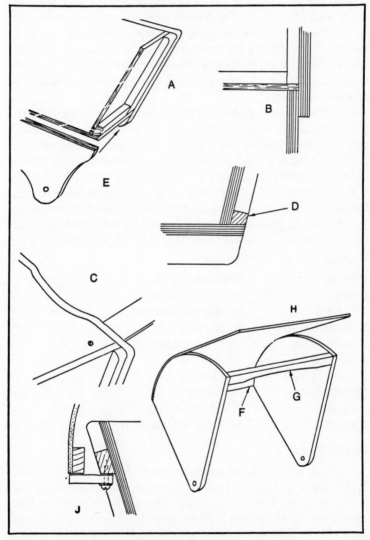

Fig. 6-21. Constructional details of the doll's baby carriage.

127

fitted. All of the pieces across should be of a length that will allow the hood to swing with a little clearance over the carriage. Make up this assembly using screws through the bolt holes into the temporary strut.

Cut the hardboard piece slightly oversize. Spring it to shape. If this is difficult, moisten it. Have some clamps ready. Put glue on the meeting surfaces and start at the bottom edge with thin nails fairly closely spaced. Clamp to the bottom frame piece. Go around the curve with more nails (Fig. 6-21H) until you can nail to the top piece, where it is advisable to grip with more clamps until the glue has set. When this has happened, remove the clamps and trim the edges. Round all exposed parts, particularly corners. Try the hood in position after the temporary strut has been removed. See that its action is satisfactory.

The hood needs to be held up and be easy for a young girl to release and lower. Position a block of wood on the center of the end, with its lower edge level with where the hood should come when it is in the up position. Shape a short piece of wood as a turn button under it, pivoting on a screw with a washer under its head (Fig. 6-21J). Make it long enough to go under the end of the hood and around its end. It can be swung back when the hood is to be lowered.

Finish the hood and handles in bright colors different from those of the rest of the carriage. That completes the woodwork.

Materials List for Doll Carriage

2 sides	9×24×⅜ plywood
2 ends	9×12×⅜ plywood
1 bottom	12×20×⅜ plywood
2 wheel frames	7×20×⅜ plywood
2 hood sides	13×15×⅜ plywood
2 handles	1½×18×¾
2 hood frames	1×13×½
framing from	½×60×½
1 handle	⅝×15 round rod
1 hood	14×30×⅛ hardboard

RIDING CRANE

This is a mobile crane on which a small child can sit (Fig. 6-23). It is mounted on furniture casters. The youngster can use his or her feet to propel it about the floor while lifting and moving loads. The child's weight on the rear platform provides stability, while he or she can alter the angle of the *jib* with one handle and lift loads with the other. *Pawls* on ratchet wheels give the young engineer more

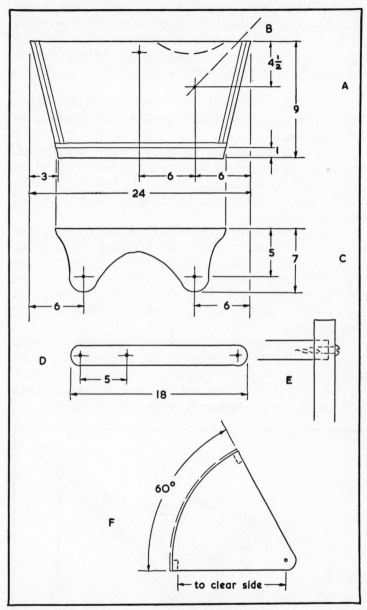

Fig. 6-22. The main parts of the doll's baby carriage.

levers to move. The toy should be strong enough to stand up to normal use. With a child sitting astride it, there should be no fear of it toppling with any load he or she tries to lift.

Some of the parts are plywood, but the control tower is solid wood. Round parts can be made from dowel rods. The four casters are the type intended to be attached with screws. They should be obtained at the start, so any adjustment of size can be arranged to suit them. The type of caster with a stem to go into a leg cannot be used.

The general drawing (Fig. 6-24) shows overall sizes. If you decide on variations, they will affect some of the information in the detail drawings.

Start by making the base (Fig. 6-25A) from ½-inch plywood. Round the rear corners and edges. Mark on the position of the control tower. Put blocks underneath for the casters. The blocks must be large enough to take their mounting plates and spread widely for stability.

Mark out the control tower sides (Fig. 6-25B) and make them to match. Drill through for the ⅝ inch dowel rod winding drums. Make the jib supports (Fig. 6-25C) and the two crosswise pieces (Fig. 6-25D). Drill a small hole centrally in the top piece to take the end of a cord. Join these parts with glue and nails or screws. Mount the assembly on the base with the jib supports projecting forward over the edge.

The jib sides look best if they are given a curved taper towards the top (Fig. 6-26A). Mark them to take a spacing block at the bottom. A short length of dowel rod serves as a spacer where the tops are pulled in (Fig. 6-26B). Make the width of the spacing block to let the assembly be an easy fit between the jib supports.

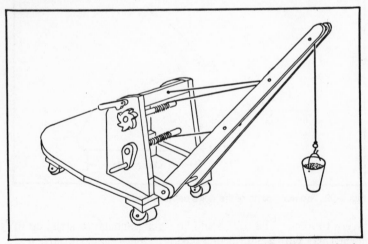

Fig. 6-23. This crane has a base on which a boy can sit while picking up a load.

130

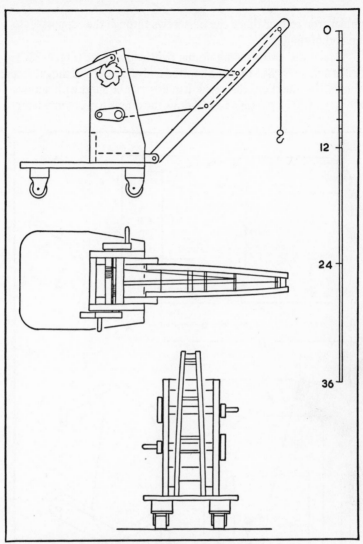

Fig. 6-24. Three views showing suitable sizes for a riding crane.

The other three crosswise pieces shown serve as guides for cords. They can be pieces of ¼-inch dowel rod, but it might be better to make them of round iron rod about 3/16 inch in diameter which can be cut from large nails. The lifting cable goes under the lower one, then over the top one and down to the load. The jib-adjusting cable goes around the middle one and back to the hole in the top piece of the control tower. The jib can pivot on another

131

similar iron rod, or there can be screws through the supports into the end of the jib.

Make the two winding drums overlong at first (Fig. 6-26C). Drill a hole in each to take the knotted end of the cord. If the ratchet wheels are glued on, the crank handles can be held with screws only, so it will be possible to withdraw the drums if necessary later.

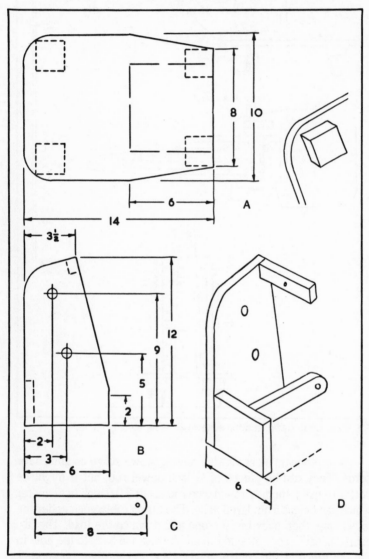

Fig. 6-25. The main parts of the crane assembly.

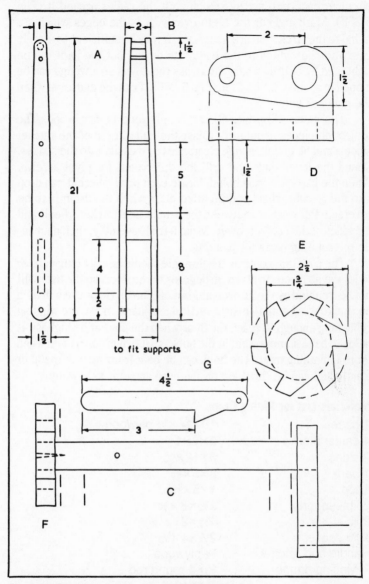

Fig. 6-26. The jib and parts of the crane's mechanism.

Make the crank handles (Fig. 6-26D) from plywood, unless you have some close-grained hardwood that will resist splitting. Glue in a piece of thinner dowel rod for the grip.

The ratchets should also be of plywood. There can be any number of equally spaced teeth, but it is convenient to divide the circumference into six by stepping off the radius around it (Fig. 6-26E). Mark and cut the teeth evenly. It is the edges which are radial to the circle that are important. It may be sufficient to merely glue a ratchet wheel to the end of its dowel, but the joint can be tightened by putting a saw cut across the dowel so a wedge can be tapped in as the joint is glued (Fig. 6-26F). Trim the end level when the glue has set.

The pawls (Fig. 6-26G) can be plywood or hardwood. The projecting pieces should fit against the radial teeth of the ratchet wheels and be given enough clearance to go easily into the spaces. Round the lever ends and drill the other ends for pivot screws. When the parts are assembled, locate each pawl where it can drop into the ratchet wheel and be lifted clear when the drum is to be reversed. Put washers between the handles and ratchet wheels and the sides of the control tower. Make a trial assembly, then dismantle the rotating parts for painting.

The cord that controls the jib angle should be only long enough to let the jib go out to about 30 degrees to the floor, so the user will not be troubled by the jib dropping out of control. He or she will then be able to wind it up to nearly vertical. Similarly, make the winding cable long enough to reach the floor when the jib is at its highest. It helps to have some weight at the hook, so it hangs down even when there is nothing on it. The hook can be bent from wire. A metal or plastic ball can be threaded on the cord above it as a weight.

Materials List for Riding Crane

1 base	10×14×½ plywood
4 caster blocks	2×2×1
2 sides	6×12×⅝
1 back	3×5×⅝
1 top	1×5×⅝
2 jib supports	1½×8×⅝
2 jib sides	1½×21×½
1 jib spacer	2½×4×⅝
Handle and ratchet	½ plywood
2 winding drums	⅝×8 round rod
2 pawls	¾×5×½

TIPPING TRUCK

This toy is one that a young child can push along. A doll can sit in the driving seat. The back may be loaded with wooden blocks or other things. They will travel safely, but when the lever at the side is pulled forward they will be shot out of the back on to the floor. The design is more functional than lifelike, but it should withstand plenty of rough use. The general construction is with parts glued and nailed together (Fig. 6-27). The drawing gives an acceptable size (Fig. 6-28), but dimensions are not very critical and can be varied to suit available wood.

If the base is made first, it can be used to mark out the sizes and positions of other parts (Fig. 6-29A). The axles may be slightly longer than the width of the base to give clearance to the wheels. The engine and seat assemblies are attached to their upright parts and to the base. Round all exposed edges and corners.

The back is just an open-ended box with a plywood bottom. At the forward end take the wood below the bottom to act as a stop for the tipper (Fig. 6-29B). The hinge piece underneath should be no longer than the width of the vehicle base (Fig. 6-29C) to give clearance for the wheels. Round the rear corners and the top edges of the sides.

The tipper assembly uses a piece of plywood. The plywood and the crossbar should be the same total thickness as the hinge bar on the back, so the back sits level over the base (Fig. 6-29D). Arrange the crossbar to extend far enough for the lever to be pulled when the plywood part of the tipper is central under the back. Glue a piece of dowel rod in a hole as the lever. Hinges can be quite small; 1-inch or 1½-inch hinges should be satisfactory. Do not let them into the wood. Put two hinges between the hinge bar on the back and rear edge of the base. Put another pair on the tipper bar. Locate this on

Fig. 6-27. This tipping truck is large enough to carry building bricks and be pushed around.

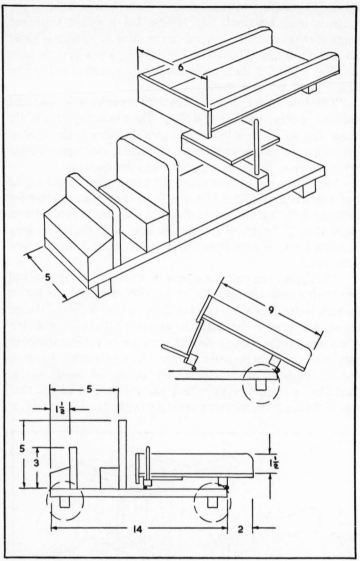

Fig. 6-28. Sizes, the main parts, and the tipping arrangements.

the base far enough forward to only just clear the piece extending
downwards as the lever is operated.

Wheels should not be more than 3 inches in diameter. Otherwise, there may not be enough clearance for the rear ones. They can
be wood, metal, or plastic. Mount them on long screws with
washers on each side of a wheel. There can be a screw eye at the

front for a pulling cord, but the youngster is more likely to want to crawl and push the truck.

Materials List for Tipping Truck

1 base	5×14×½
2 axles	¾×5×¾
1 engine	1½×5×1½
1 seat	1½×5×1½
1 front	3×5×½
1 back	5×5×½
1 back	6×9×½
2 sides	1½×9×½
1 front	2½×6×¼
1 hinge	¾×5×¾
1 tipper	¾×6×½
1 tipper	3×4×¼ plywood
1 lever	¼×3 round rod

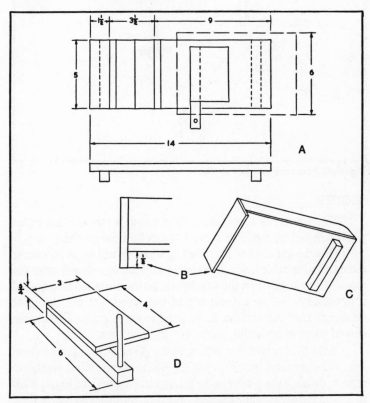

Fig. 6-29. The main parts to make before assembling a tipping truck.

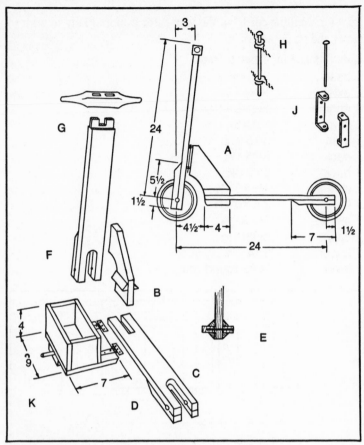

Fig. 6-30. This small scooter can be fitted with a sidecar.

SCOOTER

This scooter is almost entirely of wood. It can be fitted with a small sidecar, so a doll or other toy can be transported.

The design allows for wheels about 5 inches in diameter mounted on suitable iron rods as axles. Get the wheels and make the axles before starting on the woodwork, so the sizes can be adjusted if necessary. Before cutting any of the wood, set out the front bottom corner full-size so as to get the sizes right. The handle should come at about 80 degrees to the platform.

Make the bracket that will carry the pivot with its grain following the longer direction (Fig. 6-30A). At the bottom allow enough to project through the platform, so fillets can be glued in (Fig. 6-30B) to stiffen the joint. Make the platform (Fig. 6-30C), notched at the forward end to take the bracket, and cut away enough at the rear for the wheel. Glue and screw a thickening piece below the rear end (Fig. 6-30D). Drill through for the axle. Glue the bracket in place. Drive long screws or nails across it through the platform. Glue and nail fillets above the joint and add others below when you make the joint (Fig. 6-30E). See that the bracket is kept square to the surface of the platform when viewed from the front.

The upright handle is made in a very similar way to the platform, with the bottom cut away and thickened to take the wheel and axle (Fig. 6-30F). At the top the best joint for adding the handlebar is a mortise and tenon (Fig. 6-30G). Keep the handlebar square where it comes over the upright, but thoroughly round the projecting parts to form grips.

The simplest form of pivot is made with four large screw eyes and a rod or piece of a large nail through them (Fig. 6-30H). Another hinge can be made with two pieces of strip iron, about 1-inch by ⅛-inch section, bent to interlock and drilled for screws or bolts into the woodwork (Fig. 6-30J).

A sidecar cannot be very large, or it may interfere with the foot that kicks against the ground. A simple box with its bottom extended is shown in Fig. 6-30K. Mount an axle with a block of wood underneath. At the edge next to the platform, bevel the underside to allow for tilting as the scooter is used. Attach the sidecar with two small T hinges.

Materials List for Scooter

1 platform	5×20×¾
1 bracket	6×14×1
1 handle	5×24×¾
1 handlebar	1¼×18×1¼
2 thickeners	5×7×¾
1 sidecar bottom	7×9×¾
2 sidecar sides	4×9×⅝
2 sidecar ends	4×5×⅝

THREE-WHEEL SCOOTER

This toy is intended for a small child who may have difficulty in balancing on a two-wheel scooter. The horse's head should appeal to him or her. Some sizes depend on the choice of wheels, so get them before starting on the other parts. A diameter of about 6 inches is suitable, and they will probably have holes to suit ⅜-inch iron rod. Choose close-grained hardwood for all the wooden parts. Softwoods will soon crack.

The part that will have to take the most load is the bracket between the platform and the handle (Fig. 6-31A). Cut it with the grain diagonally for greatest strength. Any angle between 75 and 85 degrees should be satisfactory.

Notch the platform to take in the bracket (Fig. 6-31B). Join these parts with long wood screws from opposite sides, as well as glue, and choose screws that will go right through the bracket into the wood at the opposite side.

Enclose the rear axle in a slot in a block screwed under the platform (Fig. 6-31C). For most wheels there can be washers and a cotter pin through a hole at each end of the axle (Fig. 6-31D).

The handle width has to suit the front wheel thickness. If the wheel is about 1 inch thick, the head and spacer can be made to suit. If the wheel is much thicker, the bottoms of the handle sides may have to be cut away (Fig. 6-31E). The parts that make up the handle have to be arranged, so the platform will be level when the bracket is hinged to the spacer. There may have to be some experimenting.

To get a good shape for the horse's head, set it out first on paper and transfer this to the wood (Fig. 6-31F). Round the edges, particularly at the top. Be careful to drill squarely for the handlebar. Put the parts temporarily together, with the side pieces clamped to the spacer and the head, and the front wheel in place (Fig. 6-31G). Hold this against the bracket and move the spacer up or down if necessary to get the parts in the right position to bring the platform level. Glue and screw the parts together and fit the front wheel.

The hinge is made up of stout screw eyes (Fig. 6-31H), with a rod having bent ends or a bolt and nut. Note that the screw eyes on one part come between those on the other part to prevent movement up or down.

If the head is painted all over one color, the outlines may give a nice effect. It will be better to at least paint in eyes. There can be a painted harness or even leather or plastic straps.

Materials List for Three-Wheel Scooter

1 platform	6×17×¾
1 bracket	5×12×1
2 handle sides	1½×16×¾
1 spacer	1½×4×1
1 head	6×12×1
1 handlebar	¾×8 round rod

WHEELING HORSE

This is a toy that gives a toddler something to hold and push while learning to walk. The child can sit astride it and either propel himself with his feet, or someone else can push him (Fig. 6-32).

The main parts can be solid wood, thick plywood, or blockboard. Softwood can be suitable, but the head might be too

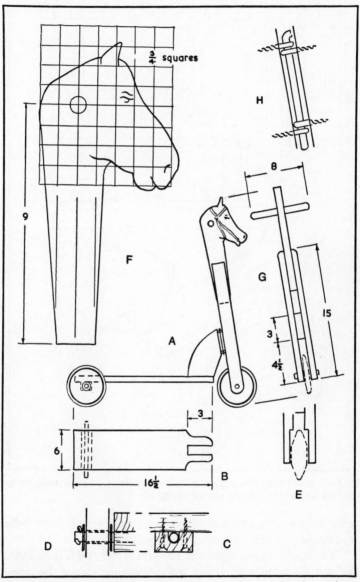

Fig. 6-31. A small three-wheeled scooter with a horse's head should appeal to a younger child.

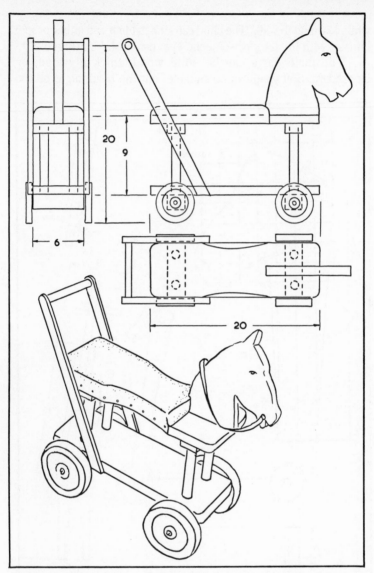

Fig. 6-32. A wheeling horse gives a toddler something to push while he is uncertain on his legs. It is big enough to ride on.

easily broken if it is common softwood. It is better in plywood, with two thicknesses glued together if necessary.

The base is a plain piece with its corners rounded (Fig. 6-33A). The seat is a similar piece, but with some hollowing at the sides (Fig. 6-33B) and a notch for the head.

142

Mark out the head with the aid of a pattern of squares (Fig. 6-34A). The piece that projects through the seat can be plain and held by screws up through the crossbar, but a dovetail arrangement is ideal (Fig. 6-34B). The head slides in from the front, and there can be one or more screws up through the seat into the overlapping part.

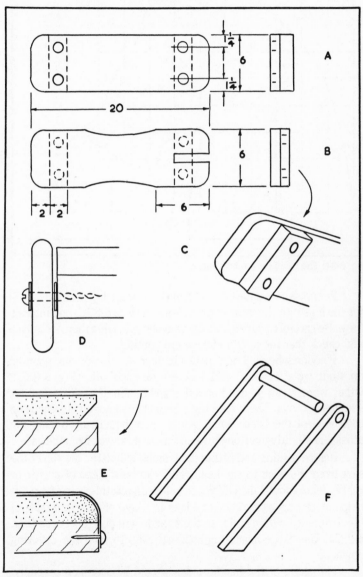

Fig. 6-33. The main parts of a riding horse.

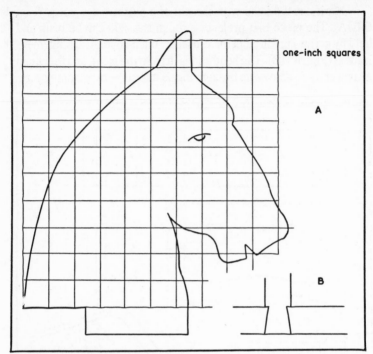

Fig. 6-34. The head for a riding horse.

Put crossbars under the seat and base at the leg positions. Drill for the legs into the thinner top crossbars (Fig. 6-33C) and into the base. Be careful to cut all legs the same length. Glue them into place and check that the seat and base are parallel.

Wooden wheels 3 or 4 inches in diameter are shown mounted on stout wood screws with washers on each side (Fig. 6-33D). Other wheels can be used on axles and mounted as described for some other toys. Make sure the wheels have enough clearance on each side of the base. Some wheels may benefit by having the crossbars slightly overlong to keep the wheels away from the base.

Before making and fitting the handle, upholster the top of the seat from the back to the head. This can be a piece of plastic or rubber foam about 1 inch thick and held with plastic-coated fabric. It helps in getting good rounded edges to shave off the underside of the foam edge with a knife, so the outside will pull to a curve (Fig. 6-33E). Use large-headed upholstery nails to hold the covering down.

The slope of the handle sides should be arranged carefully. They must be clear of the wheels at the base and cross the seat forward of the curved corners. Put a piece of round rod through holes for the handle (Fig. 6-33F).

The head should be painted and may be fitted with a harness. You can paint on the harness. A mane can be made with rope strands. A tail can be a piece of frayed rope glued into a hole, although the toy will stand up to rough use better if left without these things.

Materials List for Wheeling Horse

1 seat	6×20×1
1 base	6×20×1
2 crossbars	2×6×1
2 crossbars	1½×6×2
1 head	11×11×1
4 legs	1×9 round rod
2 handle sides	1½×24×¾
1 handle	¾×9 round rod

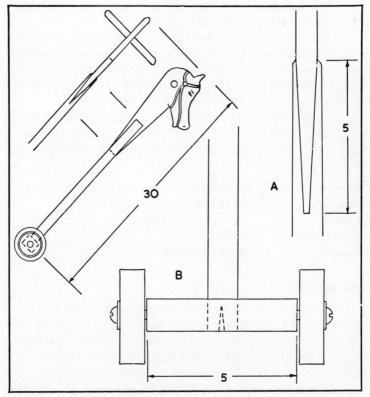

Fig. 6-35. A hobby horse is a traditional toy that still has great appeal.

145

HOBBY HORSE

Children's hobby horses go back to classical Greek days. The simplest version had something to represent a horse's head, which may have been just a bundle tied by the child. The head was attached to a stick. In many forms this merely dragged along the ground while the user walked astride it. The trailing end should run on wheels, and this example has both a shaped head and a pair of wheels (Fig. 6-35).

The head and the handle across it are the same as described for the three-wheel scooter. Mark the shape from the grid of squares (Fig. 6-31F). Cut the shape and drill for the handle. Round the edges of the head's outline. To make a strong joint, taper the part that will go into the shaft (Fig. 6-35A). Make the shaft from a piece of round rod about 1¼ inches in diameter. Alternatively, start with a square strip and plane it octagonal. Then take the sharpness off the angles. Saw the top to match the taper of the head. Make the joint with glue and a few screws driven from opposite sides. Make sure the screwheads are sunk below the surface, as they come near the places where a child's bare legs may rub.

At the other end of the shaft, glue it into a hole in the wheel block, preferably with a wedge driven into a saw cut for extra security (Fig. 6-35B). Use wood, rubber, or plastic wheels about 3 inches in diameter. Take care when assembling that the head is square with the wheel block when viewed from the end.

Much of the appeal of a hobby horse is in its appearance. The shaft and the trailing end may be any bright color, but you can use your painting skill in making the head look lifelike. You can add a mane and reins.

Materials List for the Hobby Horse

1 head	6×12×¾
1 shaft	1¼×24 round rod
1 wheel block	2×5×1
1 handle	¾×8 round rod

PUSH TRICYCLE

This tricycle can be the first wheeled riding vehicle for a toddler. He sits astride and steers, but he propels himself by pushing with his feet against the ground. There can be a single front wheel, but the design is shown (Fig. 6-36) with two close steering wheels. Sizes suit short legs. Even if the whole thing topples, the child does not fall very far (Fig. 6-37). Wheels about 4 inches in

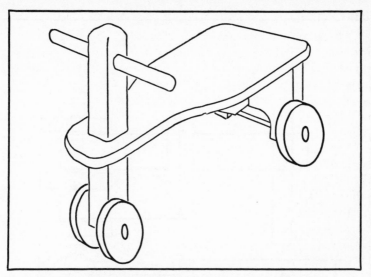

Fig. 6-36. This push tricycle is a first riding toy for the younger child.

diameter can be used, and these mount on a ¼-inch rod axle. For other sizes the dimensions may have to be altered.

Start by setting out the seat (Fig. 6-38A), as this allows you to get the sizes and positions of other parts. Notice that the front projects rather more than a semicircle to increase strength the short way of the grain. Round the outline where the child's legs may rub, then round the cross section everywhere. The pivot for steering is a piece of 1-inch dowel rod. Drill for this. A fairly close fit is advisable at this stage to allow for wear later.

The back leg (Fig. 6-38B) is the same width as the top. The easiest way to make the bottom cutout is to drill holes for the curved corners and saw into them. Mark for the axle holes on both sides and drill carefully both ways to get the holes in line. The top edge of the back leg will be screwed to the seat. Make sure it is cut squarely for a close fit. The bracket (Fig. 6-38C) is simple. It will be strongest with the grain diagonally. Round its exposed edges.

The steering assembly is made of 2-inch square wood with its corners rounded well. Drill the top part for the handle, which is a length of dowel rod with its ends rounded (Fig. 6-38D). The bottom part has a hole drilled across for the front axle (Fig. 6-38E). Between the two parts comes a piece of 1-inch dowel rod (Fig. 6-38F) and a pad which serves as a washer to reduce wear (Fig. 6-38G). Drill the upper part to fit over the dowel rod with a little to spare in the depth of the hole. Drill the part into which the rod will be glued.

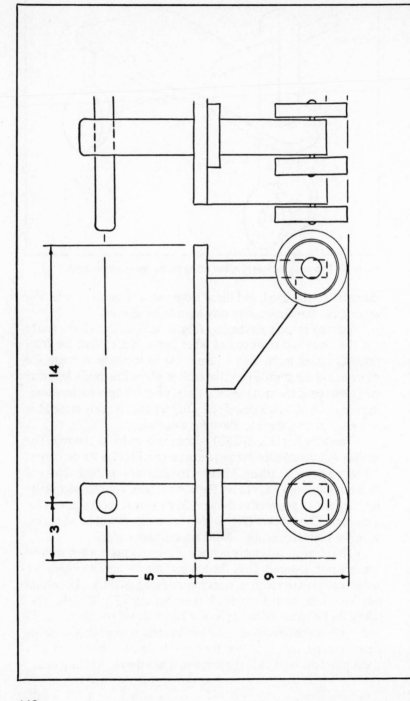

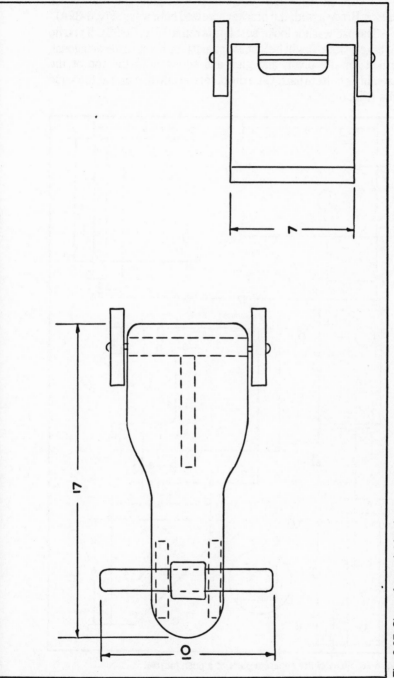

Fig. 6-37. Sizes of a push tricycle.

Attach the back leg to the seat with glue and four 2-inch screws. Brace it with the bracket screwed both ways (Fig. 6-39A).

The pad washer looks best if it is round (Fig. 6-39B). If you do not have a lathe, it will be just as satisfactory if it is made octagonal. Drill it for the pivot, and glue and screw it to the top of the assembly's bottom part. Glue the pivot rod into that part at the same time (Fig. 6-39C).

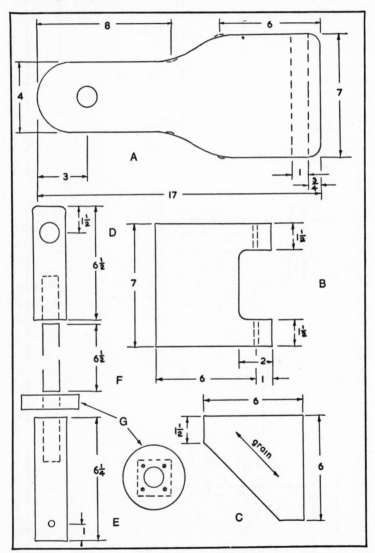

Fig. 6-38. Sizes of the separate parts of a push tricycle.

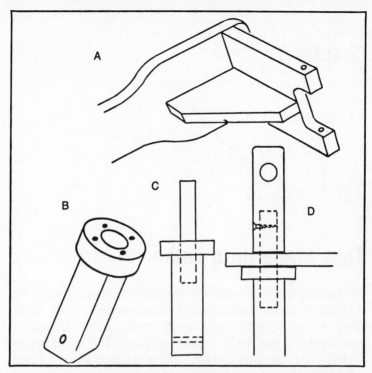

Fig. 6-39. Assembly of the back leg and steering column of a push tricycle.

Glue the handle into the top part of the assembly. Make sure the end that will be upwards is rounded and smooth, as a child's head may come against it in a fall. To put the parts together, pass the pivot rod up through the hole in the seat. Press the top part down tightly over it. Do not glue this part, but attach it with one or two screws (Fig. 6-39D). If after much use there is wear around the hole in the seat, the screws can be removed. The parts can be pressed tighter before putting screws into different positions.

Check that the axles will fit. Then paint the woodwork before adding the axles and wheels to complete construction.

Materials List for Push Tricycle

1 seat	7×17×¾
1 back leg	7×7×1
1 bracket	6×9×¾
1 pivot	1×7 round rod
1 handle	1×10 round rod
Steering assembly from	2×15×2

Chapter 7

Toys Made on a Lathe

The spinning reel that depends on the smooth coiling and uncoiling of a string is not quite such a simple turning exercise as it may seem. The narrow groove must have a smooth interior, and it is not easy to make this by turning the yo-yo from solid wood. It is better to turn the two sides separately and join them with a short piece of dowel rod (Fig. 7-1A).

YO-YO

Turning is best done on a screw center. Plane the sides of each piece that will be inwards. Cut the wood approximately round and mount it on the screw center. There is no need for the screw to enter very far, and a plywood washer can be put behind the wood if the screw is very long (Fig. 7-1B). Bring up the tailstock center to provide additional support while turning the wood round (Fig. 7-1C), but withdraw it for turning the outside to shape. Round and sand what will be the edges of the groove. Deepen the center mark by cutting in with the point of a chisel (Fig. 7-1D) to provide a good starting place for the drill later.

Remove that side and turn the other side to match. Use calipers and rule to check that parts are the same. Drill each piece squarely through the wood, preferably with a drill press. Glue in a piece of dowel rod, so the two sides are 3/16 inch to ¼ inch apart.

DIABOLO

Diabolo is a game or pastime that is at least 150 years old. It has gone through periods of revival. The diabolo is held on a thin string between two long sticks or handles. One handle is held in each hand. It can then be rolled along the string, tossed into the air, caught again, and juggled in various ways. There have been many designs, but the essential arrangement is a round section with large diameters near the ends and a small neck between them. The neck runs on the string, and the large ends have a flywheel effect to make the toy spin. The handles can be just plain sticks, but you can make turned ones.

The diabolo will often fall on the floor. It should be made of close-grained hardwood. Then it resists damage and is given weight; light softwoods are unsatisfactory.

Making a diabolo is a straightforward turning job. The only special requirement to watch is to make both halves to match in shape and weight. For the *double cone* type (Fig. 7-2A), turn the

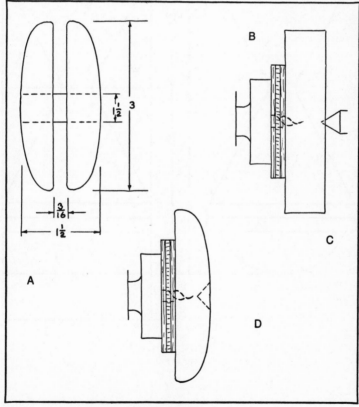

Fig. 7-1. A yo-yo is easily made on a lathe.

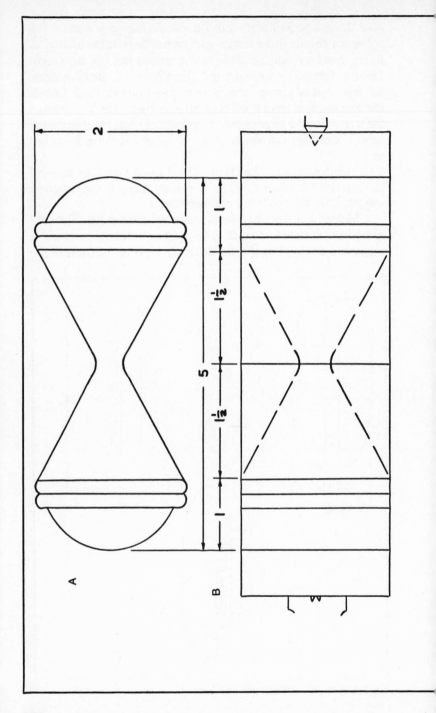

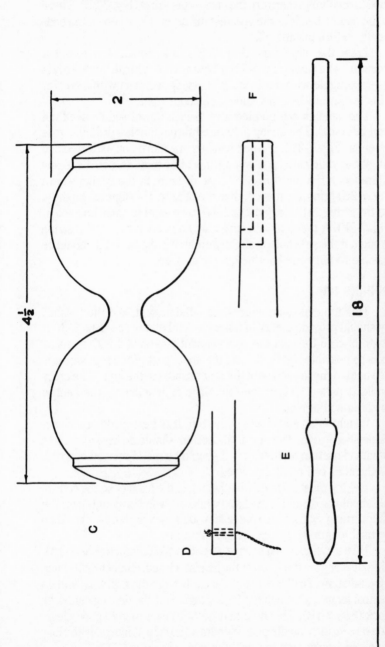

Fig. 7-2. Diabolo is a game played with a turned piece on a cord between two handles.

155

wood circular and have it overlong. Pencil the main parts while the wood is revolving, then turn the inner tapers first (Fig. 7-2B). There can be double beads at the greatest diameter. Curve down the ends equally before parting off.

Treat the other type (Fig. 7-2C) in a similar way to get it symmetrical. Diameters of either type are not critical, but the toy is easier to juggle with if it is fairly heavy. If you start with a greater diameter of 2 inches that should be about right.

The handles can be pieces of ½-inch dowel rod or need not even be round. The string is knotted through holes drilled across the ends (Fig. 7-2D). Turned handles are more sophisticated and will show your skill as a woodturner, but they do not make any difference in the performance of the diabolo. In the design shown (Fig. 7-2E) grips are shaped, then the other part is tapered slightly. For the string, drill along the end and make another small hole into it (Fig. 7-2F). A piece of thin wire may be needed to pull the string through. If the side hole is slightly greater in diameter, it should be possible to bury the knot below the surface.

SPINNING TOP

This top makes an interesting lathe project, and the finished toy should provide plenty of fun for a child of any age (Fig. 7-3). A length of cord through the cross handle is wrapped with as many turns as possible tightly around the spool part of the top, which is then held to the ground with the other handle in the hole. The cross handle is pulled to spin the top. Once it is spinning, the central handle is withdrawn.

Weight is an advantage in the top. It is best made of a close-grained hardwood. The peg at the bottom should be hard enough to withstand friction on the floor. It should be metal instead of wood. The handles can be of any wood.

The top must spin truly on the peg of the handle, so the central hole should be drilled in the lathe while the wood is mounted for the other turning. Start with a piece of wood 1 inch or more longer than the final length, so the drill can run into it.

Turn a cylinder and square its end at the tailstock (Fig. 7-4A). Without changing the wood at the headstock and, mount a drill chuck in the tailstock. Drill far enough centrally to go through what will be the final length, although not far enough to hit the driving center or chuck (Fig. 7-4B). This hole may be 5/16 inch to give good clearance on a ¼-inch handle peg. Withdraw the drill at intervals to clear chips which may clog the drill flutes.

Replace the tailstock center and turn the top to shape. The reel for the cord should be parallel. The rim above it should be curved, so it will not snag the cord (Fig. 7-4C).

Finish the top except for parting off the waste part, and thoroughly sand the wood. Painting will have to be done later, but a good hardwood looks well if it is polished with wax. That can be done in the lathe. Part off the wood to complete the top. Make a peg

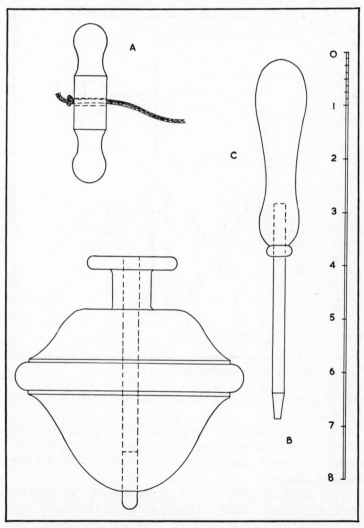

Fig. 7-3. This spinning top is started with a cord around the neck while it is held to the ground by the handle.

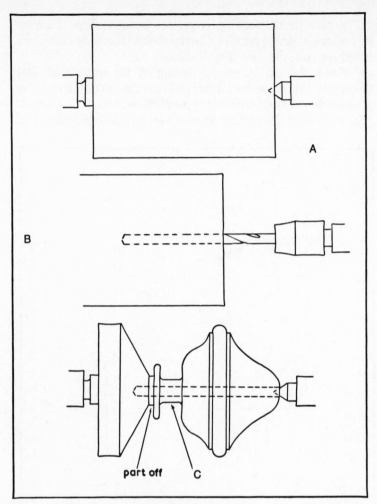

Fig. 7-4. Steps in turning a spinning top.

to go into the hole about ¾ inch and project with a rounded end. Glue it in place.

The cross handle can be just a piece of dowel rod drilled across its center, but it is shown shaped in the lathe (Fig 7-3A). The cord needs to be tough and flexible. A piece of soft synthetic braided line would be suitable.

The peg in the other handle is a piece of dowel rod. Taper its end (Fig. 7-3B), so it is easy to insert in the top. The handle (Fig. 7-3C) is made like a handle for a file or other tool. Drill it in the lathe to keep the assembly concentric, and at the end that will come close to the top turn a bead for minimum friction if the parts touch. The handle can be wax-polished in the lathe. Glue in the peg. Clean off any surplus glue around the joint before it hardens, so it cannot interfere with free turning. The top should spin successfully the first time, but it may help to rub the peg with wax.

Materials List for Spinning Top

1 top	4¾×7×4¾
1 peg	5 /16×1 round rod
1 handle	⅝×4 round rod
1 handle	1¼×5×1¼
1 peg	¼×4 round rod

CUP AND BALL

This is a toy with a long history. It was known as a *bilboquet* and was a popular amusement at the court of King Henry VIII. Many old examples have survived, and there are variations. Basically, there is a wooden ball on a cord and a cup on the end of a handle to which the cord is attached. With the handle in one hand and the ball hanging free, the toy is swung so the ball is tossed upwards. An attempt is made to catch it in the cup. Some cups were very shallow, and catching must have been difficult. The length of the cord also affects difficulty; a piece 24 inches long is about right.

In the example (Fig. 7-5A) the cup is deep and big enough to let the ball drop in easily, so a child will not be frustrated by a task that is too difficult. All of the work is done on a lathe with normal woodturning tools, except that forming the inside of the cup is most easily done with a scraping tool narrower than may be found in most tool kits. It can be made by grinding the end of a piece of steel rod about ¼ inch square to form a rounded cutting edge. There are many ways to form the handle.

Turn the ball first, as its size will control the size of the cup. Drill a hole through the ball for the cord. Counterbore its end so the knot will come below the surface (Fig. 7-5B).

Mount the wood for the main part in the lathe, so that the cup is towards the tailstock. Turn the wood cylindrical and shape all the external surfaces. There should be enough wood left to provide strength at the end of the handle, so it will not break until it is parted off as almost the last cut.

With the outside finished, cut in where the cup end will come with a parting tool or the edge of a chisel. Reduce the waste part diameter to ¾ inch or less. This gives clearance to allow a narrow gouge or scraping tool to start hollowing (Fig. 7-5C). As cutting progresses, cut into the waste part to taper it. Be careful not to go too far, so as to cause the waste to break off before you have the cut shape satisfactory (Fig. 7-5D). Remember to round the mouth of the cup before finishing the hollow. Go to the other end of the handle to reduce the thickness there.

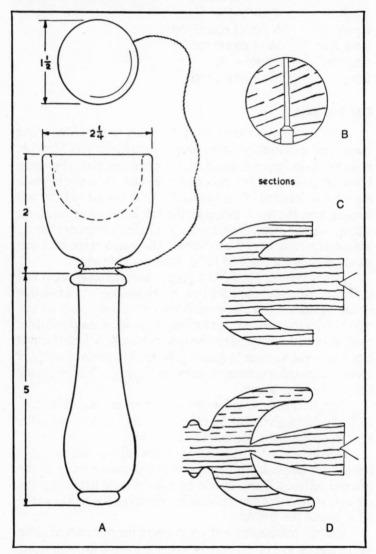

Fig. 7-5. The cup and ball make a traditional game and an interesting lathe project.

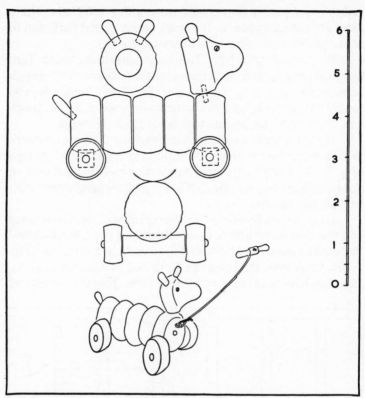

Fig. 7-6. A wobbling dog is entertaining as it is pulled along.

Continue reducing the waste part inside the cup while shaping the curve. Check the inside diameter of the cup with inside calipers to see that it will take the ball easily. Cut toward the center until the waste piece breaks off. Saw off the end of the handle from the waste at the drive end. You will probably have to clean the inside of the cup, particularly near the center, with abrasive paper wrapped around your thumb.

Start with a cord that is longer than you need. Knot it through the ball and tie it around the neck of the handle to try your skill. Knot or splice it permanently when you have discovered the length that gives the most satisfying game. This is not really a toy for painting in bright colors. If you have used attractive hardwood, it can be waxed. The wood can be sealed with a coat of varnish.

WOBBLING DOG

This pull-along toy (Fig. 7-6) will please a young child. It

161

makes an interesting project for anyone with a small lathe. Use a close-grained hardwood, so it is easy to get a good finish and to resist knocks which the toy will inevitably get.

Start by making the body. Turn all the parts in one length. Turn the wood into a parallel piece, then mark the body parts with enough between for the parting tool to enter (Fig. 7-7A). Square the end toward the tailstock, but leave some waste wood at the headstock end. Do not take the parting tool in too far at this stage.

Try to get the five parts identical by doing the same tool work to each in turn before moving on to the next stage. Round the tops (Fig. 7-7B), then slightly taper the parting tool cuts and remove sharpness from the rims (Fig. 7-7C). Clean all the parts within reach with abrasive paper.

The parts will be strung on a fiber or rubber cord. There has to be a hole through each piece to take the cord. If you have a long drill that can be mounted in a tailstock chuck, use it to drill through (Fig. 7-7D). Otherwise, the holes can be drilled as separate sections, after they have been removed from the lathe. Take the parting tool

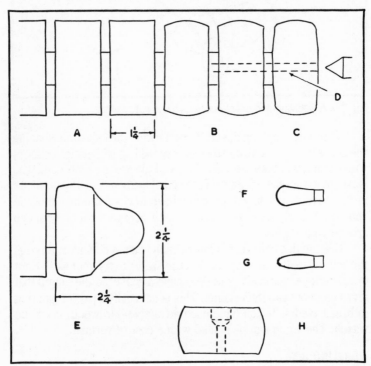

Fig. 7-7. Turn the dog parts together and make little pegs for the ears and tail.

in further at each division, but it is unwise to try to part off completely. This will result in the wood breaking and possibly becoming damaged. Instead, saw the sections apart on the bench and smooth the meeting surfaces.

The head is the same diameter as the body parts. It may have been turned on the end of the same strip of wood, but excessive length in the lathe may give trouble with bending at the parting tool cuts. Turn it on the end of a longer piece (Fig. 7-7E). Other animal heads may be turned or carved, but the toy is not intended to be very lifelike.

The head is attached to the front body section with a piece of ¼-inch dowel rod. The ears are fitted into ¼-inch holes. Drill for these parts. There is no need to be absolutely symmetrical. The head will probably look better tilted back and to one side.

Turn the ears (Fig. 7-7F) and tail (Fig. 7-7G). Glue them in place. The eyes may be round head nails, but a better type is sold for making dolls. They glue in place and will alter direction when the toy is moved. If the end sections have their holes counterbored (Fig. 7-7H), knots in the joining cord can be hidden.

Turn the wheels from one piece of wood (Fig. 7-8A) in a similar way to the body parts. They are shown with the screw holes drilled centrally. If the holes are drilled slightly off-center, the dog will wobble up and down and flex sideways as it is pulled along.

The axles are square strips. Notch the end body sections to take them (Fig. 7-8B). Use round head wood screws and washers to attach the wheels (Fig. 7-8C). Candle fat or a pencil rubbed on the screw necks, as they are inserted, will lubricate the wheels enough without being messy.

Put a screw eye in the front section for a pulling cord. There can be just a loop in the end of the cord, or it can be knotted through a piece of dowel rod. If you are using a lathe for all the other parts, a turned handle (Fig. 7-8D) is appropriate.

Paint all the parts before assembly and before adding the eyes. You can simulate mouth and nostrils with paint, but just a general brightness seems more appropriate. White with black spots looks attractive.

Materials List for Wobbling Dog

Body from	1 piece	2⅜×14×2⅜
Head from	1 piece	2⅜×4×2⅜
Wheels from	1 piece	1½×6×1½
Tail and ears from	1 piece	½×5×½
Handle from	1 piece	½×4×½

163

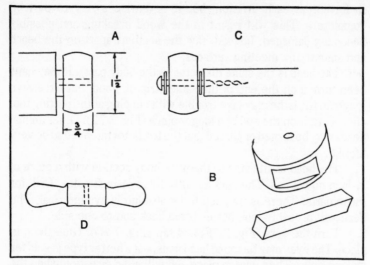

Fig. 7-8. Turn wheels and mount them on screws in crossbars notched into body parts. The handle may also be turned.

DOLL'S HIGH CHAIR

The chair (Fig. 7-9A) is shown with turned parts. It can be made with wood of square section, but turning the wood gives a lighter assembly and provides an interesting exercise for anyone with a lathe. The sizes shown allow a girl to attend to her doll while standing alongside the chair (Fig. 7-10). The flap height comes near the height of a normal table, so it is possible for the child to have the chair nearby when sitting at a table for a meal.

The seat and flap are plywood, but for strong joints in the other parts it is advisable to use a close-grained hardwood. As in the making of ordinary full-size furniture, some of the joints do not have very large glue areas. Good fits in close-grained wood ensure maximum strength.

If the sizes are altered, keep both the seat and the spread of the legs square for simplicity in construction. It is also important that the chair back and the inner edges of the arms are parallel, so the flap can swing over them from its position in front to clear the back and hang at the rear.

Make the turned parts first. Make the four legs identical (Fig. 7-11A). If there are slight variations in the curves, that may not matter. Get the overall lengths the same. The positions of the lines around the parallel parts should match, as these indicate where the rails and footrest come. Holes in the seat may be ⅝ inch, but use the chosen drill on a piece of scrap wood. Turn the tops of the legs to fit that hole.

The four lower rails (Fig. 7-11B) should have their ends turned to fit ½-inch holes. Be careful to get the beads central. A marked strip of wood to hold against the wood in the lathe when turning will help, as it can be reversed for checking.

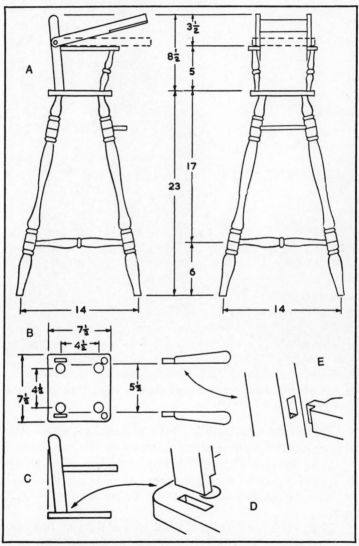

Fig. 7-9. This doll's high chair allows a girl to deal with her doll at table height. The turned parts fit into a plywood seat.

Fig. 7-10. The high chair seats a doll at a convenient height. The playpen is the one shown in Figs. 5-3 and 5-4.

The two arm supports (Fig. 7-11C) are made like the rails. The lower ends go through the seat, but the tops must be trimmed later.

Make the seat (Fig. 7-9B) from ½-inch plywood. Mark the positions of the holes for the legs on the underside, but do not drill yet. Mark the positions of the holes for the arm supports to clear them.

Make a full-size drawing of a side view of the seat, two legs, and a rail—using just their centerlines—to get the angles for drilling holes. You may get the same results by laying the parts down in the correct relationship to each other. Use an adjustable bevel set to the angles as a guide when drilling the holes. To get the spacing of the holes for the rails, wrap a piece of paper around the line where the holes come and mark its overlap. Remove it and divide the distance between the overlap marks into four. Use the adjustable bevel as a guide to the drill angle and let the holes run

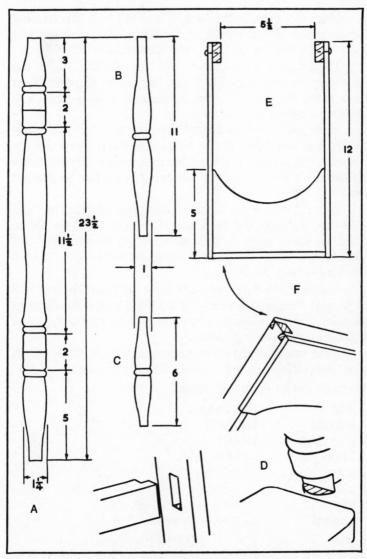

Fig. 7-11. Sizes and constructional details of high chair parts.

into each other. At the footrest level, put slots in two legs to suit the plywood thickness (Fig. 7-11D).

Drill the holes in the seat for the legs. Make a trial assembly of the parts below the seat. Cut corners off the ends of the rails, so they clear each other inside the meeting holes. Make the footrest of a length to fit into the slots in the front legs. Round its corners and edges.

Make the sides of the back (Fig. 7-9C) and the crossbar between them. At the bottoms of the sides, make tenon joints to clear the leg holes (Fig. 7-9D), with the sides 5½ inches apart.

The arms have rounded fronts and tapered backs, so they can be tenoned into the sides (Fig. 7-9E). Drill for the arm supports in the seat and the arms. Note that the supports will slope outwards slightly as well as forward.

When you are satisfied that all the parts are prepared, assemble the legs and rails with the seat and footrest. Check that the assembly is symmetrical. Stand it on a level surface and view it from all four directions, so you can make adjustments before the glue has set.

Trim the ends of the leg tops if they project through the seat. Assemble the parts that come above the seat. Make the flap to match the actual sizes. Its sides must rest on the arms. The tray must have sufficient clearance to swing over the back, pivoting on two screws (Fig. 7-11E).

Let the plywood tray in flush with the flap sides. The best joint at the front corners is a *dovetail* (Fig. 7-11F). Use round head screws as pivots. Put thin washers under the heads and in the joints, so the flap does not rub as it is moved.

Make sure all sharp edges are removed. Clean off any excess glue, then refinish all of the wood with paint or varnish.

Materials List for Doll's High Chair

4 legs	1¼×24×1¼
4 leg rails	1×12×1
2 arm struts	1×7×1
2 backs	1×9×½
2 arms	1¼×8×⅜
1 back rail	1¼×6½×⅜
1 seat	7½×7½×½ plywood
1 footrest	3×7½×⅜ plywood
1 tray	5×8×3/16 plywood
1 flap front	1×8×¼
2 flap sides	1×13×¼

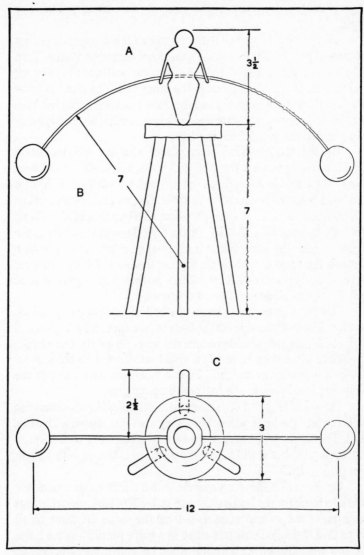

Fig. 7-12. An equilibrist or balancing man performs on his platform.

EQUILIBRIST

This is a balancing toy that was first made a long time ago in the East. It is not so much a toy to play with as one to watch. When the balancing man is given a push, he will sway from side to side and turn on his platform for a long time. A baby may be fascinated by the movement and lulled to sleep. An older child may be allowed to operate the toy, or it can serve as a moving decoration on a table or shelf.

A figure may be carved to have a more lifelike appearance, but as shown (Fig. 7-12A) it is in the usual form turned on a lathe. Turn it between centers (Fig. 7-13A). Allow some waste at the tailstock end as well as the usual piece at the other end. The foot has to be finished smooth and rounded and should not include a hole left from the tailstock center. Do some hand sanding there, if necessary, after you remove the wood from the lathe.

The balancing arm is a piece of stiff wire that will not buckle after it has been shaped. It can be hard brass, mild steel, or stainless steel. Thickness is not critical, but somewhere between 1/16-inch and ⅛-inch diameter should be suitable. Draw a curve with a radius of 7 inches on a piece of scrap plywood. Use that as a guide to bend the wire by hand (Fig. 7-12B). Drill a hole through the waist of the figure to take the wire. Some traditional examples have the wire through the arms only, held forward of the body. Other examples have the arms pivoted at the shoulders, so their angle can be altered and the figure allowed different postures.

Make the arms from pieces of wood about ½-inch by ⅛-inch section. Plane off the sides of the body to take them (Fig. 7-13B) and make their lengths suitable to take the wire. Shape the arms to the shoulders after they have been glued on. Turn two balls about 1¼-inch diameter as weights. Fit the balancing wire through the body and into holes in the balls with epoxy glue.

The stand (Fig. 7-12C) should be high enough for the balancing balls to clear the table when they swing low. It is shown with three legs. The figure will swing and rotate on a plain top with surprisingly few falls, but it will help if the platform is turned with a slight rim (Fig. 7-13C).

On the underside, draw a circle with a 1-inch radius and divide this into three for the leg positions (Fig. 7-13D). How much the legs flare out is not so important as getting the slope the same on all three (Fig. 7-13E). Draw this angle as a guide for drilling the holes for the legs. Either pack up the wood on a drill press or use an adjustable bevel as a guide for freehand drilling. Legs could be turned, but ⅜-inch dowel rods are suitable.

Circus performers and babies like bright colors. Paint the head with some semblance of hair and features if you wish, then use bright paint for other parts of the toy. The bottom of the man and the top surface of the platform may be better left plain or polished to reduce friction and allow the toy to keep moving as long as possible.

170

Materials List for Equilibrist

1 body	1½×5×1½
2 arms	½×3×⅛
1 platform	3×3×½
3 legs	⅜×8 round rod
2 balls from	1¼×5×1¼

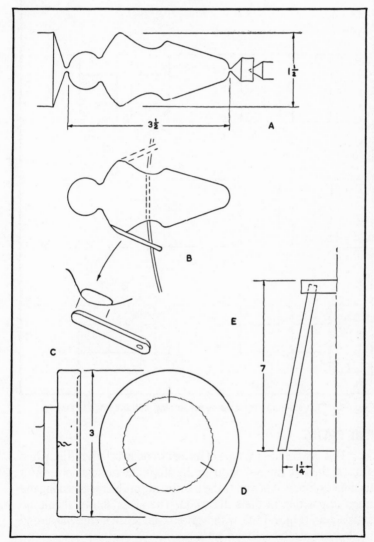

Fig. 7-13. Turn the balancing man between lathe centers, attach his arms, and put the wire through his body. Make the platform like a small tool.

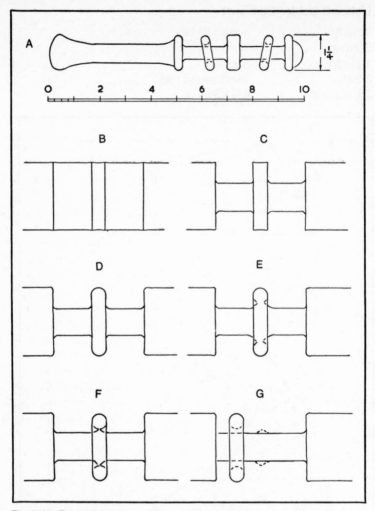

Fig. 7-14. This old-time ring rattle needs turning with the rings in stages.

RING RATTLE

This is a traditional type of turned wooden baby's rattle. When shaken, the two rings slide to hit the stops and make a noise. As a turning exercise, it presents the interesting problem of forming the rings in position in the solid wood. The sizes shown should be satisfactory (Fig. 7-14A), with a grip to suit small hands and an end too big to push far into a mouth.

Both for convenience in turning and for strength, the wood chosen should be hard and close-grained. The rings will be weak in other woods. They either will not stand up to turning or will break in use.

The general outline is a straightforward turning job, with the wood mounted between the lathe centers. Turn it cylindrical. Deal with the rings before doing much to other parts, although they can be roughed to shape. If you finish all the other parts and then make a mistake with your first attempt at turning the rings, you will have wasted that much effort.

Pencil lines around each section with a ring (Fig. 7-14B). Turn down to near the final size of the necks on which the rings will slide (Fig. 7-14C). Leave the lower corners lightly rounded. Be careful not to take anything off the top of the ring. Round the ends of the cutaway and the top of the ring (Fig. 7-14D). With the point of a narrow chisel, start cutting the inside of the ring (Fig. 7-14E).

Concentrate on the ring section. Be careful not to cut into the neck, but otherwise the waste wood left there does not matter at this stage. Cut in a little at each side until your cuts meet, and the ring is separated from the neck (Fig. 7-14F). If you have been careful with tool work, there should be no need for sanding the ring. If you think sanding is necessary, do this just before cutting right through. With the ring to one side, turn the center of the neck level (Fig. 7-14G).

Turn the other parts of the rattle to shape after cutting both rings. Be careful that the loose rings do not catch in a tool and become damaged. A ring can be held to one end of its space with adhesive tape, out of the way while the other end is finished, and then moved for work on the second end.

If a suitable clean wood is chosen, there will probably be no need for paint or varnish. One way of safely sealing the grain is to rub it with a vegetable oil, such as salad oil, to finish with a slight sheen.

Chapter 8

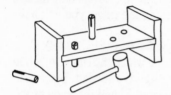

Games and Puzzles

This is an educational toy for the youngest child who is just learning to use his hands. The pegs are driven through holes with a mallet, but they touch the floor before falling out. The toy can be turned over for them to be driven back. Saw cuts across the pegs provide slight springiness to help enter the pegs in the holes and pull them out.

HAMMER AND PEG GAME

Sizes need to be large enough to give stability, yet not so big as to be heavy for the child to handle. Those shown (Fig. 8-1) should be satisfactory.

The main frame (Fig. 8-1A) has square ends. The part with holes can be simply nailed between the ends, but in use hammering might loosen the grip of the nails. It is better to cut shallow trenches across the ends (Fig. 8-1B), so the parts are joined with glue and screws from outside.

The pegs are four pieces of dowel rod, or they can be turned on a lathe (Fig. 8-1C). Saw across the ends at right angles to each other and let the saw cuts come within about ¼ inch of each other at the center. Round the ends slightly. The hole size should be such that a peg will drive in without too much effort, yet not be so large that the peg slips through. Pegs may have to be sanded to get the fit right. Allow for paint thickening the pegs slightly.

The mallet (Fig. 8-1D) is made from a piece of ½-inch dowel rod as a handle, glued into a hole in a thicker cylindrical piece for a head. If the hole has to be made without the aid of a drill press, get an assistant to sight the direction of the drill, so it goes in squarely.

Round off corners, but not excessively, as the main frame must stand level. Round the end of the mallet handle. If a bought rubber or plastic mallet or hammer is used, its face will be about twice the diameter of the pegs or, if smaller, a child may have difficulty in hitting accurately. The toy can be expected to get some hard use, so there is little point in giving it a high gloss finish. Bright colors will make it more appealing.

Materials List for Hammer and Peg Game

2 ends	4×4×5⁄8
1 center	4×10×5⁄8
4 pegs	5⁄8×2½ round rod
1 mallet head	1¼×2½ round rod
1 mallet handle	½×6 round rod

SWINGING HAMMER AND PEG GAME

This is a variation on the previous game. The user drives pegs through holes with a mallet, but instead of turning the whole thing over to drive them back, the parts with holes in can be swung to the opposite side. The assembly also makes a box in which the pegs and mallet can be stored. These pegs are the same as for the earlier game, except that the mallet should be of a size that will go in the box. Keep the pegs short, so the lower ones do not hit the bottom of the box before their tops are driven level with the board.

Mark out a pair of sides and from them get the size and angles of the end pieces (Fig. 8-1A). Drill for the pivots. These can be screws, but pieces of ¼-inch dowel rods are shown (Fig. 8-2B). Assemble these parts with a plywood bottom (Fig. 8-2C).

Make the flap long enough to be flipped over easily and narrow enough to fit easily between the sides (Fig. 8-2D). Drill the holes and round the ends before mounting between the sides. After a trial assembly with overlong rods or temporary screws, remove the flap for painting the toy. Glue the pegs into the flap holes.

Materials List for Swinging Hammer and Peg Game

2 sides	3×12×5⁄8
2 ends	1×4×5⁄8
1 flap	4×6×5⁄8
1 bottom	5×12×5⁄8
5 pegs	5⁄8×2½ round rod
1 mallet head	1¼×2½ round rod
1 mallet handle	½×6 round rod

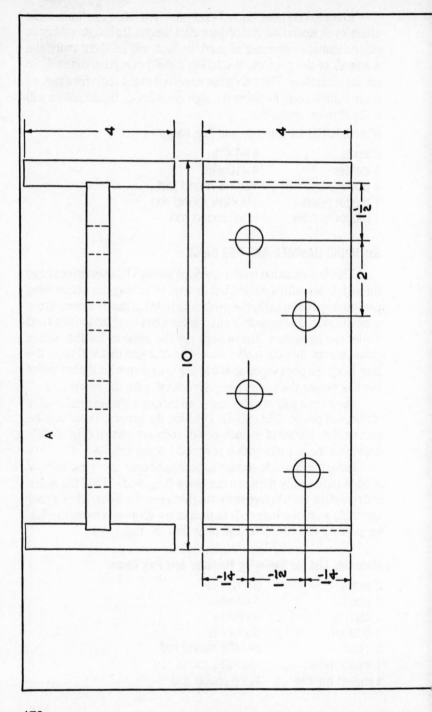

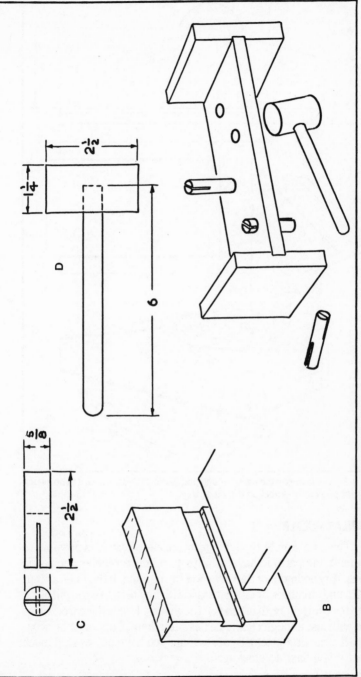

Fig. 8-1. A hammer and peg game lets a child wield a hammer harmlessly and trains him or her in control.

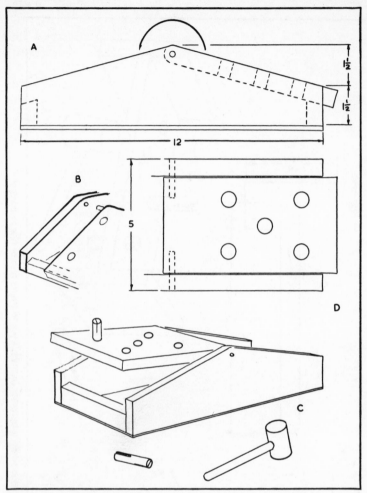

Fig. 8-2. A variation on the hammer and peg game allows the board to be swung over for pegs to be knocked the other way.

ANGULAR PUZZLE

This is a simple type of jigsaw puzzle where it is possible to assemble the parts in several ways to produce regular geometric forms. Any oddment of thin plywood can be used. If the lines are cut with a fine circular saw or a backsaw with fine teeth, there will be no need to do any more than sand off roughness. Leave the parts still to size with just enough clearance between them. Cuts must be accurate. If your first attempt goes wrong, you have not wasted much effort if you have to start again.

Mark out the standard shape (Fig. 8-3A) including the internal lines. The shapes are numbered for identification in showing the other assemblies, but putting the parts together becomes more puzzling if there are no numbers.

As can be seen (Fig. 8-3B), at least five geometric shapes are possible. Check that your parts will assemble properly. Sand off numbers if you have used them. For younger users the outlines of possible shapes, but not the internal lines, can be drawn on a piece of plywood as guides to layout.

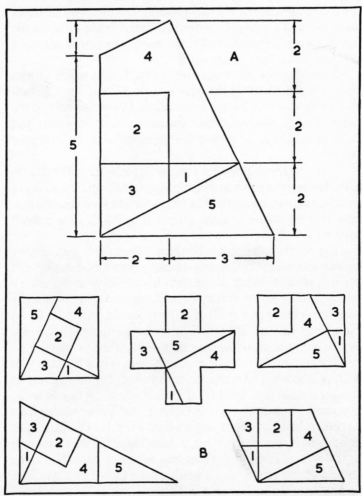

Fig. 8-3. This angular puzzle can be made from a scrap of plywood and assembled into several shapes.

CLOCK PUZZLE

A clock face is a mystery to a young child, and he wants to learn what it is all about. What better way of teaching him than with the aid of a puzzle? For a child who still has to learn numbers and the arrangement of a clock dial, the toy should not be too small. This one is shown 12 inches across, but it can be made any size to suit available materials.

The toy consists of a shallow tray into which segments can be fitted to make up a clock dial. A central disc carries the hands, and they can be moved around to any position. The disc with the hands can be loose. It is probably better to attach it to the center of the tray. Locating the positions for the numbered pieces will be a sufficient puzzle for a young mind.

Set out the size you want on paper first. Draw a square with its border. At the center of the square draw a circle; for a 12-inch square that can be 3 inches in diameter. Draw diagonals to the square. That divides the shape into four, and each one-fourth part (90 degrees) has to be divided into three to mark the 30-degree divisions.

Make the tray with a piece of plywood as the base. The rim can be another piece of plywood with the shape cut out, but it is easier to get an accurate shape if strips of about ¾-inch by ¼-inch section are mitered at the corner to make a frame (Fig. 8-4A). Glue and nail them in place.

The puzzle parts should be thicker than the frame, so they stand up and are easily gripped—½-inch plywood is suitable. With care it is possible to cut all the parts from a single sheet, using a fretsaw or a fine jigsaw. Otherwise, each part can be cut separately, using the drawing as a guide. The parts should be a loose fit, so young hands have no difficulty in lifting and moving the segments. Get the edges straight and smooth. Round all angles slightly.

The central piece can be round, although it may be made with 12 straight sides. The hands can be plywood, but they should be stronger if made from solid wood. Decide where the figures are to be painted. Use a compass to get them all the same distance from the center. Make one hand long enough to overlap the figures and the other so it does not quite reach them. Shape the points and drill for the screw before finally rounding the inner ends. Use three washers on the screw, so the hands can be turned easily without them rubbing the surface (Fig. 8-4B).

Attach the central disc to the base and make a trial assembly. Ease off any sharp or awkward parts, so there is no difficulty in using

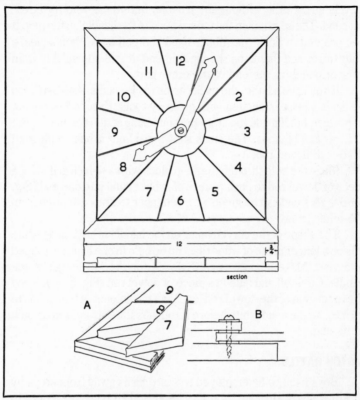

Fig. 8-4. This clock puzzle serves as a beginner's jigsaw puzzle and can be used for teaching children how to tell time.

them. Allow for the extra thickness that paint will cause, so they will still fit without trouble after painting.

Paint the tray and the disc in one color. Have all the segments another color and paint the hands to contrast with the other colors. The numbers can be painted on by hand, or it is possible to get decals to make a neat job. It is advisable to varnish over them, so they do not get scratched and removed by the hands.

POP-IN TRICK

This is a simple trick that a youngster can use to mystify his friends. The two parts consist of a hollowed block and a peg to fit in the hole (Fig. 8-5A). The hollowed part has a piece of rubber band held in its end with a peg. The object is to push the peg into the hole and hook on the rubber band. When it is pulled and released, it springs back and the two parts hit. The owner is apparently able to

181

do this every time without any trouble, but others who try never succeed. The secret is in the tapered end of the handle on the peg. If you pretend to hook the rubber band and pull back, then squeeze your finger and thumb on the tapered end, it will slip quickly from your grip and hit the end of the other part.

If you have a lathe, the trick can be made round. Both parts can be made square in section with ordinary tools. Exact sizes are not important, but if made too large the squeezing action becomes more difficult and obvious. The sizes shown are built around a piece of 3/16-inch dowel rod.

Make the hole through the main block with a ¼-inch drill. Use a piece of dowel rod to push a piece of rubber band into one end (Fig. 8-5B). That end can be given a curved taper to draw attention from the other taper.

The shape of the curved taper on the handle is best made while it is on a longer piece of wood that can be held in one hand or gripped in a vise. Make smooth curved slopes for the full length of the handle. Cut it off and glue in a piece of dowel rod (Fig. 8-5C). Keep the extension of the dowel rod less than the amount of hole it has to go into, so the handle hits before it touches the bottom. Cut a notch in its end.

MATCH RATTLE

Boys used to be employed to scare birds away from crops by making noises. Besides shouting, they used all types of devices to create noise. One of the most effective was a rattle made in the way described here. It is certainly not a baby's rattle. The rattle is more suitable for an older boy who wants to cheer on his team to victory.

The rattle is held by its handle in one or two hands, then twirled around so the body spins on its axle. While this is happening,

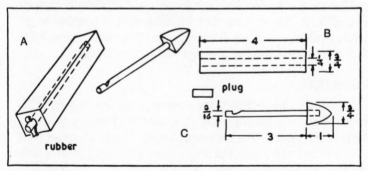

Fig. 8-5. The puzzle is a teaser until you know how to solve it.

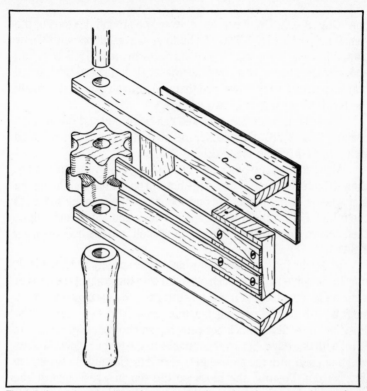

Fig. 8-6. A match rattle will produce a penetrating noise when swung vigorously.

the two tongues are lifted by the star wheels, so they spring back frequently against the sounding block and make a continuous loud chattering noise. To be effective, the body should be fairly long, so centrifugal force allows it to rotate quickly with little effort. Scaling down much from the sizes given is not recommended.

The exploded view (Fig. 8-6) shows the parts in relation to each other, but the two views (Figs. 8-7 and 8-8) give the sizes. Plywood can be used for many parts, or the whole thing can be made of hardwood.

Cut the pieces for the top and bottom (Fig. 8-7A). Mark the positions on the tongue block and the striking block on them, but there may have to be some final adjustments to get the tongues against the star wheels correctly.

The star wheels are probably most easily made as one piece, then cut apart after shaping. The materials list allows for this, but they can be cut independently. Set out the shape by drawing a circle. Divide it into six by stepping off the radius around the circumference (Fig. 8-9A). Draw curves midway and around the tops of the remaining parts (Fig. 8-9B). The hollows can be cut out with V saw cuts, followed by a gouge or a round Surform tool (Fig. 8-9C). File and sand the section to a smooth surface. Drill this and the top and bottom pieces for the dowel rod that will form an axle. Cut through the block to separate the two wheels.

If a lathe is available, a handle can be turned and given some shaping (Fig. 8-7B). Otherwise, the pivot dowel rod can be glued into a thicker handle piece (Fig. 8-7C).

Make the tongue block and the striking block. Be sure to get their heights the same. Thread the bottom on the handle. Put on the star wheels, with the teeth of one coming in line with the spaces of the other. Locate them with gaps between and above and below, then secure them with glue and screw sunk into the hollows (Fig. 8-8A).

Make the two tongues. They have to be springy and flexible. It may be possible to use ⅛-inch plywood with the grain of the outside veneers lengthwise, but it will be better to use a springy hardwood, such as ash or hickory, planed thin enough to flex sufficiently. Position the striking block between top and bottom. Note that it is level with one edge. Screw the tongues to the tongue block, so they will be in line with the star wheels. Try this assembly between top and bottom. Position the block so the tongues rest against the striking block and into hollows of the star wheels when at rest (Fig.

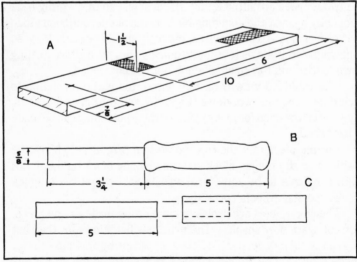

Fig. 8-7. Sizes of the main parts of a match rattle.

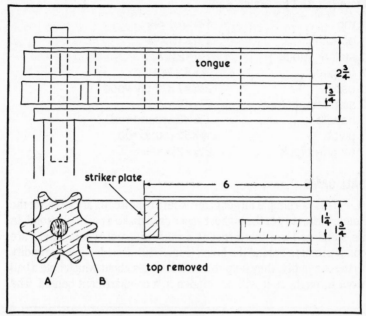

Fig. 8-8. Assembly details of a match rattle.

8-8B). Round the ends of the tongues slightly, if necessary, but they will soon wear rounded in use.

Screw the tongue block between the top and bottom pieces and try twirling the rattle. You may get a better note by moving the tongue block in or out, but whatever the position, the tongues must hit the striking block as they spring back, without becoming caught in the star wheels.

When you are satisfied that you have obtained the best performance from the rattle, loosen the screws so you can apply glue. Tighten them again. To further stiffen the rattle, nail and glue on a back piece of plywood to the top and bottom and the striking block. This will also intensify the sound, as the plywood acts as a sounding board.

As viewed from above, this rattle has to turn counterclockwise. Most users can twirl it either way, but if there is a preference for twirling the other way, assemble the parts upsidedown. The handle then comes on the other end of the pivot dowel rod, and the tongues set up their satisfying noise when the rattle is going the other way around.

You can paint all the parts. It is best, though, to leave the star wheels and the working parts of the tongues plain.

Materials List for Match Rattle

1 top	1¾×10×⅜
1 bottom	1¾×10×⅜
1 striking block	1¼×2½×½
2 tongues	¾×8×⅛
1 back	2¾×7×⅛ plywood
2 star wheels from	2¾×2×2¾
1 handle	1¾×5×round rod
1 pivot	⅝×5×round rod
1 tongue block	2½×2½×⅝

BALL GAME

This is a simple target game where rolled balls are aimed at the holes, either to get the highest score or to make a particular total. In its simplest form the target is a thick piece of wood. There are compartments behind the holes (Fig. 8-10). Besides giving rigidity to the assembly, they help to avoid disputes about which hole a ball went through, as it will be trapped in a compartment behind. The

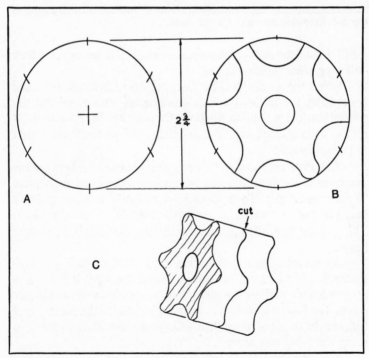

Fig. 8-9. This is how to set out the operative part of a match rattle.

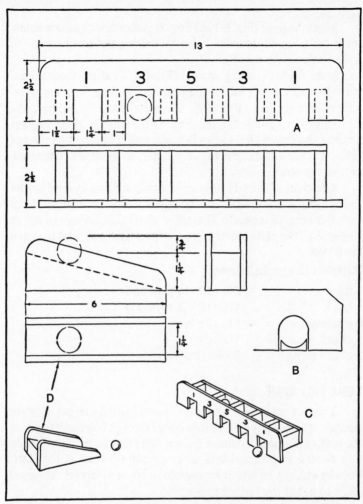

Fig. 8-10. A ball game can be played on a table or floor using parts that are easy to assemble.

balls can be rolled by hand, but a chute is shown that is more appropriate with small balls. It can be moved about a set distance, and there is some skill in sighting it to get a ball on the right course.

The sizes given are intended to suit balls of ¾-inch diameter, with a moderate clearance through the holes. The game is played with three or five balls. Get them before starting construction and modify sizes to suit. Obviously, more clearance makes the game easier. This may be advisable for young children, so they are not discouraged by rarely scoring anything.

Make the front (Fig. 8-10A) first. It is shown with square holes, but it can be given rounded holes by drilling and sawing into the drilled holes (Fig. 8-10B).

Make the back and the spacers (Fig. 8-10C) all the same height. Mark the back and front for the spacers, so they fit in squarely. Assemble with nails. Round all the parts that will be upwards. Finish by painting and put numbers over the holes, with the highest score at the center. If a target is made with a different number of holes, it is advisable to cut an odd number, so there is a central one for the top score.

The chute (Fig. 8-10D) is most easily cut and tapered on the end of a longer piece, which can be gripped in a vise or with a clamp over the edge of a bench. The sides stand high enough to act as guides. Nail the parts together, round the edges, and paint to match the target.

Materials List for Ball Game

1 front	2½×13×¼ plywood
1 back	1¼×12×¼ plywood
6 spacers	1¼×2×½
1 chute	1¼×6×1¼
2 chute sizes	2×6×¼ plywood

TABLE BALL GAME

This is a game where balls are rolled toward a target of seven numbered holes. Any balls that do not go through holes will run over the back of the table, so these and any balls that go through drop on to a sloping surface and back to be picked up again at the start. Besides straight rolling, it is possible to bounce balls off the raised sides to get at the further holes.

The board is intended to be used with balls about ¾ inch in diameter (Fig. 8-11). It can be made larger to suit bigger balls, or it can be made much smaller for use with ball bearings or similar smaller balls. It can be lengthened to increase difficulty, but as shown it should satisfy young users and not be too big for storing.

Construction is with ½-inch plywood and ¾-inch square strips for stiffening joints. Mark out one side (Fig. 8-12A) and use this as a guide for making the other parts. Make sure there is enough clearance for the size of balls to be used.

The playing surface has a pattern of 1¼-inch holes (Fig. 8-12B) laid out by drawing a circle and stepping off the radius around the circumference. Frame around the underside with strips glued and nailed on (Fig. 8-12C). Make the back and front pieces (Fig. 8-12D). Get their lengths from the width of the playing surface.

Assemble the back and the playing surface between the sides. From this assembly get the size of the sloping surface. Supporting pieces under it need not go right down to feather edges (Fig. 8-12E). Fit this and the front parts between the sides to complete the game. Round all exposed edges. Paint the parts that are accessible. If you wish to paint the underside of the playing surface or the top of the sloping surface, that will have to be done before final assembly. Be

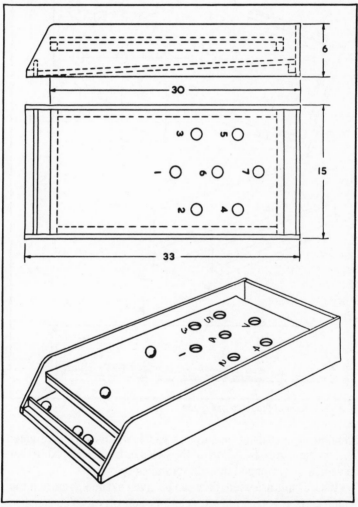

Fig. 8-11. In this ball game the balls that drop through holes return to the start.

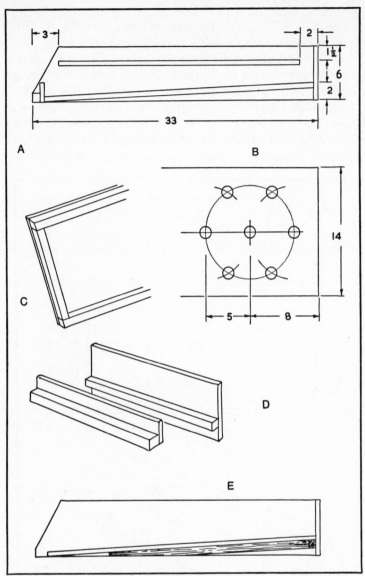

Fig. 8-12. Details of the table ball game.

careful not to get paint on surfaces which will have to take glue. Paint on the numbers in front of the holes or use decals. Note that the scores are arranged in order of difficulty.

If hard balls are used, they can be given a quieter return if the sloping surface is covered with cloth or soft plastic. You can also line the sides with plastic to give an effect something like that of a billiard table's cushion.

Materials List for Table Ball Game

2 sides	6×33×½ plywood
1 playing surface	14×28×½ plywood
1 sloping surface	14×32×½ plywood
1 back	6×14×½ plywood
1 front	2×14×½ plywood
4 stiffeners	¾×27×¾
4 stiffeners	¾×14×¾

SLIDING BLOCK

This is a toy or trick that a young child can control and use to mystify his friends. A block or ball is threaded on a cord with handles at the ends. When the block is held vertically and allowed to slide under its own weight, it will slip down or stop as commanded, either by the operator or his audience. The secret is the tension of the cord. When the cord is stretched taut, the ball will stop. When it is relaxed, but not enough to be obvious, the block will slide.

The block is a piece of wood in the form of a cube with its corners removed to show octagonal faces (Fig. 8-13). Alternatively, a ball can be turned on a lathe. It is not easy to make a perfect sphere, and the block looks better than an irregular ball. There is an advantage in weight, so a piece of fairly dense wood should be used.

The exact angle used for the hole is not critical, but it may be advisable to do the drilling first before shaping. Test the action in case the first attempt is not to your satisfaction. The drill should be of a size that will allow the cord to pass easily. Mark the centers of opposite sides and drill squarely in for about ⅛ inch. These dents are to give the drill a true start when it enters diagonally. If a drill press is used, tilt the block on packing (Fig. 8-13A) and set the stop to give the correct depth. If drilling is done freehand, it helps to mark the depth with a piece of adhesive tape around the drill. Use a piece of thin wire attached to the string to pull it through. If you do not get a desired result with the first hole, you will not have wasted much wood or effort if you have to start again.

To shape the cube neatly, mark diagonals on one face. Measure half a diagonal and use this from each corner in all directions along the edges (Fig. 8-13B). Join these marks to get regular octagonal outlines. Remove the corners by careful chiseling, then sand the block to remove any roughness and sharpness.

The handles are simple strips of wood (Fig. 8-13C) with holes for the cord. Round their edges and ends. The length of cord depends on the user. It can be of a length to hold between the outstretched hands or it may be longer, so the bottom handle is held to the floor by a foot. The top handle is held high by one hand to give a long fall and more scope for stopping and starting.

Materials List for Sliding Block

1 block	2×2×2
2 handles	¾×5×⅜

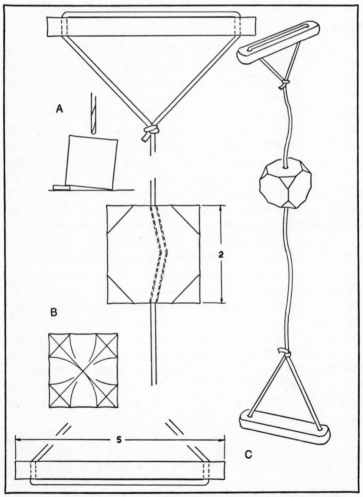

Fig. 8-13. The sliding block can be made to slide or drop as commanded.

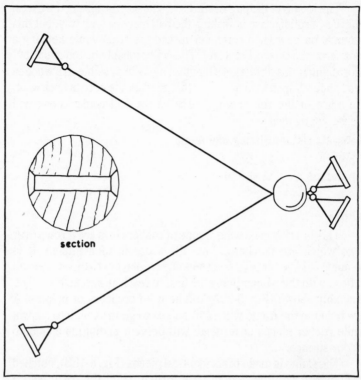

Fig. 8-14. Two players make the ball slide from side to side by spreading and closing their arms.

SLIDING BALL GAME

In this toy two cords pass through a hole in a ball (Fig. 8-14). The ends of the cords are held by two players. With the ball near one end, the player at the other end brings his hands and the cord ends together at the same time as the other player keeps the cords tensioned and spreads his arms quickly. The effect is to cause the ball to shoot along the cords to the other end. The action is reversed, and the players can keep the ball traveling backward and forward quickly.

Construction is very similar to the sliding block trick. The ball maybe a sphere, or it can be a square block with octagonal faces, either about 2 inches across. Drill a hole through the center large enough to pass a double thickness of cord easily. Countersink the ends of the hole fairly deeply and sand inside the hole to remove any roughness. The four handles are the same as for the sliding block trick.

The length of the pair of cords depends on the size of the users. There is a satisfaction in making the ball travel a long way, but this depends on how far a child can spread his arms while keeping a tension on the cords. Try 8 feet. This will probably be too much, but shortening is possible where lengthening is impossible. If a wooden bead about ¾ inch in diameter is threaded on the cord at each knot, the noise of the resounding smack as the ball comes along will please young users.

Materials List for Sliding Ball Game

| 1 ball | 2×2×2 |
| 4 handles | ¾×5×⅜ |

QUOITS

This is a ring game where rope or rubber rings are thrown over pegs which are numbered, and the score is then totaled. It is common to have three or five rings and for players to throw them all in turn, with the winner being the first to reach an agreed total. The assembly shown (Fig. 8-15A) can be used outdoors or indoors. A few holes in the frame will allow spikes to go through into a lawn, while rubber pieces underneath will prevent sliding on a smooth indoor surface.

The frame is made of six identical pieces (Fig. 8-15B), notched to fit into each other, so surfaces match. Glue the parts before drilling at the center of each joint for the pegs. If a lathe is available, the pegs can be shaped and shouldered to fit the holes (Fig. 8-15C). Otherwise, use pieces of ¾-inch dowel rod. Whichever pegs are used, it helps to saw the ends and glue in wedges during assembly (Fig. 8-15D).

In use the frame is placed with one corner toward the thrower, so the easiest peg to ring will be the front one. That should be the lowest score. Paint on numbers or use decals to indicate the values of each peg (Fig. 8-15E).

The rings can be rubber or plastic. In the traditional form of this game they were made from rope, which has less tendency to bounce off. Use rope about ¾ inch in diameter. It can be old discarded rope which is not used for anything else. As each quoit is made from one strand, a length of three-stranded rope will make three quoits. Start with an unlaid strand about 10 times the intended diameter (about 5 inches for the size game described here). Do not disturb the kinks, but start to wrap around in these kinks (Fig. 8-15F) until you have made a total of these circuits to produce an endless rope

(Fig. 8-15G). Cut of any surplus and bind over the joint with several turns of thread or thin string.

Materials List for Quoits

6 frame strips	2×24×1
9 pegs	¾×6 round rod

TABLE SKITTLES

This is a game in which nine skittles standing on a platform have to be hit by a ball swinging on a cord from the top of a post (Figs. 8-16 and 8-17). The ball is swung around the outside of the post, so it hits the skittles on the return. The skill comes in judging the path of the swinging ball. Each player normally has three tries, and the skittles are not stood up again until a player has swung three times. If a player knocks all of them over with one and/or two swings, they may be stood up again for the second and/or third tries. The maximum score possible, although extremely unlikely, is 27 with three swings. Most players will not knock over all nine skittles with three swings.

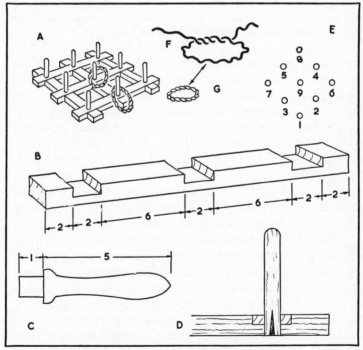

Fig. 8-15. Rope quoits are used for an outdoor ring game.

195

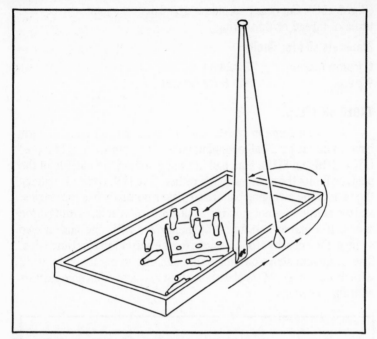

Fig. 8-16. Table skittles are exciting for the whole family.

Many sizes are possible, but those shown (Fig. 8-18) will suit adults playing with children. The skittles or ninepins may be turned on a lathe. If the skittles are bought, the measurements of the game may have to be adapted if they are of a very different size.

The tray is a simple box with a plywood bottom glued and nailed on. Simple screwed lapped joints will be satisfactory (Fig. 8-19A), although you can use dovetails (Fig. 8-19B). The diamond-shaped platform is just a square box with the plywood bottom upwards (Fig. 8-19C). This is another place where you can use simple laps or dovetails at the corners. Fit the diamond centrally with screws or nails up through the bottom of the tray.

There is some advantage in getting a satisfactory swing if the post is long, but that shown is about the same as the diagonal of the tray, making it convenient for storing. At the bottom of the post, cut it to half lap over the side of the tray and allow for two 3/16-inch screws (Fig. 8-19D) with washers and butterfly nuts. A good fit at this joint is necessary to prevent the post from wobbling.

Taper the post to square at the top and round the upper parts (Fig. 8-19E). The pivot on which the ball and cord swings must turn smoothly. In the type shown (Fig. 8-20A), a turned wood disc has a groove around it to take the cord and a piece of metal tube set into it and to revolve on a wood screw and washers. If a disc cannot be turned, something similar with eight sides will do. An even better pivot can be made with a small ball race set into the disc and fitted over the screw.

The ball must be heavy, so it should be made of hardwood. Most rubber balls are unlikely to have enough weight. The wood

Fig. 8-17. Table skittles will provide fun for any age.

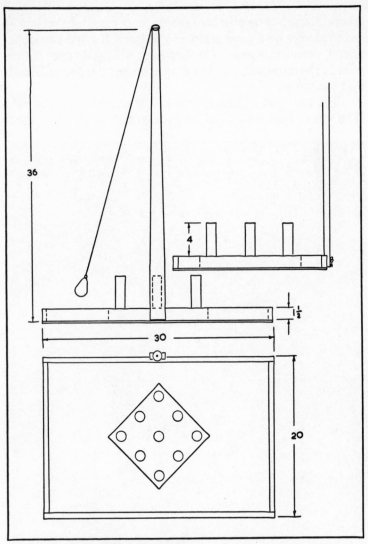

Fig. 8-18. Sizes of a table skittle game.

ball can be about 2 inches in diameter and drilled for the cord to go through it (Fig. 8-20B). If you turn the ball, make it pear-shaped with a screw eye for the cord (Fig. 8-20C).

If you turn skittles, make them double-ended. Hollow the ends so they will stand firm (Fig. 8-20D). Bought skittles may be single-ended, and you can turn them that shape if you prefer the design (Fig. 8-20E).

Use braided cord about ⅛ inch in diameter. Experiment with its length before finally securing it. When swung, the ball must be able to knock down any of the skittles. It should be able to do this if you get the cord length so that the center of the ball comes near the center of the middle skittle, when you hold the cord taut.

The ball and the falling skittles tend to mar each other and the rest of the game, so any finish should be tough. Gloss paint will soon damage. The skittles and ball can be waxed or oiled. The rest of the game is finished with matte paint and allowed to soak in.

Paint circles of the size of the skittle's ends on the diamond-shaped platform. They are always replaced in the same positions.

Materials List for Table Skittles

1 base	20×30×¼ plywood
2 sides	1½×30×⅝
2 ends	1½×19×⅝
1 diamond	9×9×¼ plywood
4 diamond sides	1½×9×⅝
1 post	2×36×¾
9 skittles	1½×4×1½
1 ball	2×3×2

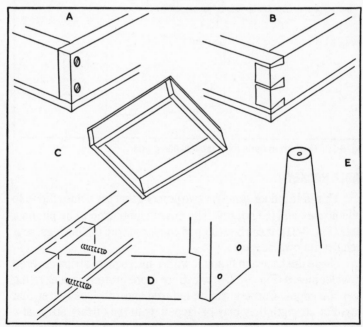

Fig. 8-19. Details of a table skittle board and post.

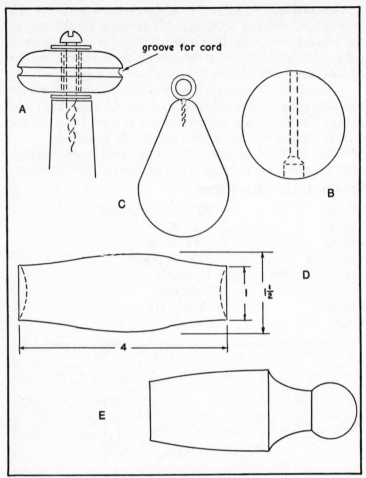

Fig. 8-20. The turned parts for a table skittle game.

TABLE HOCKEY

This is an indoor game for two persons that has some affinity to field hockey and ice hockey. The board is intended to be put on a table (Fig. 8-21). It can be stiffened and fitted with folding legs, so it includes its own supports.

Shape the base and frame it with 1-inch square strips covered by wider pieces (Fig. 8-22A), which are there to stop the puck rising over the edges. Corners can be mitered and will look better that way. For strength they may be lapped, with the thicker strips at a corner overlapped one way and those above them lapped the other way, so nails or screws through the parts will lock the joints.

Allow for goals at the ends, which are shown 9 inches wide (Fig. 8-22B). The gaps can be narrower, but 9 inches should suit most children. Cover the goals with strips that overhang inwards to trap a rising puck.

With a goal gap unprotected, the puck can be driven through so fast that it does damage elsewhere. Make cloth bags to go behind the goals and attach them with tacks. The puck can then be released by pushing the bag inside out.

The puck is just a plywood disc (Fig. 8-22C). Take the sharpness off the edges, but do not round them excessively. It may be worthwhile making a few spares.

The hockey sticks are plywood (Fig. 8-22D) and intended to be used one-handed, but the handle is long enough to keep a hand out of

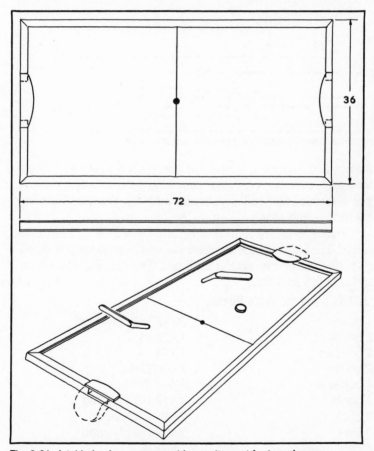

Fig. 8-21. A table hockey game provides excitement for two players.

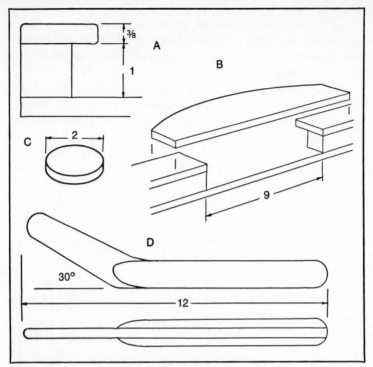

Fig. 8-22. Details of the table hockey board and sticks.

the way of the opponent's stick—at least most of the time. Thicken the handle with strips each side and round them in all directions. A grip something like a full-size hockey stick can be made by binding the handle with string.

Paint the surface of the board green. Draw a line and dot at the center. The border can be any color you wish, but paint the puck in a color that shows it up against the board. The sticks will look most authentic if varnished.

Materials List for Table Hockey

1 base	36×72×⅜ plywood
2 borders	1×72×1
4 borders	1×14×1
2 borders	1½×72×⅜
4 borders	1½×14×⅜
2 goals	3×12×⅜ plywood
1 puck	2×2×⅜ plywood
2 sticks	3×12×⅜ plywood
4 stick handles	1×9×¼

PIN TABLE

This is a game of skill. The object is to trap the steel balls in the pin circles. The basic table is shown with a separate cue that gives more control over the thrust put on each ball than the more common spring action. A spring arrangement is also shown. There is a storage compartment for the balls and cue. The game will appeal mainly to an older child and his parents. The sizes given (Fig. 8-23) make it suitable as a family game. Although it may be made more

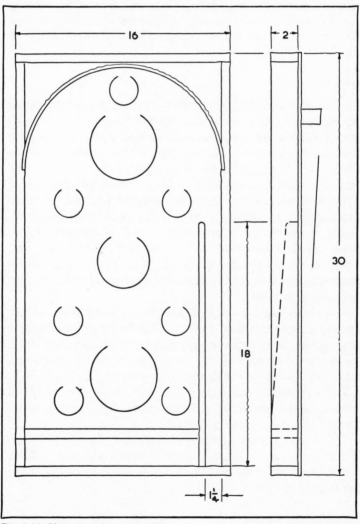

Fig. 8-23. Main sizes for a pin table.

compact by scaling down, a smaller table is less effective and does not permit the use of as much skill.

It is the size of the steel balls that controls the size of the game. As shown, the balls needed are between ⅝ inch and ¾ inch in diameter. It is normal to play with 10 balls, but you need a few spares. With these go the sizes of pins to make the cages. For this size game they should be about 1 inch long, and they look best if they are brass or steel bronzed over. Art shops have special brass pins with neat partially conical heads. Patterns are made by weaving wire around an arrangement of nails. They can also sell you a gauge to control the amount of projection of each nail as you drive it. You need about 150 pins.

Parts

The general assembly is straightforward, except for the curved top. Make up the framework, using whatever joints you favor at the corners. Glued and screwed joints are satisfactory, but you can form dovetails or other joints. Have the plywood base ready, but do not attach it yet. At the points where the curved part meets the sides, mark the ends of the notches (Fig. 8-24A). The curved part is a piece of thin plywood cut so the outside veneers have their grain across to give maximum flexibility. Some ¼-inch plywood may bend sufficiently. If you can get thinner material, use it. Springing this to shape will show how much to trim out of the frame sides (Fig. 8-24B). Aim to get a flush finish for the ball to run around. Attach the bottom and glue the curved part into its notches and to the top. Use fine nails if necessary.

The ball guide is a simple strip held in place by glue and nails or screws through the bottom (Fig. 8-24C). If the pin table will always remain level, the storage compartment may be left open. If the table will be turned on edge for storing or carrying, there should be a sliding lid. This might fit a plowed groove in each part (Fig. 8-24D). A V groove will be satisfactory (Fig. 8-24E). Groove the end of framing and the partition (Fig. 8-24F). Make the lid to suit, with a thumb notch at its end (Fig. 8-24G).

The cue can be just a length of dowel rod or, if you have the use of a lathe, it can be turned with a hollowed end (Fig. 8-25A). Alternatively, cover the end with a disc of rubber or cloth like the end of a billiard cue.

Constructional Details

If a spring plunger is preferred, there has to be a round rod

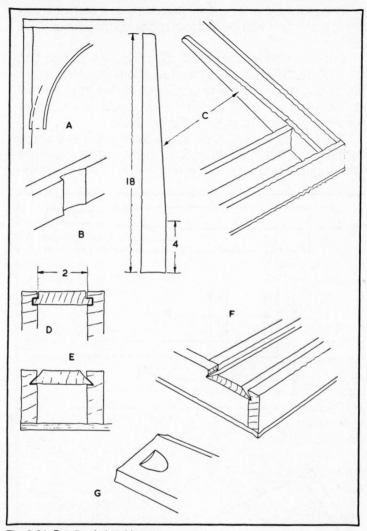

Fig. 8-24. Details of pin table parts.

sliding through the end and a guide in the ball alley (Fig. 8-25B). How far along to put the guide depends on the spring available. The rod may be a piece of dowel rod, or it may be plastic or metal of about ⅜ inch in diameter. Fit a knob to the end (Fig. 8-25C). There has to be a compression spring that will slide easily over the plunger. To allow enough movement and control, the spring should be about 3 inches long and stiff enough to shoot the plunger forward when the knob is released. Slide it over the plunger and put a peg or nail through the rod at the end of the spring (Fig. 8-25D). You may have to experiment with the choice of spring and the position of the peg.

In use the table has to be tilted, using a strip across toward the far end (Fig. 8-25E), but you may like to complete the table and try it with temporary packing before settling on the height of the final packing. When you fit it, its lower edge should be either well rounded or planed to an angle that stands level.

The successful action of the struck ball depends on it hitting something that will make it rebound after traveling around the curve. It can be a spring steel nail (Fig. 8-25F). A better arrange-

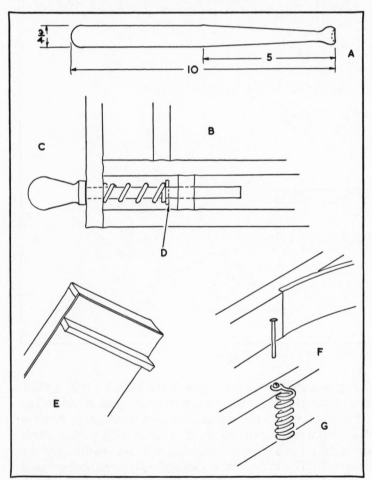

Fig. 8-25. Constructional details of a pin table.

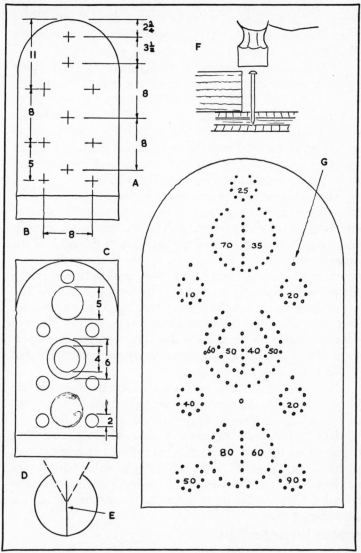

Fig. 8-26. Steps in arranging the layout of nails on a pin table.

ment is made from a small tension spring. Cut off one looped end and bend the other over to screw into the top of the frame side (Fig. 8-25G). Position the stop about 1 inch down from the end of the curve.

The layout of the nailed cages is best done full-size on paper (Fig. 8-26), which can be put on the base and the nails driven through it. Each nail position can be marked through with an awl before discarding the paper. Do your general painting or varnishing before driving any nails, but leave numbering until later.

Details of the design are not as complicated as they may appear if tackled systematically. Draw a centerline and on it mark the centers of the main cages (Fig. 8-26A), with other lines across to mark the centers of the side cages (Fig. 8-26B). Draw all the circles on which nails have to be driven (Fig. 8-26C). The openings are all found by projecting lines from the circle centers at 30 degrees each side of vertical lines (Fig. 8-26D). In the large circles there are center divisions almost to their tops (Fig. 8-26E).

The spacing of nails or pins must be related to the size of the ball to be used. The gaps must obviously be less than the ball diameters, but not very much so. With ⅝-inch balls, space the nails about ½ inch. In each circle drive the nails at the sides of the openings and the tops of the divisions, then work around the circles from there. A piece of wood ¾ inch deep, or slightly less, can be held alongside each nail in turn to set the height (Fig. 8-26F).

Besides the nails in the circles, there can be single ones set ahead of some of the circles as hazards (Fig. 8-26G). You will probably want to try the game at this stage, and you may find it worthwhile leaving out the hazard nails until experimental shots tell you the best places to put them.

Rolling steel balls can quickly wear away numbers that are painted on. You can use decals or other applied numbers, but they need protecting with several coats of varnish.

Balls that reach the bottom do not score. Make your own rules. You may allow for them to be picked up and used again until every ball has scored. Similarly, if the ball rebounds so hard that it runs back into the starting alley, decide if it can be used again or has to be discarded. Continue the game in turn until someone reaches the agreed target total.

Materials List for Pin Table

2 sides	2×30×⅝
2 ends	2×16×⅝
1 base	16×30×⅜ plywood
1 guide	2×18×½
1 division	2×15×⅝
1 block	1½×16×1
1 lid	3×15×½
1 curve	2×18×⅛-¼ cross-grain plywood
1 cue	⅝×10 round rod

Chapter 9

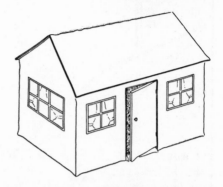

Dollhouses and Playhouses

The size of most dollhouses is necessarily restricted because of available space. Although a girl may enjoy arranging furniture, most of the dolls she plays with are too big to be used with the house. A simple playroom can be made in proportion to the dolls, so the child can decorate and furnish it to suit her favorite dolls. She can improvise furniture from cardboard boxes painted or covered with paper, and there will be plenty of uses for scraps of fabric and other oddments.

DOLL'S PLAYROOM

If space is restricted, the playhouse can be made to fold flat (Fig. 9-1). It is an open-sided box with the parts hinged together. The sizes shown are suggestions, and they can be adapted to suit the particular dolls and available materials. The box can be nailed together rigidly, but it is shown with the two ends folding underneath and the back folding forward on to the bottom.

Make the bottom of plywood or hardboard, framed around underneath. The back can be framed all round, but it will probably be stiff enough to only need strips across the ends. It will stand on top of the bottom (Fig. 9-1A). Make the ends the same width as the bottom and to the same height as the back, when arranged to overlap the bottom (Fig. 9-1B). Round the corners that will be outwards.

The simplest hinges are pieces of fabric-backed plastic—of the type used for upholstery. Cut strips the full length of the joints. Glue

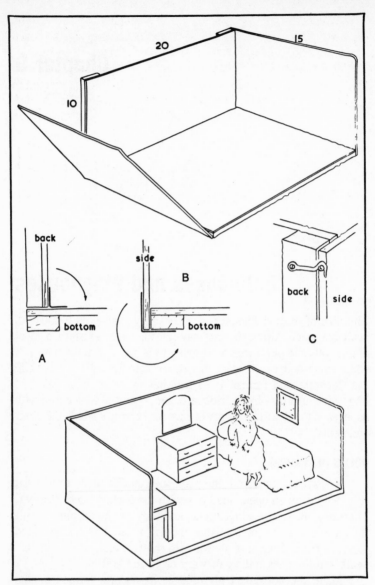

Fig. 9-1. A doll's playroom is open-fronted, so a girl can arrange the interior as she wishes.

it on and reinforce with tacks. If about ¼ inch is allowed for each glued surface, that should be strong enough. The back folds on to the bottom (Fig. 9-1A). The fabric folds back between the ends and the bottom (Fig. 9-1B).

When the room is assembled, the sides and back have to be linked together. This can be done with a hook over a screw at each corner (Fig. 9-1C).

Paint the outside with a neutral color, so attention is not drawn to it. The floor may be stained inside. The walls can be painted to simulate a normal room finish, or they can have paper pasted on. A baseboard painted around the bottoms of the walls will help to give a realistic effect.

Materials List for Doll's Playroom

1 bottom	15×20×¼ plywood
1 back	10×20×¼ plywood
2 ends	11×15×¼ plywood
2 bottom frames	1×20×½
2 bottom frames	1×15×½
2 back frames	1×10×½

SMALL DOLLHOUSE

The size of a dollhouse has to be a compromise between one which is large and spacious and one that does not take up much room. There has to be a reasonable proportion between the size of the house and the size of dolls and furniture that may be used in it. A child may not notice small discrepancies of scale, but large differences will spoil her enjoyment of the toy. Some suppliers of dollhouse furniture and dolls to go with it use a scale of about one-twelfth, or 1 inch represents 1 foot. There are also supplies of metal and plastic doors to this scale, as well as scaled-down paper printed with stone or brick patterns, and with suitable designs for inside walls. This house (Fig. 9-2) suits this scale and has internal accommodation sufficient for the young owner to equip the rooms with all the usual things (Fig. 9-3). The overall sizes are as small as can be expected to provide sufficient scope for rearranging furniture and dolls. The roof lifts off in two sections.

If ready-made doors and windows are to be used, get them first as they will control the sizes of openings to be cut. Some of the parts may have to be adapted to make best use of them. For simplicity and ease of construction, most of the parts can be made of ⅛-inch hardboard, although ¼-inch plywood can be used with little difference in total weight. With hardboard there may have to be reinforcing strips at most joints, but with plywood some joints can be pinned directly into the panel edges.

The key piece on which most of the other sizes are based is the main partition (Fig. 9-4A). Even if hardboard is used for the other parts, plywood for this part and for the base will provide rigidity. The front and back of the house are the same height, but the ridge comes forward of the right-hand wall position to allow for the roof overhanging it. The design allows for door openings without doors inside, as a child may find them a nuisance. They are all 7 inches by 3 inches. The top of the window in this panel is level with the tops of the doors, and its depth and width should suit a plastic window or be cut as shown. For neatness the windows around the house should all be the same height, although they may be different widths.

Use the partition as a pattern for making the left-hand wall, which will have the same outline but no openings. A full-size house may have more windows, but in a dollhouse you have some walls with no openings to help with the arrangement of furniture and wall decoration.

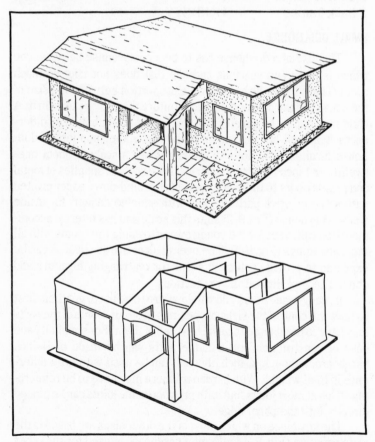

Fig. 9-2. This small dollhouse has a lift-off roof for access to the interior.

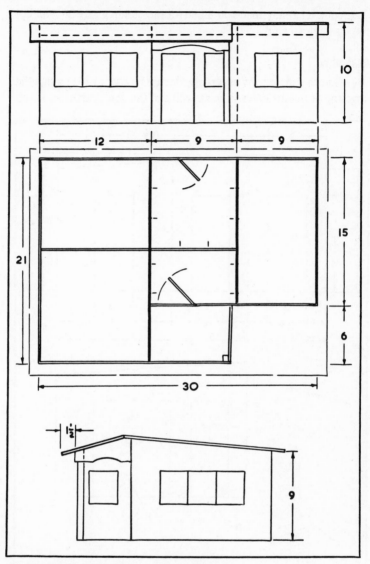

Fig. 9-3. Sizes and layout of a small dollhouse.

Use the partition as a guide for marking the shorter wall on the right. That may have a longer window at the same height as the others (Fig. 9-4B). The other partition with its doorways is the same size (Fig. 9-4C).

Back and front walls are simple rectangular pieces, some with windows. The front doorway can be slightly larger than the internal

213

door cuts. If a ready-made door and its surroundings are bought, cut the opening to suit.

Assembly

Before starting any assembly, decide how you will arrange the crossing of the inside crosswise wall and the main partition. If you

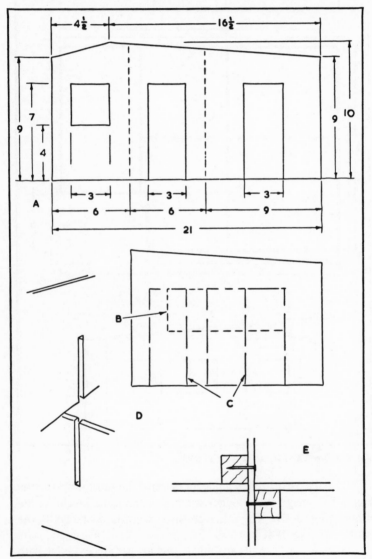

Fig. 9-4. The main inside wall and joint details for a small dollhouse.

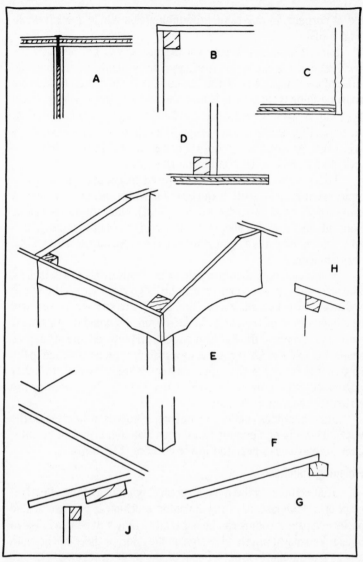

Fig. 9-5. Detail work on a small dollhouse.

use stiff plywood, it may be satisfactory to cut half out of each piece (Fig. 9-4D). Hardboard will not be stiff enough for that method. The alternative is to add stiffening strips to separate crosswise pieces, so they can be glued and pinned in place (Fig. 9-4E). With T joints in plywood, it should be possible to get satisfactory joints with glue and panel pins or thin nails into edges (Fig. 9-5A). With hardboard and at corners, in any case, stiffening strips inside are advisable (Fig. 9-5B).

Join all the parts. Check squareness as you go. See that the lower edges are all level. Arrange a base inside by making the internal parts narrower. Then the outside walls can be nailed to a plywood floor (Fig. 9-5C). It may be better to put the house on a base which extends a little all round and is kept to the full width at the porch (Fig. 9-5D), so as to support a post there. There will have to be a few strengthening pieces between the walls and the base, but they do not have to be continuous all round.

There does not have to be a covered porch, but appearance is improved if you have one. It can be made with a corner post and two pieces of plywood or hardboard (Fig. 9-5E). Mark the sloping piece from the partition and shape the undersides of both pieces. Carefully square the parts as you assemble them. Any error here will be very obvious.

The roof panels should overhang the walls by about 1½ inches. The large main panel should reach the ridge right across the house and be cut to make a *miter joint* (Fig. 9-5F). Round the edge that will be exposed beyond the porch. Make the smaller panel with a similar overhang and plane the mitered edge. Stiff plywood might keep its shape, but at the ridge there can be a stiffening piece attached to the large panel on which the other may rest (Fig. 9-5G). If the other edge needs stiffening, add a strip to that (Fig. 9-5H). Cut away the strips to easily fit over walls.

Put other blocks under the roof panels to locate them inside the walls. There is no need for continuous framing. It should be sufficient to put blocks near the lower corners (Fig. 9-5J).

Finishing Touches

That completes the main structure, but much of the effectiveness of a dollhouse is in the finishing touches. If you use scaled patterned paper, rooms can be papered as they will be in a full-size house. You may use a wood design on the floor, or there can be cloth stuck on to simulate carpets. Paper on the roof can have a tile design on it, and a plain paper might go underneath. For the outside there will be a choice of brick, stone, or wood markings. All the paperwork should be done before the addition of metal or plastic door and window assemblies. If these are intended to be attached with fine nails, it may be difficult to obtain any small enough. Needlework pins can be cut off. In hardboard some of them should be left long enough to go right through a small amount. The ends can then be turned over inside.

If the house is to be completed without paper and prepared doors and windows, this is the stage where you do the painting. High gloss is inappropriate. For most parts it is better to finish with semigloss or flat paint. Hardboard will have to be treated with a special primer to prevent it from absorbing an excessive amount of paint. For a painted finish on hardboard you may choose to assemble the outside walls with the smooth surfaces inward. The back pattern shown outwards can then be painted a stone color, and it will give an appearance sufficiently near that of a stone or cement surface. The inside surface can then be painted to give the smoothness of a plastered or paneled wall.

Windows can be unglazed, but it is better to use clear transparent plastic, which will do no harm if broken. Frame around the outside with strips tacked or pinned through (Fig. 9-6A). The strips can be plywood or hardboard, but they are easier to use if they are solid wood. Instead of the same section pieces all round, the top may be shaped and the bottom made wider to represent a sill (Fig. 9-6B). The larger windows look better if the "glass" is divided into panes. That can be done with thin pieces of stiff wire held in place by the framing (Fig. 9-6C).

The main problem to be overcome in making tiny doors is hinging them. It is possible to get very small hinges, but they are meant for jewel boxes and similar things. It is difficult to use them on dollhouse doors and have them sufficiently inconspicuous. It may be better to use cloth. Thin plastic-coated fabric may be the neatest, but ordinary woven cloth is easier to disguise under a few coats of paint. Frame around the doorway and trap the cloth under the side framing (Fig. 9-6D). The framing need not be severely plain, particularly at the top, although in this house, with the doorway partly hidden under a porch, your decorative work there may not be appreciated. Panels and other detail on the door are best indicated by paint. It is possible to cut or scratch lines into the plywood to show through paint, so that it looks like a built-up door instead of a single piece of plywood. Put a small knob on the outside. A round head screw might do.

Some sort of a catch to keep the door shut may seem desirable, but at this scale anything you use can be out of proportion. It is better to rely on friction. A bent nail across an inside corner will act as a stop (Fig. 9-6E). Friction to hold the door can be provided by a tiny piece of soft rubber or a scrap of Velcro fastening tape glued under the top of the doorway, where it will not be noticed (Fig. 9-6F).

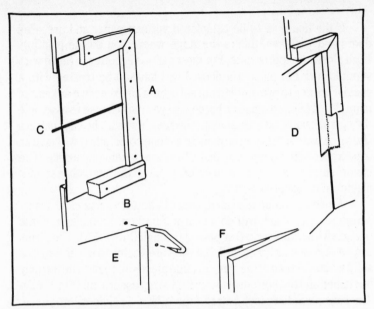

Fig. 9-6. Window and door details for the small dollhouse.

Paint the door, its frame, and the window frames before assembly. These are parts that can be painted with gloss paint, so they stand out against the main walls.

A girl gets much of her enjoyment out of arranging and rearranging the inside of the house. It may be better to leave all the rooms plain. You may wish to build in a few blocks to represent things like kitchen counter tops and a bath. A constructional advantage is that those blocks may take the place of some of the narrow strips needed to join hardboard walls to each other and to the base.

Materials List for Small Dollhouse

1 main partition	10×21×¼
1 end wall	10×21×¼ or ⅛
1 end wall	10×15×¼ or ⅛
1 inside wall	10×15×¼ or ⅛
1 crosswise wall	10×21×¼ or ⅛
1 back wall	9×30×¼ or ⅛
1 front wall	9×12×¼ or ⅛
1 front wall	10×18×¼ or ⅛
1 roof	17×33×¼ or ⅛
1 roof	8×21×¼ or ⅛
1 base	24×33×¼
framing from	½×60×½

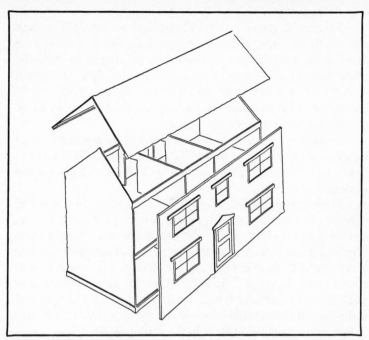

Fig. 9-7. A two-floor dollhouse with a removable front had good access to the inside.

TWO-FLOOR DOLLHOUSE

When a dollhouse is made on one floor, its appearance may be more like what a girl is used to seeing, but it takes up space and usually has to be moved for storage and use. Access to the rooms and furniture has to be from the top. If the house is made on two floors, the space it occupies in your room is less. It can be given a fairly permanent position against a wall in the girl's bedroom. She will appreciate being able to get at things inside from the front, which gives her a more natural view. This form also lends itself better to electric lighting.

This dollhouse (Fig. 9-7) has a roof that lifts off and a front that can be removed. The only windows and a door are in the front, so when this is removed the main part is a solid-sided box. This is easily constructed, and it gives the owner a chance to arrange things around the walls without restrictions. It also allows the installation of fireplaces, stoves, and kitchen equipment without having to shape around window openings. The back is completely closed, except that there can be access to the space under the stairs for a battery to serve electric lighting.

The size shown (Fig. 9-8) will suit furniture and dolls of about one-twelfth full-size. The stairs have a scale depth of tread more than the real thing, but that is necessary to avoid having to make the house deeper back to front. The back wall is already as far as most children will be able to reach inside a room. There is no attempt to indicate uses for particular rooms, and the child will probably be glad to rearrange things occasionally.

It will help if you use the wood that will be the front to draw the locations of other parts as well as its own openings (Fig. 9-9A), but do not cut it to size yet. If the bottom edge is planed straight, you can work from that.

Make the pair of ends (Fig. 9-9B). The roof slope is about 30 degrees. The bottom is a plain piece between the ends, with its surface 1 inch up (Fig. 9-9C). The two inside walls are the same (Fig. 9-9D). Check their sizes against the ends. They may have nails or screws up through the bottom, but there may also be stiffening pieces under the stairs (Fig. 9-9E). Allow for pieces going across under the the upper floor at back and front and across under the roof at the front. If the material to be used for the back is not stiff enough to keep its shape, include a strip there (Fig. 9-9F).

Put supporting strips for the upper floor across the end and inside walls. Do not make the upper floors yet. They may need a slight adjustment in size, as you assemble the parts after making the stair assembly.

The stair treads are made of pieces of 1-inch square strip cut diagonally and glued to a piece of plywood (Fig. 9-10A). Let the glue set, then make the bottom to fit the floor (Fig. 9-10B) and the upper end to come against the landing (Fig. 9-10C). Mark where the stairs are to come on the two walls, then glue and nail the treads and the landing in place. Fit this center assembly to the bottom and fit all the other parts, with the back last. Have this slightly oversize so you can adapt it, if you have to manipulate the other parts to get them square and lock them in place as you nail on the back. If there is to be access to the space under the stairs, deal with that before attaching the back.

Front and Roof

The front fits into place at the bottom into a slot (Fig. 9-11A). This *plinth* is continued around the end walls with matching pieces to give the effect of stone foundations. Put a step across below where the front door comes (Fig. 9-11B). At the top the front is held back by the overhanging roof (Fig. 9-11C).

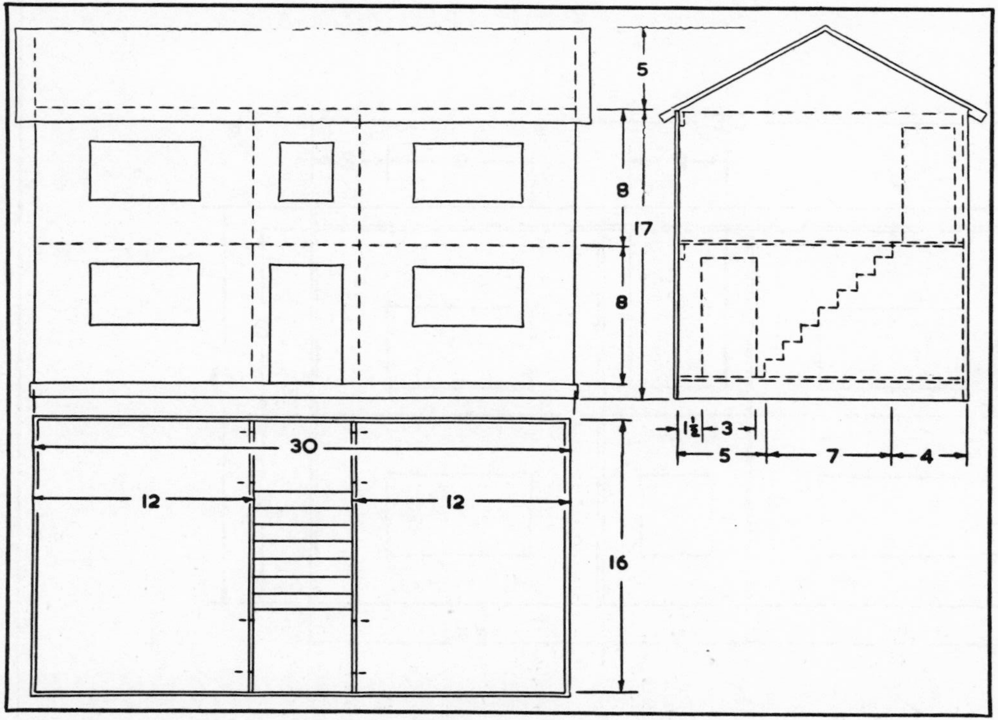

Fig. 9-8. Sizes of a two-floor dollhouse.

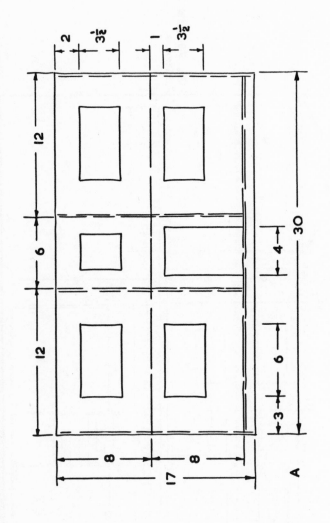

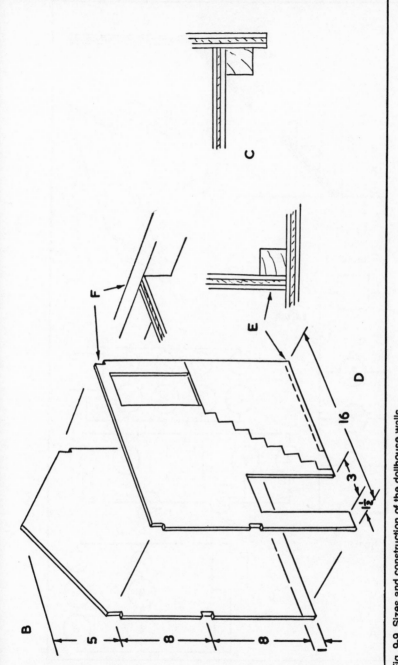

Fig. 9-9. Sizes and construction of the dollhouse walls.

223

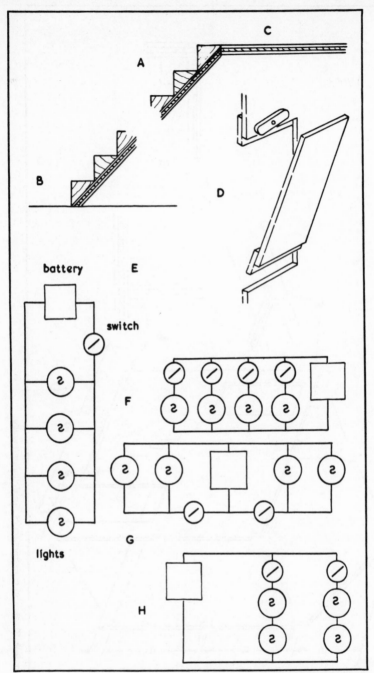

Fig. 9-10. Staircase and hatch details, with wiring circuits for lighting.

Cut the front to fit. Make the openings. The windows and doors can be bought plastic or metal ones, as described for the small dollhouse. Alternatively, they can be made as described as the alternative for that house. If the windows are reasonably large, there can be a good view of the interior, particularly if lighting is provided. With all of this work on a board that can be removed, it is easier to use your skill in making imitation decorative framing around the door and windows. The inside of the front can also be dealt with by arranging papering, curtains, and other things. Make sure the front door swings easily over the house bottom when the front is in place.

The roof is made of two pieces, joined together (Fig. 9-11D) and resting on the ends of the house. Allow for about 1-inch overhang all around. Stiffen the front and back edges with pieces that fit easily over the front and back walls (Fig. 9-11E). To keep the roof in shape, fit one or two intermediate formers. They need not come down to the wall level (Fig. 9-11F).

The finish can be as you wish, with brick or stone design paper outside or a paint finish. You can paint or paper inside and fit carpet to the floors and stairs.

Electric Lighting

Electric lighting can be with small lamps and holders fed from a flashlight or other battery under the stairs. Access through the back is probably simplest with a lift-out panel that hooks on at the bottom and is held by a turn button at the top (Fig. 9-10D).

Although it is possible to get lamps and holders that can be arranged inconspicuously, even if they are rather overscale, switches tend to be too obviously out of proportion. It may be better not to attempt to mount them on room walls. It is better to switch lights on and off from outside. Then the front does not have to be opened. You can arrange a light in each room, with one switch to control them all, or each room light may have its own switch. That means more wiring to be hidden. If the upstairs lights are arranged on the rear wall and the downstairs ones near the centers of the ceilings, nearly all of the wiring can be outside the back of the house where it will not normally be seen. The wiring is then brought through holes to the lamp holders.

Remember to connect the lamps in parallel if they are the same voltage as your battery. If one switch is to control all lights, it goes in either line to the battery (Fig. 9-10E). If you want a switch to each light, you can loop one line to the switches (Fig. 9-10F). If you want to switch both downstairs lights together and both upstairs lights

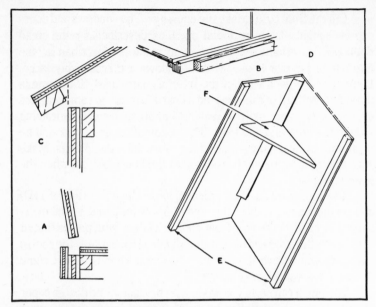

Fig. 9-11. Front and roof details for the two-floor dollhouse.

together, treat as two circuits (Fig. 9-10G). If you get lamps of half the voltage of the battery, pairs may be wired in series instead of parallel. Upstairs and downstairs lights may then be used in pairs (Fig. 9-10H). You must not switch these lamps singly, or they will burn out immediately.

Wire can be fairly fine for neatness, but do not make it any longer then necessary. Otherwise, lights will lose brightness. Putting switches near the rear of one end wall will be convenient. They will not need much wire.

Materials List for Two-Floor Dollhouse

1 front	17×30×⅜ plywood
1 back	17×30×⅛ hardboard
2 end walls	16×22×¼ plywood
2 inside walls	16×16×¼ plywood
1 bottom	16×30×¼ plywood
2 floors	12×16×¼ plywood
Stairs from	1×50×1
6 stiffeners	¾×30×½
framing from	½×70×½
2 roofs	12×32×¼ plywood
1 roof ridge	1×32×1
2 roof formers	4×15×¼ plywood

DOLLHOUSE FURNITURE

If you make a dollhouse, you should make at least some of the furniture for it. This creates a problem of scale. There has to be a compromise. If you make the house one-twelfth full-size, it may seem simple to use the same scale for the furniture. If all you are making is a display model, you can use your skill to make furniture which is as exactly proportioned as you can manage it. Such fine work will not stand up to handling by a child.

For instance, most tables are about 30 inches high. You can make the height of your model 2½ inches, which is one-twelfth of it, but what about the size of legs? The correct section to scale of a 3-inch leg is ¼ inch. That might just be strong enough if you use the right wood, but a chair leg is usually less than 2-inch square section. Making that to scale will certainly produce a chair that will soon have broken legs, even with careful use as a toy. If you have to go overscale for some things, it is advisable to make other things overscale if the general proportions of furniture are to look right.

You can safely go a little oversize in general measurements without this being obvious. At one-twelfth scale, the table can be 3 inches high instead of 2½ inches. The usual 16-inch chair height can then be 1¾ inches or 2 inches instead of 1⅓ inches, and thicker legs will not look so much out of proportion. Generally, ¼ inch should be regarded as the normal minimum cross section, although legs can taper to rather less.

If furniture is to stand up to much handling, the finer parts should be close-grained hardwood. Plywood about ⅛ inch thick will do for tabletops, seats, closets, and similar things. It is unwise to use anything thinner, but the plywood can be made to look thinner by tapering from the underside and rounding edges. There are some places where veneers can be glued to a flat front to look like drawer fronts or doors. Handles, which do not have to function, can be represented by nails that are not driven fully in. When painted, they will look sufficiently realistic.

Balsa and Plywood

An easy wood to work is *balsa*. It can be bought in thin sheets. Shaping is easily done with a knife and by sanding. Unfortunately, there is not much strength in balsa, so it is unsuitable for unsupported use over much area. It can be used glued to other wood, where its thinner sections will give a better-proportioned appearance. For model aircraft use, there are treatments that strengthen the wood. These are like clear lacquers, and they may be used on balsa in doll's furniture to provide some strengthening. Do not expect balsa to come up to the strength of the more usual woods. Treating balsa in this way, and covering it with several coats of paint, should make it reasonably durable in a child's hands.

Domestic pins can be pushed into balsa. They can be used to temporarily hold down a thin sheet while you cut it, as well as for holding it in place while gluing.

Plywood made from hardwoods is useful. If you can get 1¼-inch thick beech plywood made of five veneers, instead of the usual three, you can use this as a basis for nearly all the furniture you wish to make.

Most joints in toy furniture can be plain glued and nailed ones, but in a few places parts can be notched together. If you want to show your skill, you can attempt cabinetwork joints. Besides the finest nails and panel pins, domestic needlework pins can be cut off and used as nails. Useful small nails are sold as *gimp pins* and are intended to be used for fitting the tapelike gimp at the edges of upholstery. They have bigger heads in proportion to their thin sections than other small nails have, and this helps in holding small parts together.

In a typical plywood assembly, the opposite legs and their joining rail can be cut (Fig. 9-12A) and joined with crosspieces. Where the thickness does not show, as in these pieces (Fig. 9-12B), it is always wise to use a thick piece for strength. A plywood top is glued and nailed on. If you have to use thicker plywood, taper the edges to give a lighter appearance (Fig. 9-12C).

Construction

Stools can be made in the same way as the table. For a plywood chair, cut opposite sides to include the back and legs (Fig. 9-12D). Upholstery is done with a square of cloth (Figs. 9-12E and 9-12F) glued and pinned around the edges. The back looks best with some shaping (Fig. 9-12G).

Solid wood legs can be tapered slightly, but leave some parallel section at the top. For a table, there can be a solid block to give the appearance of rails around the edges. The legs are nailed and glued into notches (Fig. 9-13A), and the top is put on (Fig. 9-13B). The same method can be used for a chair, but the rear legs may be shaped to give the back a slope (Fig. 9-13C). A piece of thin wood with cloth glued over it will make an upholstered back (Fig. 9-13D). As chairs should be in sets of four, decide on the method of construction. Make all the similar parts of all the chairs at the same time, so they match.

Many items, particularly if you are working to a small scale, will have to be made solid. Although they may appear to have doors or drawers, these do not function. Much can be done with paint to make a just plain block of wood look like a chest of drawers or other furniture. A little shaping helps. Cutting back at the bottom makes a plinth (Fig. 9-13E). It may be easier to do this with another piece of

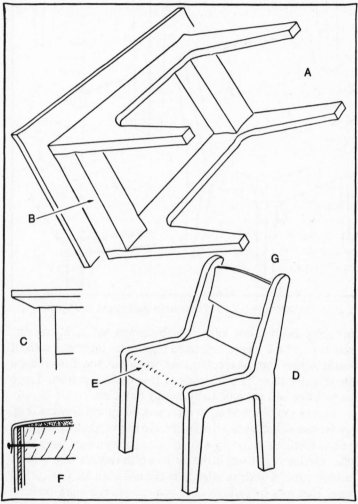

Fig. 9-12. Dollhouse furniture requires careful construction.

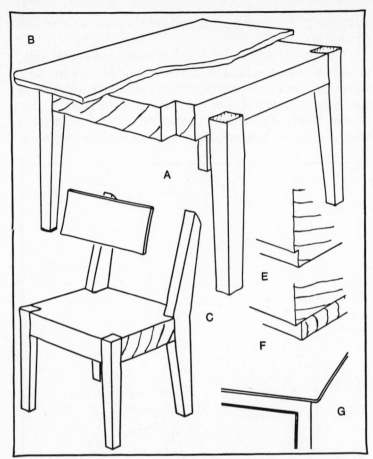

Fig. 9-13. The dollhouse table and chair have solid blocks for strength.

wood (Fig. 9-13F). For kitchen or bathroom furniture, working surfaces may be Formica laminated plastic. Its thickness without wood backing is about correct to scale, when glued on to overhang a little (Fig. 9-13G). Choose a plain or less obvious pattern. Large bold patterns will not look right on tiny furniture.

Veneer can be glued on to represent doors and drawers (Fig. 9-14A), with suitably placed nails to make knobs. Another way is to scratch in outlines. If you want to indicate a paneled door, use a knife along a straightedge to cut in the outlines of the panels (Fig. 9-14B). For lines parallel with an edge, you can use a marking or cutting gauge. That may be sufficient, or you can make a more realistic effect by careful cutting toward the lines on the panels (Fig. 9-14C) with light chisel cuts.

A bed can be just a block of the right size wood. Its covering can be taken to the floor all round to hide it. A bed head is a shaped piece of plywood at one end (Fig. 9-14D). Put a matching piece at the foot, if you wish (Fig. 9-14E). If you want to get away from a solid piece of wood, the bed can be made more like an inverted box. It can be cut away to give the effect of legs (Fig. 9-14F).

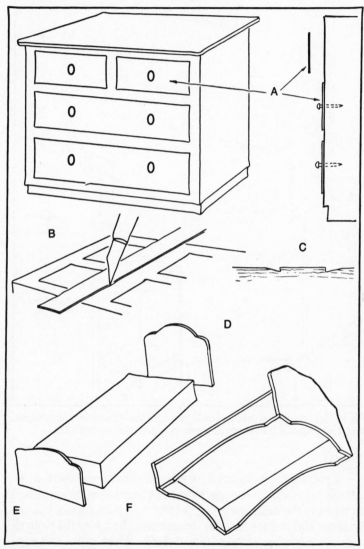

Fig. 9-14. Some dollhouse furniture is solid with details added, or it may be built up.

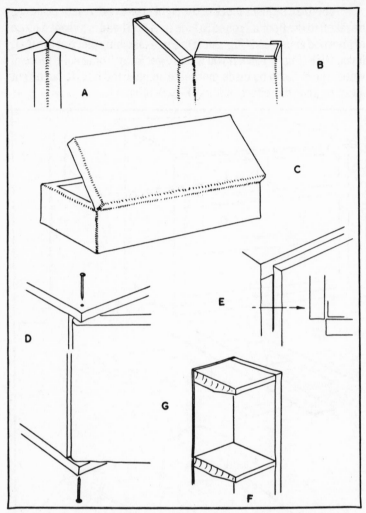

Fig. 9 -15. Cloth may be used for covering and hinges. Pins will also form hinges. Wood may have to be thinned at edges to appear slimmer than it is.

Hinges

If you want to make furniture with doors that open, there are no suitable hinges small enough. Fabric can be glued on, as suggested for doors in the dollhouses (Fig. 9-15A). In some furniture you can avoid the abrupt edge showing through paint by taking the cloth all over the adjoining surfaces (Fig. 9-15B). If you make a storage chest, it can be covered all over with cloth. The part forming the hinge would be inconspicuous (Fig. 9-15C).

232

For an upright door, it helps to let the top and bottom overhang. Pins or thin nails can be used as hinges (Fig. 9-15D). Round the door edge for clearance as it opens. If the door can stand forward of the edges, there may be a cloth hinge inside, but the door will not swing out further than square to the opening. If a child tried to force it further, something would have to break. This makes a neat arrangement with the top and bottom of each door overlapping on a clothes closet (Fig. 9-15E).

If a dresser is to include a mirror, it can be made from aluminum foil, preferably a new flat piece. Wrapping material may be smoothed out.

Shelving, as in a bookcase, is difficult to make to a small scale. Edges can be tapered to look thinner (Fig. 9-15F), but the upright sides will have to be of thin material. Stiffness can come from the back, which may be veneer or even stiff card (Fig. 9-15G).

Upholstered Furniture

More fully upholstered furniture is actually easier to make. If you want to produce a chair in which no wood shows, a surprising amount can be done with padding on a fairly plain base. The back and the sides may be plywood attached to a slightly tapered block (Fig. 9-16A). Do some shaping of the outline and take off all angular edges.

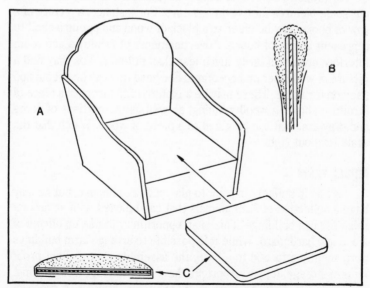

Fig. 9-16. Upholstered furniture can be based on simple forms.

Pieces of plastic foam, cotton batting, or anything soft and pliable may be wrapped around the wood and held in place with adhesive tape (Fig. 9-16B) to give the rounded effect you want. This can be done on the block to make the seat, but it is easier to get the right shape if you make a lift-out "cushion" (Fig. 9-16C).

The covering material for this and any other upholstered furniture should be chosen to give a scaled appearance. The material used for covering full-size furniture will look out of proportion. This cloth intended for dresses is more appropriate, particularly if it has a tiny pattern or is a plain color and a fine weave. Experiment with stretching the cloth over the chair. Use glue and pins around the edges. If you want to simulate leather, it is possible to use flexible plastic. Much of that does not stretch very well, and you may be limited in the amount of compound curvature you can give it. Moderate heat will make some plastics more flexible, and you can get the shape you want before the plastic has cooled.

Most furniture you make will be freestanding. It may then be moved around as the girl rearranges rooms, or she can take it out for play away from the dollhouse. There may be an advantage constructionally in building in some furniture. A combined dresser and clothes closet can also be your way of reinforcing the joint between a floor and wall. Besides doing this, the furniture itself will be stronger.

Study color advertisements in magazines. You may want to cut out some pictures for use on furniture. For instance, a picture of a row of books may be glued to a block of wood and put on a shelf to represent a rack of books. Advertisements of furniture and room interiors are necessarily much less than full-size. You may find a picture of wallpaper or a decorated bed head that can be cut out and used on furniture. There may be a picture of the front of a piece of furniture showing wood graining, as well as the outlines of doors and drawers, that can be glued to a piece of wood. Watch that the scale is about right.

MODEL FARM

A boy is unlikely to want to play with a dollhouse, but he may have a collection of farm animals that can be used with an assortment of farm buildings. This is an opportunity to use up offcuts of wood and hardboard. While it is possible to arrange farm buildings permanently attached to a base, the assembly may present problems of storage. It may be better to have the buildings freestanding. The young farmer can arrange them to suit himself. A piece of

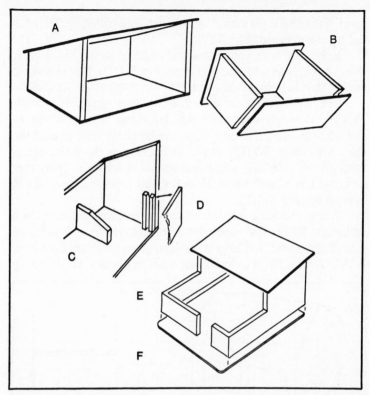

Fig. 9-17. The basic structures in a model farm can be arranged with sloping roofs.

hardboard or plywood can be painted green or brown to simulate the ground in the yard and on which the buildings may be arranged. It may be advisable to surround this with strips that look like walls or fences, but from a mother's point of view they are the means of keeping playthings within bounds. A few openings serve as gateways to admit vehicles.

Scale will have to be approximately correct. Measuring animals and vehicles and relating them to the probable dimensions full-size will give you an idea of suitable sizes, but do not expect to find all the toys of matching scale. Sheds for tractors should be of a size to admit them. If animals are to go into a building, it should look right.

The basic building is an open-fronted shed wih a sloping roof (Fig. 9-17A). It should be large enough to admit tractors or to serve as a garage for the farm motor vehicles. It may be smaller to serve as a shelter for animals. Cut two ends to match, with a back between them. If the roof is plywood, it should not need stiffening. The base can be of hardboard (Fig. 9-17B).

If the shed is for cows, divisions might be put in (Fig. 9-17C). You can construct a lift-out part door (Fig. 9-17D). Do not make it deeper than half the height, or it will not come out of its guides.

The development can include an enclosed open part in front. This is particularly suitable for pigs, but it may be proportioned to suit other animals. The roof slope can be either way. Extend the shed sides (Fig. 9-17E). Leave an opening at the front, either centrally or to one side, so the animals can be driven in. There may be a door hinged with fabric. Make the base large enough to take in everything (Fig. 9-17F).

A larger building on two levels has its construction more like a dollhouse. This can have space for animals or vehicles below. Loose gear, drums of oil, and bags of corn can go on the upper floor (Fig. 9-18A). Access might be by outside stairs or a ladder, but the young

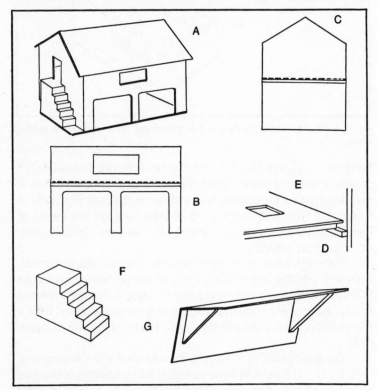

Fig. 9-18. A two-floor barn adds interest to a model farm. A lift-off roof gives access.

236

farmer will find it more convenient to lift off the roof. A ridge is shown, but a simpler construction is to have a single slope.

Use the front as a guide to sizes (Fig. 9-18B) and make the two ends to match (Fig. 9-18C). Put strips around to support the upper floor (Fig. 9-18D). There can be a hole at one end, where the young farmer can haul up bags or other things with string from a truck below (Fig. 9-18E).

Cut outside stairs from a solid block of wood (Fig. 9-18F). Attach the stairs to the end near a suitable door opening. Openings in the wall below should be of a size to admit the farm vehicles and tractors.

Make the roof in a similar way to that on a dollhouse, but arrange the formers so they just come inside the end walls (Fig. 9-18G). Unless you are making a very large building, you will probably not need to include a ridge or other lengthwise piece. The ridge and other similar joints in small buldings can be strengthened with adhesive tape stuck inside.

A loading ramp is just a solid block of wood cut wedge-shaped and at a height to allow things to be wheeled up and on to the back of a truck or trailer (Fig. 9-19A). A number of wood strips painted to look like stone walls can be used to divide up the farm or fields. Have them the same height and thickness, but provide many lengths (Fig. 9-19B). There can be smaller pieces with plywood panels to go with them. They can be used like building blocks. Buildings may be put together to suit the young farmer's current needs (Fig. 9-19C).

A pond or lake can be made for ducks by using aluminum foil or a metal mirror to represent the water. Mount this on a piece of hardboard with a plywood border. Cut this to an irregular outline (Fig. 9-19D). To avoid an abrupt edge, either bevel the plywood (Fig. 9-19E) or make up the edge with plaster or one of the modeling clays that set hard (Fig. 9-19F).

A real farm is not usually brightly colored. A gloss finish may not be very authentic, although it may have more appeal to children. Walls of buildings can be white or a stone color. Floors could be brown or green to look like earth, mud, or grass. Roofs may be red or black. If flat paint is used for large areas, small areas may be done in contrasting brighter colors.

GARAGE

This is a toy that can be used with model cars. It serves as a maintenance shop, a filling station, and a parking lot. The sizes given are intended mainly as a guide to proportions, and they may

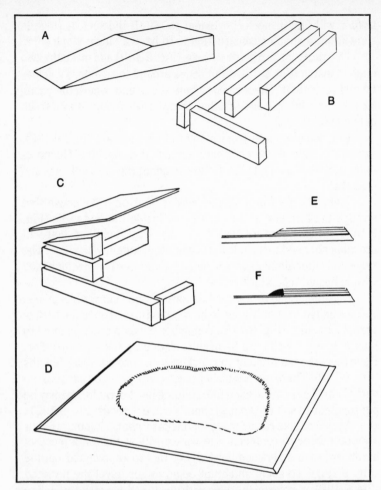

Fig. 9-19. A farm ramp is a simple block (A). Strips will form walls and fences (B). Blocks can be built into different structures (C). A pond has a raised border (D-F).

have to be modified to get the scale correct in relation to the model cars. For the smaller cars the garage may be made much smaller, but if kept true to scale for the smallest toy cars, the garage may be too compact for easy use as a toy. Keeping the proportions rather full may be preferable. A boy will play happily with cars which an adult can see are very small in relation to the garage. If the cars are oversize, use of the toy may become impossible.

The garage is made with a flat roof (Fig. 9-20) having a ramp at the back to allow cars to be pushed up for parking there. The building has an open front, so it can be used for display or as a maintenance shop. Under the canopy there are pumps, and there is space at the side for parking. With the sizes shown (Fig. 9-21), most of the parts may be plywood, although some of the thicker ones can be particle board. Hardboard will not have enough stiffness, so the top and base should be plywood.

Start by making the sides and back. The front is a narrow strip between the top edges of the sides. If the top is cut, it can be used as a guide to size and squareness of the assembly (Fig. 9-22A). The platform over the ramp at the rear may be part of the top, although it can be separate and added later.

Cut the piece for the base wide enough to take the walls around the outside of the building (Fig. 9-22B). At the rear the ramp wall extends high enough for protection on the ramp (Fig. 9-22C). The ramp is nailed between it and the back of the building (Fig. 9-22D).

The walls around the parking space on the roof go over the building walls (Fig. 9-23A), except the front piece is on top. Arrange it far enough out for nails up into it to miss those going down into the front (Fig. 9-23B).

The pump island also braces the top and base, so make it a good fit. Arrange pieces of dowel rod as pillars (Fig. 9-23C). The pumps will have to depend mainly on painting for their appearance, as they are just plain blocks of wood (Fig. 9-23D). Hoses can be insulated sleeving intended for electrical wiring.

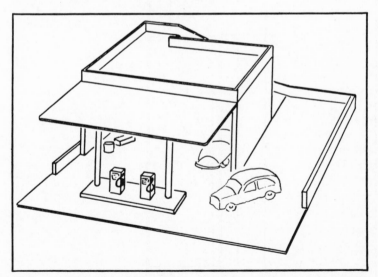

Fig. 9-20. This garage and filling station has a shop below and parking on the flat roof.

239

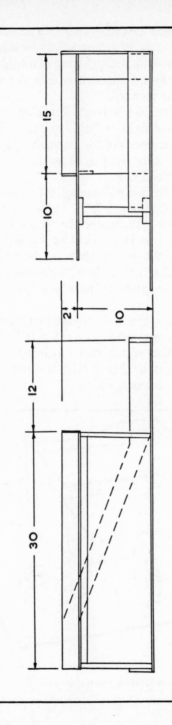

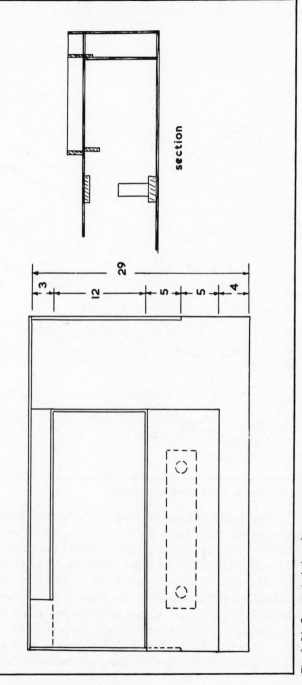

section

29
3
12
5
5
4

Fig. 9-21. Suggested sizes for a garage.

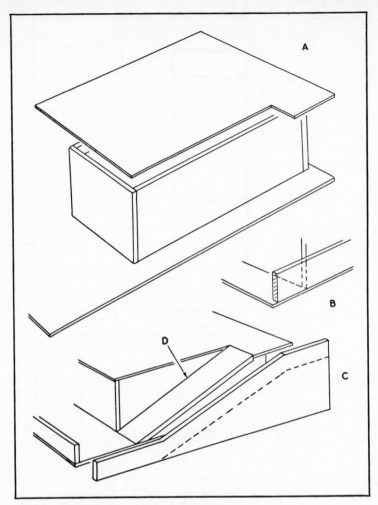

Fig. 9-22. Constructional details of a garage.

The base and shop floor of the garage may be gray. Walls can be a lighter gray or white. The ramp and parking space may be gray or brown. Most filling stations are brightly colored, even if some of the quality deteriorates as the place gets older. Model advertisements may be obtained from some oil companies, or it may be possible to cut suitable ones from magazines. The name of the proprietor may be displayed prominently. The pumps should be painted in appropriate colors. Dials and other details may be best drawn on paper and then stuck on. You can give the base a rough stone or concrete effect by sprinkling fine sand on the paint before it dries. The surplus is then brushed off after the paint becomes hard. Paper with a brick or stone design that is intended for dollhouses may be used around the outside of the building.

Materials List for Garage

2 sides	10×12×½
1 back	10×30×½
1 front	2×30×½
1 top	25×30×¼
1 base	29×42×¼
1 ramp	3×26×½
1 ramp wall	12×42×¼
2 ramp walls	3×20×¼
1 island	4×21×¾
1 island	4×21×½
2 island pillars	1×10 round rod
2 roof walls	3×15×½
1 roof wall	2×30×½
1 roof wall	3×30×½

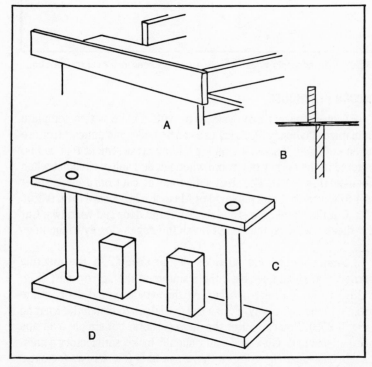

Fig. 9 -21. Suggested sizes for a garage.

243

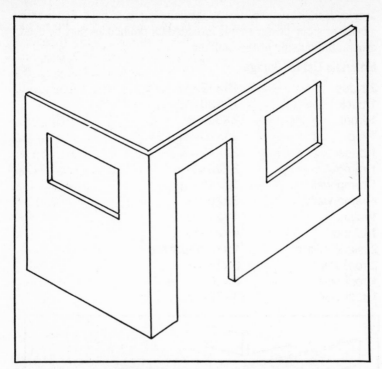

Fig. 9-24. An indoor playhouse is really a folding screen for the corner of a room.

INDOOR PLAYHOUSE

A proud parent may want to provide a child with a complete miniature playhouse. A playhouse can be bulky and difficult to store when not used. This is a simpler folding arrangement that can be erected in the corner of a room when needed and packed flat when not used (Fig. 9-24). The sizes shown can be cut from a single sheet of 4-foot by 8-foot thin plywood or Masonite hardboard (Fig. 9-25).

Cut the sheet across and mark out the door and windows. Cut out these openings, but do not finish the edges closely to the lines yet.

Frame around the outsides of the sheets. At the meeting corner, you should set back the framing on the narrow part (Fig. 9-25A) to give a neat overlap. At the windows and door, frame around in the same way. Finish the cut edges to match the framing (Fig. 9-25B). You can miter the strip corners, but simple overlaps are satisfactory. Glue and nails should make satisfactory joints, except that near the corners there can be a few screws for extra strength.

Three 3-inch hinges can link the parts (Fig. 9-25C). Round the outer corner of the house after a trial assembly. There should be some way of securing the house to the room walls, so it cannot be pushed away in use. A simple way that only involves driving two screw eyes into the walls is to have hook and eye fasteners (Fig. 9-25D) arranged diagonally.

The finishing of the playhouse depends on your artistic ideas. There can be just a plain coat of paint, or you can make it look more like a house with suitable outlining of wood or brick patterns, and appropriate framing painted around the door and windows. Inside there can be paint to match the room walls. This is not really the type of toy to be given a swinging door or glazed windows. Keep it as basic as possible.

Materials List for Indoor Playhouse

Sides from 1 piece hardboard or plywood 48×96
Framing from 8 pieces   1×60×1

SMALL PLAYHOUSE

This is a compact playhouse that may be disassembled and stored flat (Fig. 9-26). Its size makes it feasible to use indoors, yet it is large enough for outdoor use. It is a basic structure with little decoration added, but it gives a child all he needs to pretend he is in his own private home. You can remove one end and use the house as a garage for a pedal car or bicycle. The window can be used for displaying puppets.

If the house will not be left out to get wet, the panels can be Masonite or other hardboard. Exterior or marine plywood will be stronger and better able to withstand exposure to the weather. The framing is shown on the outside of the panels. If the strip wood is stained or painted dark and the panels between are painted a light color, there will be a *Tudor* effect. If that is not wanted, the house can be made with the framing inside, so the exterior is smooth. The standard arrangement will allow reversing if care is taken in measuring so peg positions match.

The ends control the sizes of other parts, so start by making one end (Fig. 9-27A). How the framing is assembled depends on what you want to do. With stiff plywood behind the frames, it may be satisfactory to merely butt the parts together (Fig. 9-27B). If you are using hardboard or more flexible plywood, corrugated metal fasteners will add strength (Fig. 9-27C). Better joints will be lapped (Fig. 9-27D). If you want to display your craftsmanship, they can be

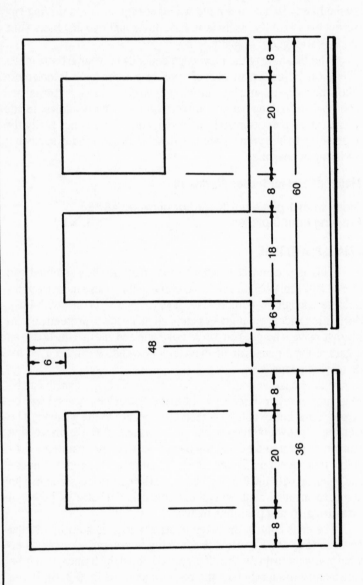

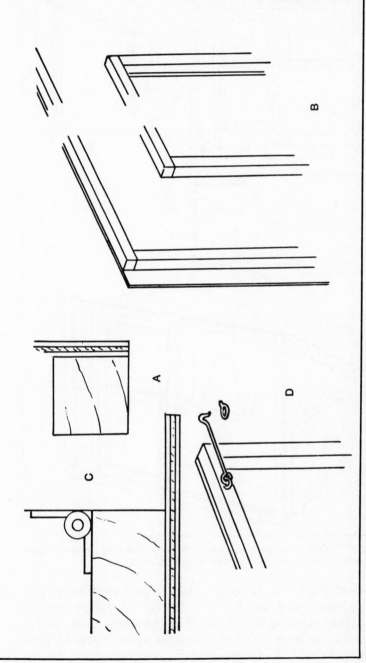

Fig. 9-25. Sizes and constructional details of an indoor playhouse.

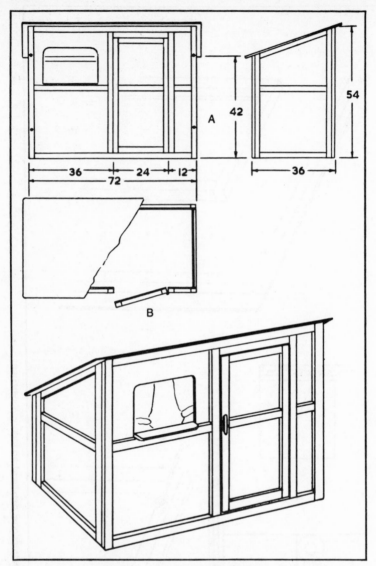

Fig. 9-26. This small playhouse has its framing outside and is of a pegged construction that allows it to be taken apart and stored flat.

tenoned (Fig. 9-27E). In any case attach the panels with enough glue and plenty of nails, possibly with a few screws near the corners.

The front panel (Fig. 9-26A) should be as high as the front of the ends, but there is no need to bevel its top edge (Fig. 9-27F). If you cannot get a panel wide enough to cover in one piece, join two pieces behind the central door post. Note that the bottom framing piece is not cut away at the doorway. Arrange the intermediate horizontal member at the same level as the ones on the ends.

Cut out the window opening with rounded top corners. There is no need to frame it, but round the exposed edges. Add a piece to form a sill on the crosswise piece (Fig. 9-28A).

Arrange the height of the back, so its top clears the roof (Fig. 9-27G). It should be sufficient to frame around the back and put one rail across its center. If more stiffening is needed, add a central vertical piece.

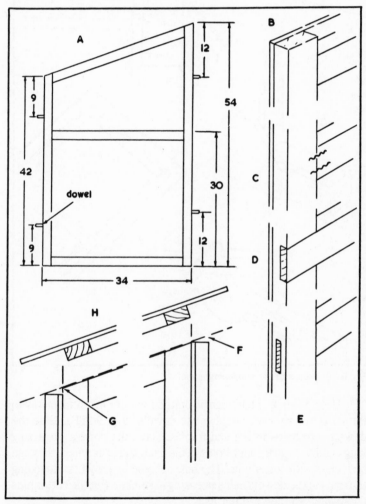

Fig. 9-27. Size and some suggested methods of framing the small playhouse.

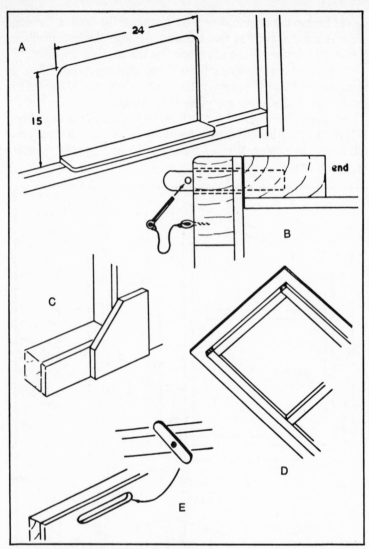

Fig. 9-28. Details of the small playhouse.

Back, front, and ends can be bolted together in a similar way to the larger playhouse. You can use dowels (Fig. 9-28B). Glue the dowels into holes in the end frames. Have the dowels projecting long enough to go through holes in the front and back where they can be locked with cotter pins. The holes should be easy fits. Rounding the ends of the dowels helps in easing assembly. Put the cotter pins on strings, so they are not lost.

Frame the door (Fig. 9-26B) in a similar way to the main panels. Make it an easy fit in the opening, with ample clearance above the framing piece crossing at the bottom. Hinge at the side nearer the end. Triangular pieces at top and bottom corners will form stops (Fig. 9-28C). A wooden turn button inside (as suggested for the larger playhouse) may be a good fastener, or you may fit a normal door catch. Put a knob or handle on the outside.

Make the roof panel large enough to overlap about 2 inches all around. Put framing around at a spacing that will drop inside (Fig. 9-27H). Arrange two crosspieces intermediately (Fig. 9-28D).

Under most circumstances the roof should stay in place under its own weight, but to guard against it blowing off or being knocked off there should be some securing arrangement. One way is to have a turn button at each end to engage with slots cut near the center of the top of the end frames (Fig. 9-28E). Round the overhanging edges and corners of the roof.

Paint the whole thing brightly. If the framing is on the outside, then paint that black or a dark color to contrast with the lighter colored panels. The roof may be red, while inside a light color will make the house seem larger. No floor is shown, but one can be made with framed plywood to drop inside. Normally it will not need securing, but it can be attached to the back and front with dowels and cotter pins. Securing it in this way will provide stability and hold the house in shape.

Materials List for Small House

1 front panel	54×72×¼ plywood
3 front frames	2×72×1
4 front frames	2×54×1
1 back panel	42×72×¼ plywood
3 back frames	2×72×1
3 back frames	2×42×1
2 end panels	34×54×¼ plywood
2 end panels	2×54×1
2 end frames	2×42×1
6 end frames	2×36×1
1 roof	42×76×¼ plywood
2 roof frames	2×72×1
4 roof frames	2×42×1
1 door panel	24×50×¼ plywood
2 door frames	2×50×1
3 door frames	2×24×1
1 window sill	2½×24×½

PLAYHOUSE

A house that can be assembled and left in the yard for long periods permits children to play and keep many of their toys in a place they can call their own. With a simple bolted construction, it is possible to dismantle it to store flat in the garage during the winter. The ends and sides of this house can be taken apart, and the hinged roof lifts off. If there is a wooden floor, that can be lifted out. It depends on the maker's inclinations as to how elaborate the house is finished. You should concentrate on a substantial construction, so it will stand up under heavy use by children.

The house is shown with a door and two windows in a long side and a window in one end (Fig. 9-29). The back and the other end can be plain or given windows. Much depends on the situation, but plain areas of the interior walls allow for decoration, temporary shelves, and hanging pictures.

Sizes are based on standard 48-inch by 96-inch sheets of plywood, with the width of the ends 48 inches and the height to the eaves the same. Other sizes can be varied. All of the main framing is intended to be strip wood about 1¼ inches square. Get enough of this at the start. The fitting of some parts depends on this width and may have to be varied if the wood is a different size.

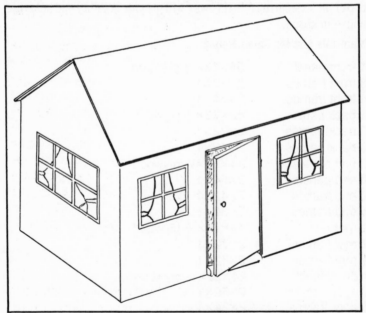

Fig. 9-29. This is a more roomy playhouse for outdoor use.

Start by laying out an end the full width of the sheet, with the roof slope starting at 48 inches high (Fig. 9-31A). This can be marked at 30 degrees, but the height shown (Fig. 9-30) gives about the same angle. Frame all round and where the window comes, take the strips right across (Fig. 9-31B). Cut the opening before framing, but do not trim the edges level until after the strips have been glued and nailed on. Letting the framing strips merely butt against each other should be satisfactory, but you can halve the corners if you wish (Fig. 9-31C).

Make the other end a companion to the first, with or without windows as you wish. If there are no windows, include two crossbars for stiffness at equal spacing in the height.

Mark out the front side, allowing for overlapping corners, which will be drilled for bolts (Fig. 9-31D). Arrange windows and a door, but for stiffness allow for the framing to cross the bottom of the door opening (Fig. 9-31E). Let the strips framing the tops and bottoms of the windows extend to the upright framing (Fig. 9-31F). It is not impossible to fill the window openings with clear plastic *glazing*, but it is advisable to leave them open. To give a neater effect, frame them with strips that project slightly (Fig. 9-31G), either all the same or with an extra width at the bottom to form a sill (Fig. 9-31H). Do the same around the door opening, but at the bottom there will be a wider step. Leave this until after a floor has been made.

The back should match the front. If it will not have any windows in it, add enough framing to give it stiffness, probably two strips each way (Fig. 9-31J). Notch the crossings, even if you do not halve the ends and corners. There is no need to bevel the top edges of front and back framing, but the plywood may have to be beveled so the roof will fit closely (Fig. 9-31K).

Drill the corners for coach bolts; ¼-inch diameter should be sufficient. Let the square necks pull into the ends. Use washers under the nuts inside (Fig. 9-31D). The number of bolts needed depends on the stiffness of the sheet material, but four at each corner should be satisfactory. The end ones are fairly close to top and bottom corners. Sun and rain may cause warping of panels if there are not enough bolts to restrain them.

Floor and Roof

Put the sides and ends together. When the children have tried the house for size, make a floor. In some positions the house may be used without its own floor, but besides giving a smooth independent

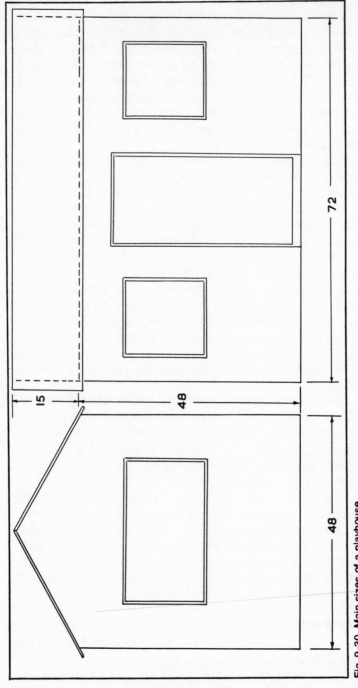

Fig. 9-30. Main sizes of a playhouse.

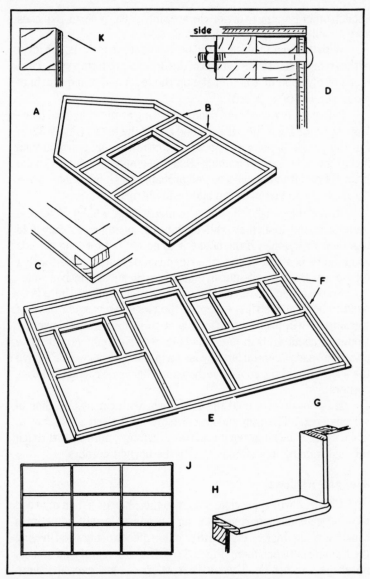

Fig. 9-31. Constructional details of the parts of a playhouse.

interior, it helps to keep the house in shape. Cut a piece of plywood to a size that will drop inside the framework easily. It does not have to be a precision fit, but should be squared. Use enough framing to stiffen it underneath. The amount of framing depends on the stiffness of the plywood, but besides going around the edges, having enough other framing to divide the area into squares about 16 inches across will probably be right (Fig. 9-32A).

With the floor in place, it will be necessary to make up the level of the framing across the bottom of the doorway to form a step. Put a piece of plywood on top to make up the level and round a strip of wood outside (Fig. 9-32B).

Allow for plywood roof panels meeting at the ridge and overlapping about 1½ inches at each end and at the eaves (Fig. 9-32C). Put the panels in place temporarily. Get inside and pencil around inside the side and end framing. Use these marks as guides to the fitting of roof framing, but you will probably find it advisable to test occasionally as you make up and fit the strips.

At the ridge make the edges to match (Fig. 9-32D). When the framing is finished, they will be hinged together, so they fold together for storage. If the house is to be left out for long periods when there is a risk of rain, the ridge can be waterproofed with a temporary strip of self-adhesive plastic strip about 2 inches wide.

Frame around to fit easily inside the wall framing. There is no need to bevel any strips, except at the ridge. To prevent the roof warping, it will probably be sufficient to include strips down the slopes at about 18 inch intervals (Fig. 9-32E). Only very flexible plywood needs a central lengthwise strip each side as well. Remove the sharpness of the roof's overhanging edges and round the lower corners.

It is possible to hold the roof down with catches or clips of various sorts. The roof should certainly not be left loose, but to make it safe and childproof it is better to arrange more bolts through the end framing in a similar way to the upright corners.

Door and Windows

Children will appreciate a door to their house. When plywood is otherwise unsupported, framing on one side will sometimes cause warping. Make a door with two thin pieces of plywood, having the framing between them (Fig. 9-33A). For the sake of appearance, miter the top corners. The bottom corners can just overlap. There should be enough stiffness if you have two equally spaced intermediate crossbars.

Give the door plenty of clearance at the bottom. It need not have such a close fit around the edges as you would give to a furniture door. Hinge it to swing outwards. There should be a stop and a simple fastener. You may fit a catch with a knob at each side, or there can be just a piece of wood as a turn button inside (Fig. 9-33B).

It can be operated from outside by reaching through a window opening.

You may leave the windows as openings. For children's use, it would be wrong and dangerous to put glass in them. One alternative is to use Plexiglas acrylic plastic or other rigid transparent plastic, but even that may be dangerous if broken. It may be better to use a semiflexible transparent plastic. To the child it will have as much appeal as a real window, and it also prevents rain and animals from getting inside.

A simple way of fitting is to stretch the plastic over the inside of a window opening and closely tack thin strips of wood around it (Fig. 9-33C). If it seems a rather large expanse of comparatively weak unsupported plastic, there can be light bars across (Fig. 9-33D).

It is possible to make opening windows. The wide end window can be made into a pair hinged at the sides. Make up frames to fit the

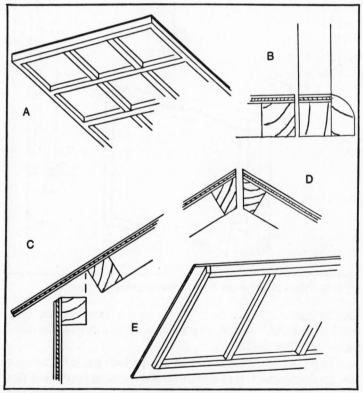

Fig. 9-32. Floor and roof details of a playhouse.

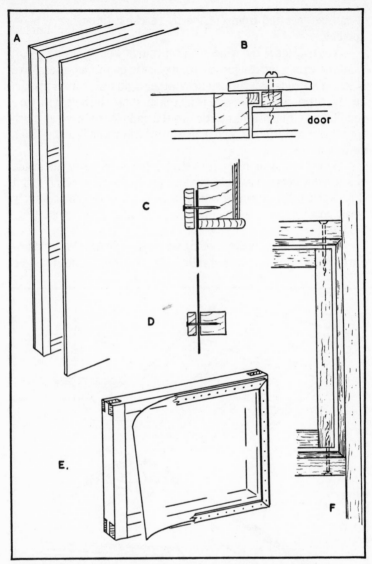

Fig. 9-33. This is how to make the door and windows of a playhouse.

opening and attach the clear plastic to the inner surface (Fig. 9-33E). Ordinary hinges may be used, or screws through the framing will do (Fig. 9-33F).

There are few projections on any part so far. If flatness for storage is important, it is unwise to add anything permanent that will interfere with packing. It is possible to arrange things like shelving inside by resting it across framing. Pictures or a mirror can go against the plywood, if thickness is kept less than the framing. Most other things inside are freestanding furniture, but some things can be arranged to clip or fasten temporarily in some way to the walls. The young owners will likely lay carpets and decorate walls, but these things will not affect packing away for the winter.

Externally, much can be done to make the house lifelike by painting. A few bright colors will probably be as effective in a child's eyes as a lot of detail. If you want to make the little house attractive to an adult, you can spend as much time as you like simulating *cladding*, bricks, window frames, and other details in paint.

Materials List for Playhouse

2 sides	48×72×⅜ plywood
2 ends	48×65×⅜ plywood
2 roofs	30×76×⅜ plywood
1 floor	48×72×⅜ plywood
2 door panels	18×42×¼
2 door frames	¾×42×¾
4 door frames	¾×12×¾
side framing from	11 pieces 1¼×72×1¼
end framing from	11 pieces 1¼×48×1¼
floor framing from	6 pieces 1¼×72×1¼
roof framing from	9 pieces 1¼×76×1¼
window framing from	7 pieces 2¼×30×⅜
door framing from	3 pieces 2¼×48×⅜
door step from	1 piece 2½×18×1⅞

Chapter 10

Activity Equipment

Any youngster likes to gain height, either by climbing on something or, preferably, by finding some way of walking tall. A young child may be frightened at a height, so it is best to modify first attempts to walk tall and not go straight into making high stilts.

STILTS

Instead, there can be a pair of pattens (Fig. 10-1A). Sizes are obviously adaptable, but those shown will suit small feet and give a feeling of height without being too high. Make sure opposite sides match. The lower surfaces are mainly flat, so a child can stand still without toppling. Round the ends so he or she can walk with a fairly normal step. Nail the parts together. Drill through for the ropes, which should be knotted at a height so the child can pull upwards and walk without having to stoop to keep the ropes tensioned and the pattens in place.

Stilts will suit an older child, although short and low ones can be made to serve as a transition from the pair of pattens. There are two possible ways of holding stilts when using them. Some children hold them with the shafts in front. The hands grip them near the top. There is better control if the shafts go behind the armpits and extend slightly behind the shoulders (Fig. 10-2). Hands grip low enough then to provide a slight pull upwards to help keep the feet in place.

The usual stilt shaft goes through in one piece (Fig. 10-1B). Length should be modified to suit the height the child wants to be and to get the tops high enough to go behind the shoulders. Any excess there does not matter.

When making the foot block (Fig. 10-1C), it helps to use a piece of hardwood with the grain diagonally for maximum strength. Do not

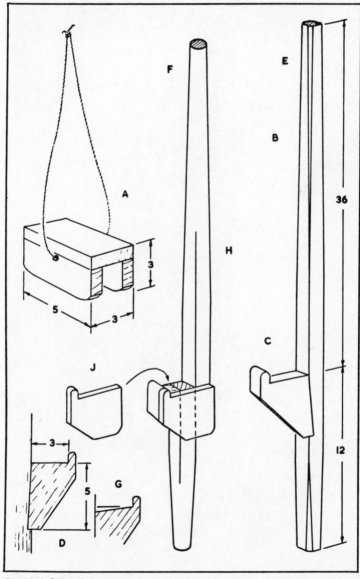

Fig. 10-1. Stilts allow a youngster to show his or her skill in walking above ground level.

Fig. 10-2. Stilts can be made at any height and are easiest to use if the shafts come higher than the shoulders.

make this notch very deep (¼ inch maximum is enough), or the shaft may be weakened. The shafts can be softwood for lightness. Start with a square piece, but taper to the ends, either octagonal (Fig. 10-1E) or to fully round (Fig. 10-1F). Some stilts have blocks that are flat across their tops, but it helps to keep a young foot in place if the end is raised. The top might also slope upwards slightly to keep the foot towards the shaft (Fig. 10-16). Attach the blocks to the shafts with glue and long screws driven through the shafts into the blocks.

The other type of stilt (Fig. 10-1H) is built up. One advantage of this construction is that it gets the shaft supporting the foot more directly under it. The upper and lower parts of the shaft overlap about 4 inches. A short piece makes up the width. Glue these parts together. Make two ½-inch plywood cheeks (Fig.10-1G) to go each side and attach them with glue and 1½-inch by 8-gauge screws. When the glue has set, trim the parts to match and round the edges.

There is a risk of stilts slipping on wet or polished surfaces. This risk can be reduced, and the stilts can be made quieter, by putting rubber pads on the bottoms. Pads intended for screwing to shoe heels are suitable. There can also be sheet rubber attached to the blocks where feet will come. If shoes with heels are worn, there is little risk of slipping.

Materials List for Stilts

2 patten tops	3×5×⅝
2 patten sides	2⅜×5×⅝
2 plain shafts	1⅜×48×1⅜
2 plain blocks	4×7×1⅜
2 built-up shafts	1⅜×40×1⅜
2 built-up shafts	1⅜×12×1⅜
2 blocks	1⅜×5×1⅜
4 blocks	4½×5×½ plywood

SLED

Whether a sled, sleigh, or toboggan is worth making depends on what sort of winter you experience. If there is a possibility of snow settling, something to allow a child to coast downhill or be pulled along on flat land is very attractive. This sled (Fig. 10-3) is of simple construction and is a size that may be right for two small children, or big enough to allow an older child to either sit or lie on it.

For lightness the wood used can be softwood, but for long and rough use it is better to use hardwood. If snowfalls are brief and a

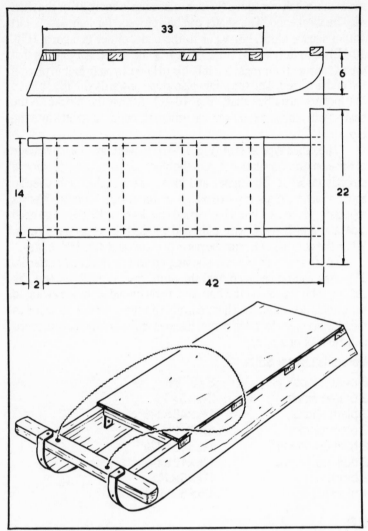

Fig. 10-3. A strong sled.

sled may be rarely used, it can be finished without the metal runners. The wood will soon wear away without them, and the runners let the sled travel more easily in any case.

Mark out the two sides. The forward curve may be drawn freehand, but bring it to near upright at the top to give enough wood for attaching the crossbar. Notch that crossbar in slightly (Fig. 10-4A), but the others go in their full depth (Fig.10-4B). The ends of the front crossbar will be gripped as a handhold when the user lies prone, or they become footrests when he sits. Round the ends and the projecting parts. Drill two holes for rope.

Assemble these parts with waterproof glue and screws. See that the angles are square and that the sides stand upright and without twist in relation to each other. Use exterior or marine grade plywood for the seat. Glue and nail it in place. Cut it just a bit too

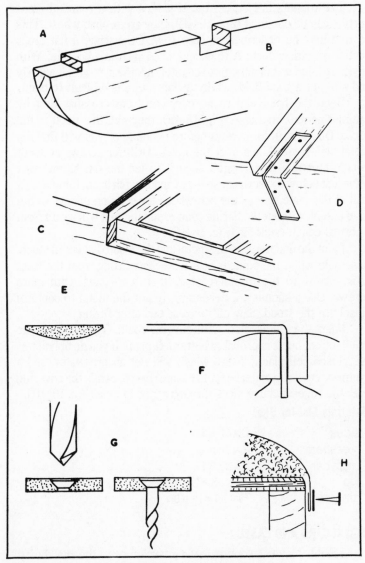

Fig. 10-4. How to make the sled, fit runners, and pad the top.

large, then put it on with the front edge level with its crossbar, but plane the other edges true after assembly. Remove all sharp edges from the seat.

There can be considerable sideways loads on the sled if it skids sideways or turns over, and this puts strain on the joints. They can be stiffened with wood inside (Fig. 10-4C), but another way is to use small shelf brackets under the corners of the seat (Fig. 10-4D).

The runners are strip iron. If pieces with a rounded cross section can be obtained (Fig. 10-4E), they are probably best. This section may be described as *hoop iron*. Otherwise, a flat cross section is satisfactory. A thickness of ⅛ inch is advisable. With anything thinner it is difficult to countersink the screws adequately and still get a good hold, while thicker metal is difficult to bend.

Bend the front end to go over the front crossbar first by hammering over in a vise (Fig. 10-4F), then pull the metal to the curve. Do not drill for screws before bending, or you will find the metal bends with kinks over the holes. Drill for screws at about 4-inch intervals. Countersink enough to let the flat screwheads come just below the surface, so they cannot catch in anything. Use a drill of the same size as the screwhead for countersinking, so the head is sunk without the flaring countersinking that will result from a normal countersink bit (Fig. 10-4G).

Paint the underside of the metal and the wood that it will touch. Assemble while the paint is still wet. Start fitting from the front back. Screw to the front crossbar, then work back with more screws. Use a hammer, if necessary, to get the metal to conform closely to the wood. Saw off the rear end after fitting.

Paint the whole sled with several coats. The seat can be upholstered, but it is probably better left plain. If you do upholster, use closed cell plastic foam, which will not absorb water, and a synthetic covering material for the same reason. Strain the covering over the edges and use tacks through strips of tape (Fig. 10-4H).

Materials List for Sled

2 sides	6×45×1
4 crossbars	2×15×1
1 crossbar	2×23×1
1 top	14×33×½ plywood
2 runners	¾×54×⅛ iron

CHALKBOARD AND EASEL

Schools may use sophisticated alternatives to the chalkboard and easel, but they still have a place for portable equipment on traditional lines, such as was used in the old-time one-room school. A smaller version of the easel and chalkboard is convenient for a child to use at home while standing or sitting on a stool, and it folds flat for easy storage (Fig. 10-5).

The board needs to be flat with smooth surfaces. Plywood should be satisfactory, although there are some manufactured boards equally suitable. It is better to avoid the coarse grain of fir plywood, unless you are prepared to do a considerable amount of sanding to smooth it. Shape the board with truly square corners, then round the corners and edges slightly. Even with apparently smooth surfaces, sand them across the grain to remove any glaze and make them as mat as possible. If the grain is obviously open, fill it by rubbing in a prepared filler. Otherwise, even with many coats of paint, chalk particles will penetrate and affect the appearance and clarity of the board.

Use a matte paint. There are special paints intended for chalkboards, but any paint that dries without the slightest sign of gloss will do. Although black is the traditional color, modern thinking favors dark gray or gray-green. Apply several coats, until there is little sign of the wood's texture showing through. Do this before starting on the easel, so time can be allowed for paint to dry.

To get the sizes and angles of the easel, set out a half-width (Fig. 10-6A). Set an adjustable bevel to the angle between rails and sides, then use this unaltered at all joints and leg ends. Mark out the legs. Round the ends slightly in cross section, so as to minimize marking of the floor covering. Remove sharpness at the tops.

The rails can be cut to the inside lengths between the legs and joints made with ⅜-inch dowels (Fig. 10-6B), or mortise and tenon joints can be used (Fig. 10-6C). When assembling this frame, do it on a flat surface. Check that it does not twist as you pull joints together with clamps. Measure diagonals to see that it is symmetrical. Leave it to set under weights if necessary.

The rear leg is a T-shaped assembly (Fig. 10-6D), having the top rail hinged with a pair of 2-inch hinges to the top rail of the front assembly. Make the joint with dowels or a tenon. A good joint should have enough strength to withstand normal use. If you think additional support is needed, glue blocks in the angles (Fig. 10-7A) or put a thin plywood gusset on the rear of the joint (Fig. 10-7B).

The support for the board should be given a rabbet to make an easy fit on the board edge (Fig. 10-7C). If you do not have the facilities for doing this, two pieces of wood can be joined (Fig.

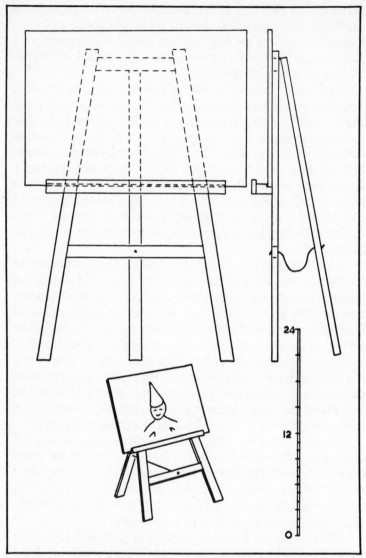

Fig. 10-5. A chalkboard on its easel can be used just like school.

10-7D). Add a lip to the front edge to prevent sticks of chalk from falling off. Round the exposed ends and attach the support to the legs with glue and screws from the back.

With the rear leg attached by its hinges, close it to the front. Drill through the rail and leg for a cord to limit the opening of the easel. Experiment with the length of cord to get a satisfactory

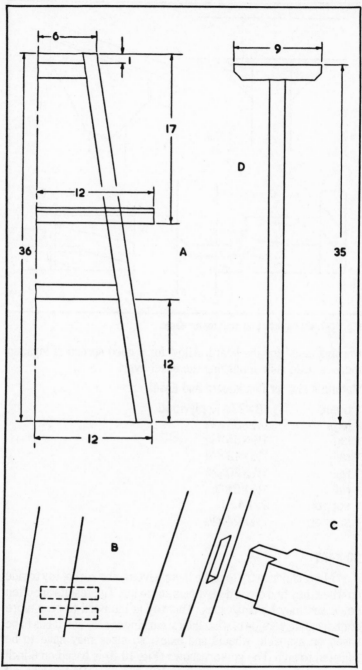

Fig. 10-6. Sizes and construction of an easel.

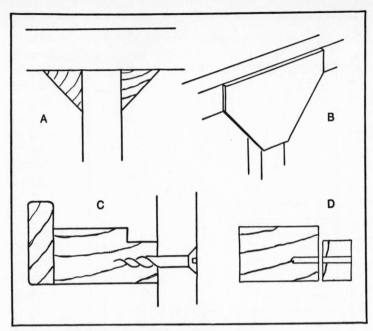

Fig. 10-7. Chalk rack and strut for an easel.

working angle for the board. Allow for a good spread of legs, so there is little risk of pushing the easel over.

Materials List for Chalkboard and Easel

1 board	18×27×½ plywood
2 legs	1½×38×¾
1 leg	1½×35×¾
1 rail	1½×12×¾
1 rail	1½×20×¾
1 rail	1½×9×¾
1 support	2×24×1
1 support	1½×24×½

GO-KART

Many children try to make themselves some sort of toy to ride on when they find discarded wheels and axles. The results are often crude and may be dangerous. This toy is intended to be a more craftsmanlike version of what they are trying to achieve. It has to be based on available wheels and axles, so sizes may have to be adjusted to suit. The go-kart shown (Fig. 10-8) is based on 6-inch diameter wheels and axles about ⅜ inch diameter. Rod may be cut for axles. The wheels can be secured by drilling the ends to take split pins. If there are existing axles with fitted ends, the width of the kart will have to be adjusted to suit. The seat should be wide enough to take the child, but not so wide that he can slide far sideways. Check his leg length. He steers with his feet while his legs are slightly bent. To give him control, his back should then be pressed against the seat back. If the go-kart is to be used for different children, or if it will have to accommodate the same child after he has grown, the chassis can be made longer than originally necessary. A hole for the pivot can be put nearer the seat to suit shorter legs. Then it can be moved to another position as the child's legs get longer.

The chassis has to take the main loads, so choose a strong board without flaws like cracks or knots. Taper to the front (Fig. 10-9A) to give foot clearance and round the edges. Notice that the front projects forward of the footrest. This is to give maximum bearing surfaces between the moving parts. On poorly made karts, slackness developing due to wearing surfaces is a common weakness.

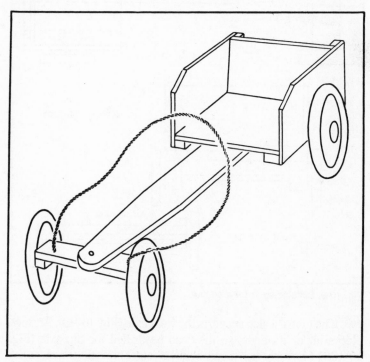

Fig. 10-8. A go-kart has great appeal for children.

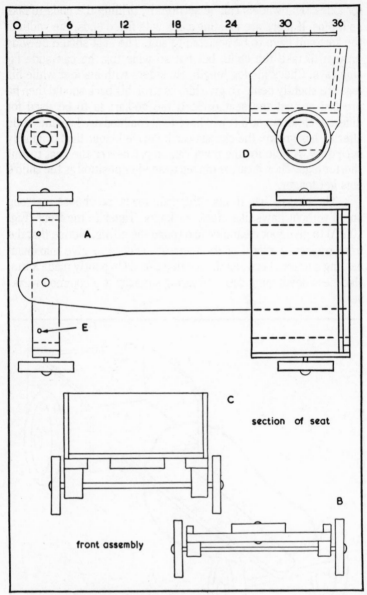

0   6   12   18   24   30   36

D

A

E

C

section of seat

front assembly

B

Fig. 10-9. Suitable sizes for a go-kart.

The footrest also supports the front axle (Fig. 10-9B). Arrange blocks under its ends, so they can be drilled for the axle (Fig. 10-10A). Mark and drill the two blocks before attaching them, so the holes match and are drilled squarely. Put two pieces of ¾-inch square strip across the tops to act as outer foot stops and keep feet away from the wheels (Fig. 10-10B).

The pivot is a bolt about ½ inch in diameter. Have its head underneath. It can be a coach bolt with a square neck to pull into the wood or a plain head with a washer under it. Arrange a large washer

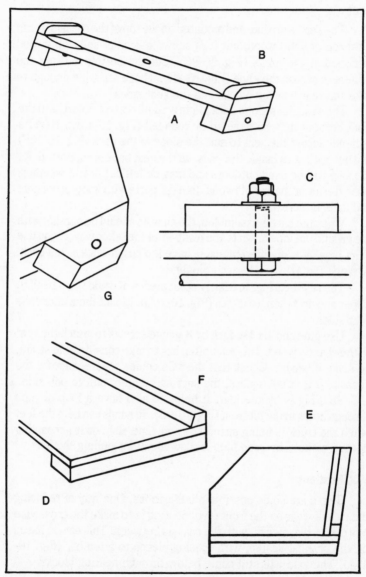

Fig. 10-10. Steering arrangements and seat construction for a go-kart.

above the chassis. Either use one of the stiff types of locking nuts or tighten two ordinary nuts against each other to lock them (Fig. 10-10C). If you do not, the assembly will soon develop a wobble. The alternative to direct rubbing is to make a sheet metal or thin plywood washer as large as the bearing surfaces.

Seat

The seat is boxlike and mounted on the top of the chassis. It can be made of solid wood, but it is shown as comprised of plywood stiffened at the joints (Fig. 10-9C). Cut the bottom and put the stiffeners across the ends (Fig. 10-9D). These are wide enough to take the rear bearing blocks and the seat sides.

The seat sides slope back slightly to increase comfort, and the front corners may be beveled or rounded (Fig. 10-10E). Bevel a stiffener across the seat to suit the slope of the back (Fig. 10-10F) and put stiffeners inside the ends, so the seat back is supported. As the kart will be used outdoors and may be left out in wet weather, use exterior or marine plywood. Join the parts with waterproof glue and nails or screws.

When the kart is assembled, the chassis should be parallel with the ground or slope down to the front—not the other way. If you use pairs of wheels of different sizes, have the larger ones at the back. Arrange the axle height accordingly.

The rear bearings are fairly stout pieces of wood (Fig. 10-9D). Taper and drill them to match (Fig. 10-10G). Mount them under the seat sides.

Use glue and six 1½-inch by 8-gauge screws to attach the seat to the chassis wood. This joint often has to take considerable strain, so make it secure. Check that the axle comes squarely across the chassis. If it is not square, the kart will tend to pull to one side.

Steering is by the feet. It helps to also have a loop of rope through holes in the footrest (Fig. 10-9E), so hands can help the feet when the truck is being pushed by someone else, or it is coasting down a slope. The rope loop is also useful for pulling the kart.

Modifications

There are some possible modifications. One way of reducing the risk of wear on the front pivot bearing is to make the crosswise footrest in two pieces, with the chassis between. This can be based on the original design, with spacing pieces to a top bar (Fig. 10-11A). The axle will still come below through bearing blocks.

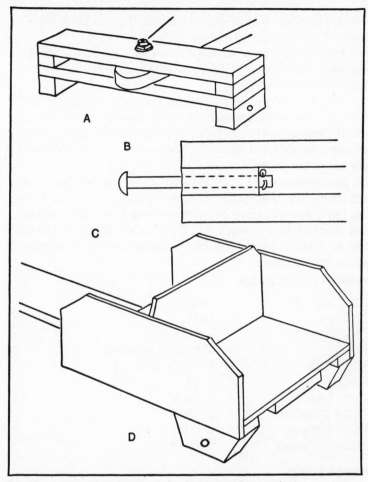

Fig. 10-11. Alternative steering and a double seat for a go-kart.

Some wheels can be mounted on stub axles or even long bolts. The axles can come between the crosswise parts (Fig. 10-11B) through the spacing blocks. This lowers the front, and the rear bearing blocks can also be shallower. Let the pieces be wide enough for the axles or bolts to go through and have a good hold. Otherwise, wear will occur soon in a short hole, so the wheels begin to wobble. If a nut cannot be used inside, drill through the axle for a split pin.

It is not difficult to adapt the seating so two children can use the kart, with one sitting backwards and pushing the kart with his feet on the ground. Make the seat with its back upright. Extend the bottom and sides to form another position (Fig. 10-11C). Have a longer chassis, so the double seat is supported by it.

Move the axle supports back. Otherwise, the weight of the rear child behind the original axle position may be enough to tilt the new rear edge (Fig. 10-11D).

Round all edges, particularly around the seat. Round well where the feet will come on the footrest. Ribbed rubber or other nonslip material can be put over these edges. Some padding in the set may be appreciated, but do not have a loose cushion, which may slip just at the wrong moment.

If the wheels and axles are used ones, you can clean their bearing surfaces and repack them with grease. If they are to be repainted, remove greasy dirt with kerosene or a degreasing fluid first. Paint all the woodwork with bright colors. Even if you do not take the colors to the undersides, use some paint there as a protection against moisture.

Materials List for Go-Kart

1 chassis	6×36×1
1 footrest	3×17×1
2 foot bearings	1½×3×1½
1 seat	10×16×½ plywood
2 seat sides	8×12×½ plywood
1 seat back	8×16×½ plywood
2 rear bearings	3×9×2
2 seat stiffeners	2×10×1
1 seat stiffener	¾×16×¾
2 back stiffeners	¾×9×¾

INDOOR SLIDE

This slide can be used by a toddler indoors (Fig. 10-12), and it can be taken outside as well. The height is not enough to be frightening, and a tumble from the slide should not be serious. It has enough weight and stability to stand up to normal use (Fig. 10-13), but for storage it dismantles into three parts: the central tower structure, the steps, and the slide.

Construction is shown with mortise and tenon joints, but doweled joints can be substituted. Plywood panels at the sides give rigidity and prevent the child from falling out. They are shown let into grooves. If you are unable to cut grooves, the plywood can be glued and nailed to the surfaces.

Start by making the legs and the rails which go with them to enclose the plywood. All legs are the same, except the pair at the slide side have a deeper rail to give stiffness across (Fig. 10-15A). Groove the parts to suit the plywood. The groove may continue below the lower rail position, although it will not be used there (Fig. 10-14A). The lower joints are plain stub mortise and tenons (Fig. 10-14B), but at the top corners they go through. The tenon has to be cut back to clear the groove (Fig. 10-14C).

Prepare the crosswise rails (Fig. 10-14D) and the feet (Fig. 10-14E), which extend 9 inches each side and are tapered on their top surfaces. Assemble the opposite sides with their plywood panels. Check that they match each other and are square and flat. When the glue has set, assemble the crosswise rails and the feet to them. Check that the tower stands firmly and upright. Check diagonals, including the shape when viewed from above.

Make the platform to fit closely against the insides of the side plywood panels and come level with the crosswise rails. Round the top corners of the sides. Take off sharpness everywhere that the slide will be handled, particularly the parts above the level of the platform.

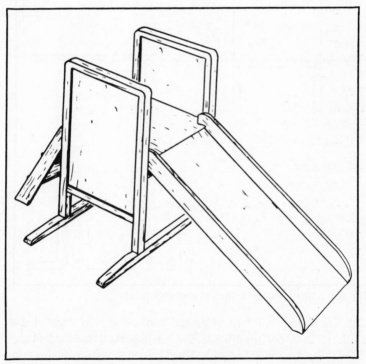

Fig. 10-12. A small slide will provide amusement and adventure for a small child indoors.

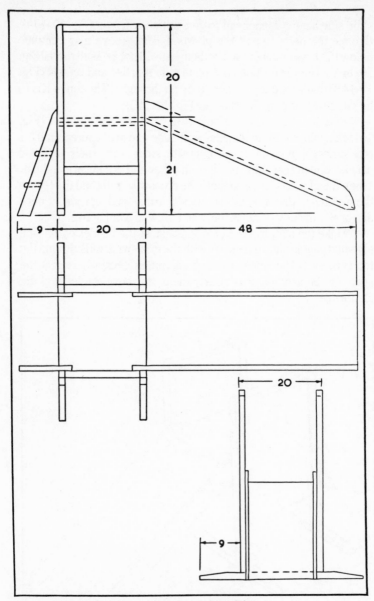

Fig. 10-13. Sizes and three views of an indoor slide.

The ladder has two steps and hooks over the edge of the platform. In this or any other ladder it is important that the feet are lifted the same amount at each step. The distance from the floor to the top of the first step should be the same as to the next step, and the same as the distance from the top of that step to the top of the platform. In this case, 21 inches is easily divided to give three 7-inch spaces (Fig. 10-15B). Draw the ladder side full-size to get the parts right. Let the steps into the sides (Fig. 10-15C), with screws to strengthen the joints. Round the edges of the steps.

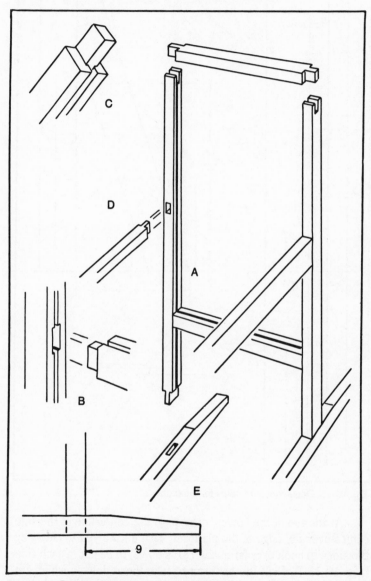

Fig. 10-14. Details of the tower of an indoor slide.

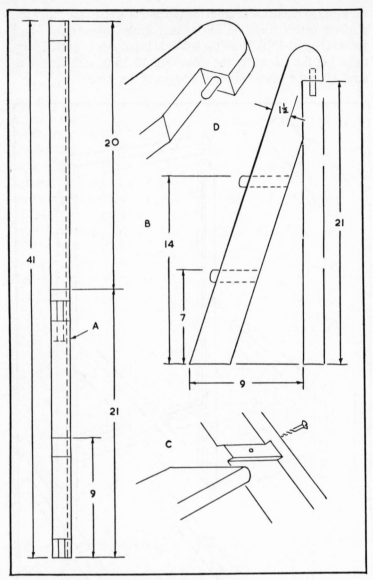

Fig. 10-15. Detail measurements for the indoor slide.

At the top of the ladder, draw it so the centerline of the side comes over the edge of the platform. That allows you to cut away the sides to hook over far enough for a dowel to be put in each side (Fig. 10-15D). Drill the platform to take these dowels which are glued into the ladder sides. Make sure the joints are tight.

Draw a side view of the slide full-size (Fig. 10-16A). The surface of the slide is plywood let into grooves in the sides (Fig. 10-16B). If you wish to avoid grooving, the plywood can be put between separate pieces (Fig. 10-16C). If that is done, there will have to be a block added at the top to take the dowel at each side.

The top edge of the plywood should come level with the surface of the platform. If it does not seem stiff enough, put a strip of wood across underneath between the sides. At the top, notch the sides over the platform, so there can be dowels similar to those at the ladder (Fig. 10-16D). The child's hands will rub along the sides of the slide, so thoroughly round the edges and ends. The sides and plywood need not go to thin edges of the bottom. It will be stronger if the full thickness of plywood rests on the floor (Fig. 10-16E).

Make a trial assembly. See that the ladder and slide fit comfortably between the legs and will do so after you have painted. With all the parts joined, check that there are no sharp edges exposed. The finish can be paint. If you have used hardwoods, the slide will

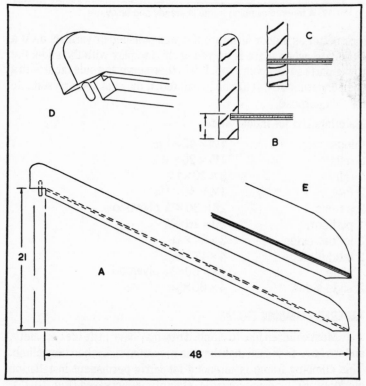

Fig. 10-16. Details of the slide.

Fig. 10-17. A tapered climbing frame is steady and enjoyable.

look better as indoor furniture if it was polished or varnished. At a later date, when there is no young child to play with the slide, the tower part can be given a top. It will then serve as a side table with a shelf underneath. If it has been painted, it may not seem as suitable for this purpose.

Materials List for Indoor Slide

4 legs	1½×42×1½
5 rails	1½×20×1½
1 rail	3×20×14
2 feet	1½×40×1½
2 panels	20×36×¼ plywood
1 platform	20×20×¾
2 ladder sides	3×24×¾
2 ladder steps	4×17×¾
1 slide	18×60×¼ plywood
2 slide sides	4×60×¾

TAPERED CLIMBING FRAME

Most children like to climb. They may have little idea of safety, and we have to insure that there is minimum risk when they climb. This climbing frame is intended for fairly permanent installation outdoors. By tapering inwards, stability is increased (Fig. 10-17).

282

Even if not attached to the ground, there is little risk of it being pulled over, but it is shown with points to press into the ground. An alternative is to drive separate short posts upright into the earth and bolt or lash the frame legs to them. If the frame is to stand on a hard surface, there can be metal brackets to bolt into the concrete. If there is no satisfactory way of holding the frame to the ground, or if it is only for temporary use in that position, attach crossbars to the bottoms of the legs at the ends. Weight them with bags of earth or sand.

Sizes can be varied, but those shown (Fig. 10-18) will suit most children of the age and size that will use the climbing frame.

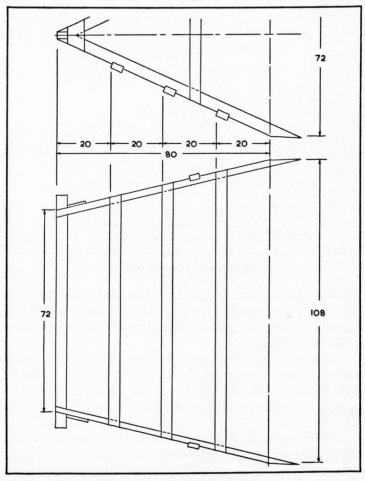

Fig. 10-18. Suitable sizes for a tapered climbing frame.

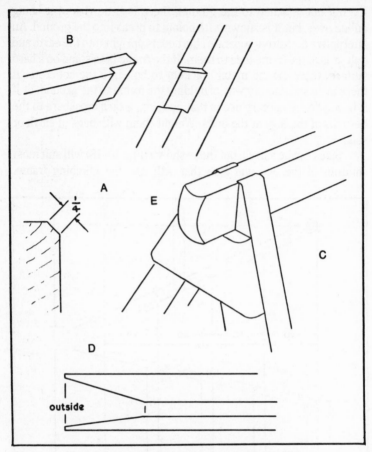

Fig. 10-19. Constructional details for a tapered climbing frame.

Whatever size is adopted, make a scale drawing of just the main lines. This gives you the vital angles. Set adjustable bevels to the angles in side and end views or make plywood templates to these angles for marking joints.

As shown, nearly all the parts are pieces of 2 by 4s. The wood should be planed. Make good bevels along the edges by planing to about ¼-inch widths (Fig. 10-19A). Sanding should not be necessary, but if there are any places where the grain has torn up, remove the roughness.

The parts are notched into each other at all crossings of rails and legs. Do not cut out much; ⅜ inch is sufficient depth for each notch. Mark the crossing angles (Fig. 10-19B) from your adjustable bevels or templates.

At the tops of the legs, notch into each side of the top rail about ¼ inch. Stiffen the joints with a gusset piece nailed across the outside (Fig. 10-19C) in a very similar way to the construction of a sawing trestle.

How much you allow for driving into the ground depends on the hardness of the ground. The drawings show a depth of about 12 inches. In very sandy soil it may be better not to taper the ends, so as to resist the legs going in too far. For harder ground, taper from the outside in each direction (Fig. 10-19D) for easier driving than if an all-round taper is used.

Soak the wood in a preservative before assembly. If soaking is impossible, brush on preservative several times, including inside the joints. Assemble with long screws or nails, preferably rustproof types. Drill for each nail through the top parts to prevent splitting. Finish with heads on or below the surfaces.

Round well all exposed ends and edges (Fig. 10-19E). This may be done with a Surform tool or rasp. There is no need for a cabinetmaking finish, but there must be no rough parts on which a child can be hurt.

Although the climbing frame is shown as made from prepared lumber, it can be made from natural poles if 3-inch diameter ones are available. Peel off all bark and smooth over any knots or other blemishes. Small lengthwise shakes or cracks should not affect strength. If the wood has been newly felled, allow sap to dry out before use, if possible. Woods like oak are very durable without preservatives, but softwoods should be treated with preservatives.

Materials List for Tapered Climbing Frame

4 legs	4×92×2
3 rails	4×84×2
2 rails	4×96×2
2 rails	4×108×2
2 rails	4×50×2
2 gussets	9×16×1

FOLDING CLIMBING FRAME

A climbing frame is a fairly bulky thing, and it may be a nuisance when it is not being used. This climbing frame (Fig. 10-20) is a cube of about 4-foot sides, but it can be folded in one direction to a thickness of about 9 inches. Rigidity is obtained by two platforms which can be put inside in various positions to give the young climber different levels. There are no loose nuts and bolts or other fastenings. There is enough weight and stiffness in the assembly to be safe for one or two small children, without fixing it down. The only risk of tipping would come if a crowd of larger children made an assault on one side.

There are two full-width assemblies (Fig. 10-21A) which are rigid. Folding sides are made up of four half-width frames (Fig. 10-21B). The platforms (Fig. 10-21C) rest across opposite pairs of rails in the folding parts. To fold the climbing frame, there are hinges outside between the narrow parts and inside between them and the wider parts (Fig. 10-21D). If a climbing frame of a different size is to be made, the widths of the folding parts must be arranged so they do not quite meet at the center when folded. The frames are

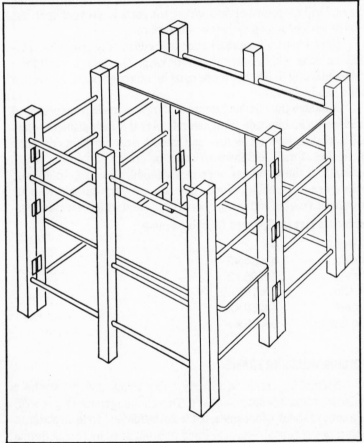

Fig. 10-20. This climbing frame with platforms can be folded flat when not needed.

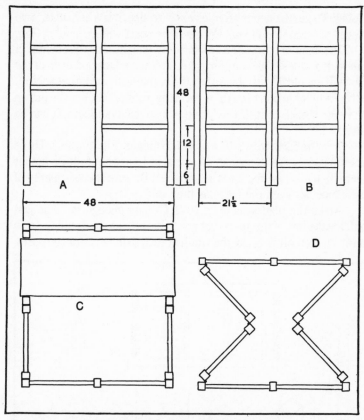

Fig. 10-21. Sizes and method of folding the climbing frame.

shown with rails across at 12-inch intervals in the narrow frames, but in the wider frames there are gaps. These allow the child to get inside easily, but he still has the rails the other way that are close enough for him to climb.

Construction is straightforward, but it is important that parts are assembled squarely and parallel. One side should be an exact match with its partner on the opposite side, so assemble one over the other. The 10 posts should be marked out together, with all the hole positions squared across and their centers marked with a gauge. Drill squarely, preferably with a drill press. The center posts of the wide sides will have to be drilled through for some rails, but for the others drill as deeply as you can without the point of the drill breaking through (Fig. 10-22A).

Cut the rails slightly short, so a long one or a slightly shallower hole will not prevent the parts from being pulled to size when gluing. To get the narrow frames exact to size, it is a help to cut two pieces of scrap wood to put between the posts when clamping (Fig. 10-22B). Similar pieces can be used between the sides and center of the wide frames. Take any sharpness off the edges and ends of the posts. It should be possible to use the climbing frame either way up. If you want to protect the floor covering, rubber feet may be put on one end of each post. If the frame is also used outdoors, it can be inverted.

Join the parts with 3-inch or 4-inch hinges (Fig. 10-22C). Three at each corner are advisable, so a total of 18 are needed. Do not let them in, but screw them to the surfaces. Be sure there is plenty of clearance between the parts as they fold.

Make the platforms (Fig. 10-21C) long enough to come just outside the line of the posts, but not so long that a child pulling down on an end can tilt it. Make the width of each to fit between the posts,

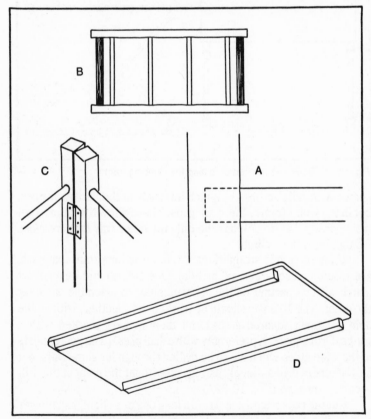

Fig. 10-22. Assembly details for climbing frame parts.

Fig. 10-23. A yard swing may also include a ladder.

but try them in several positions to check that they can be moved around. Round the corners. Put pieces under the long edges (Fig. 10-22D). They stiffen the plywood and act as stops, as they fit between rails at their ends.

If you have used hardwood, a varnish finish will be best. Otherwise, paint the posts. Rails can be left plain to provide a grip for hands and feet.

Materials List for Folding Climbing Frame

14 posts	2×48×2
4 rails	1×48 round rods
4 rails	1×25 round rods
16 rails	1×21 round rods
2 platforms	18×50×½ plywood
4 stiffeners	2×48×1

SWING

Most young children welcome an opportunity to swing. This structure is intended for fairly permanent use outdoors (Fig. 10-23). The size shown allows for two swings, or there is the alternative of a climbing frame or ladder in place of one swing (Fig. 10-24). If space is limited, the same construction can be used to make a narrower structure for just one swing.

The framework gets much of its rigidity by having the legs thrust into the ground. If a ladder is used, that also goes into the ground. Making the ends of the stand as inverted Vs that slope inwards also contributes to stability and resists any tendency for the structure to become shaky in use, shaking may occur due to the swinging loads if only upright supports are provided. It is unwise to make any child's swing freestanding. The action of swinging even a light child puts loads on the assembly and can move or tilt it if it is not fastened down.

Much of the assembly work is very similar to that of the tapered climbing frame, and reference to those instructions will help you with this project. As with the climbing frame, set out to

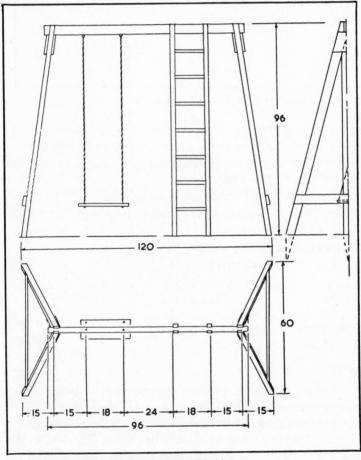

Fig. 10-24. Suitable sizes for a swing and ladder.

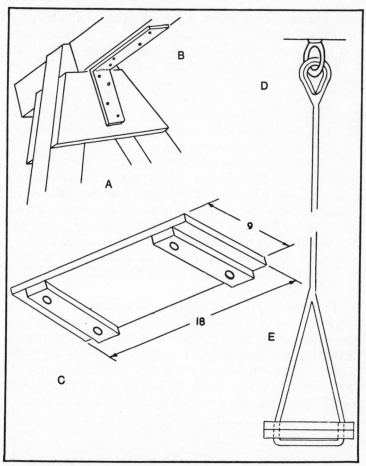

Fig. 10-25. Constructional details for a swing.

scale the main lines, so as to get the angle for cutting the joints at the sloping legs.

Make the legs similar to those of the climbing frame, with the braces across the ends notched in slightly. At the tops, notch the legs into the beam, but put the stiffening gussets inside and outside (Fig. 10-25A). If the legs are securely planted in the ground, the joints may prove strong enough. Strip metal brackets can be added as a further guard against movement (Fig. 10-25B). Shelf brackets may be adapted. They can be made from strips of ¼-inch by 1½-inch steel extending about 6 inches along each arm.

The swing(s) should be hung from ring bolts going through the beam. It is unwise to merely tie around the beam. Suitable bolts are

⅜-inch in diameter and long enough to go through a 4-inch thickness. Put a large washer under the nut to spread the load on the wood. For the strongest assembly, drill bolt holes for a very close fit. The bolt has to be driven through, so there is no risk of later movement.

The swing seat is a plain board (Fig. 10-25C). If it is thick waterproof plywood, it may need no other preparation. If the seat is solid wood, two battens underneath at the hole positions will prevent warping and strengthen the seat.

If synthetic rope is used, it will not suffer from exposure to the weather. Natural fiber rope has to be treated with preservative. Choose rope at least ½ inch in diameter, so a child can grip it easily. Ideally, the rope is spliced around a metal thimble at the ring bolt (Fig. 10-25D) and again spliced where the parts join above the seat (Fig. 10-25E). If you are unable to splice, knotting will be satisfactory although not so good looking. More information on splicing and knotting can be found in my book *Practical Knots & Ropework* (TAB Book No. 1237).

If a ladder is to be used instead of a second swing, notch the sides into the beam (Fig. 10-26A). This prevents movement and helps support the beam. Point the bottom to go into the ground. Mark out for the rungs to be equally spaced (Fig. 10-26B). Holes do not have to go right through. If you have the use of a drill press to make the holes squarely to the surfaces, the greatest accuracy comes from drilling right through both sides at the same time.

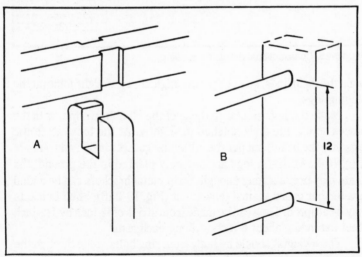

Fig. 10-26. The top of a ladder and spacing of rungs.

Treat the wood with preservative. Assemble with rustproof nails or screws. As there are no permanent lengthwise pieces to hold the lower parts of the structure in shape, you may nail on some temporary crossbars to hold the shape until you have the legs firmly embedded in the ground.

Materials List for Swing

1 beam	4×96×2
4 legs	4×120×2
2 braces	4×60×2
4 gussets	9×16×1
1 swing seat	9×24×¾
2 ladder sides	4×110×2
7 ladder rungs	1¼×18 round rod

OUTDOOR SLIDE

Children get their most fun and sense of adventure out of something high—at least in relation to their own size. A slide has its most appeal if it gives a ride down to ground level from a platform higher than children's heads (when the children are on the ground). Children have little sense of danger, and adults have to see that the apparatus can be used safely.

This slide (Fig. 10-27) is best mounted with the upright parts set in concrete (Fig. 10-28A). If permanent installation in this manner is impossible, the legs can be cut at ground level, and wide feet are added (Fig. 10-28B) braced with plywood gussets. Treat the slide supports in a similar way. The slide should not be used completely freestanding. It is better to temporarily peg the feet to the ground or hold them down with weights like bags of sand.

Use wood planed all around and select straight pieces for the long posts and slide sides, as any twist or warp cannot be pulled out with connecting wood. Mark the heights and positions of other parts on the vertical posts. If you have sufficient floor space to set out a side view of the tower full-size, that helps in getting the positions of other parts. Otherwise, it is possible to lay down the marked vertical post and put the other pieces of wood that form a side in position so as to get their lengths, angles, and positions.

At the top the platform rests on supports (Fig. 10-29A). The front one projects 1 inch and will also come under the slide (Fig. 10-29B). The tops are best joined with open mortise and tenon joints (Fig. 10-29C). The other parts are joined with plain mortise and tenons.

Fig. 10-27. An outdoor slide is a more permanent installation.

Mark out the ladder sides to give even step spacing between the floor and the platform top. Drill right through for the rungs and wedge them as you glue them in place (Fig. 10-29D). Put diagonal braces between the centers of the ladder sides and near the bottoms of the vertical posts (Fig. 10-28C).

If the posts are to go into concrete, soak the bottoms in a preservative. Mark what will be the ground level on them.

If there are to be feet, cut off the posts at ground level and tenon them into the crosswise feet. Put plywood gussets on each side of the upright posts and on the underside of the sloping posts (Fig. 10-28D).

The platform can be a piece of thick waterproof plywood or manufactured board. The width can be made with several pieces of solid wood.

The slide show is drawn at 30 degrees to horizontal. The exact angle is not critical, although making it too steep will bring the child down too fast. A very shallow slope may not be sufficiently exciting.

At the top the sides are screwed inside the upright posts (Fig. 10-30A). Round these ends thoroughly, so there is nothing rough where a child is lowering himself or herself onto the slide. At the bottom cut the ends of the sides to a long sweeping curve. The amount of curve to give depends on the plywood used. Try bending the plywood and draw that curve (Fig. 10-30B). The curve is intended to let the user swing outwards and land on his or her feet.

The length of the slide is more that the length of the common 8-foot plywood sheet. Longer plywood is obtainable, but that does not matter if you have to join two pieces. Let the long piece extend up from the bottom, so the joint comes on a flat part. Glue and screw the plywood under the sides. Put stiffeners across at intervals, arranging one under the plywood joint (Fig. 10-30C) if there is one. The number of stiffeners needed depends on the inherent stiffness of the plywood. Arrange one at the bottom of the slide.

Where the slide meets the platform, pack up the extending edge of the platform support (Fig. 10-30D). Blend platform and slide edges by rounding them slightly, if necessary.

Arrange diagonal braces from near the center of the slide to the vertical posts (Fig. 10-28E). Do not take the brace ends to the edges of the slide sides. Cut them back and round them, so they are clear of hands sliding on the sides.

At the bottom attach supports on each side to keep the end of the slide about 6 inches off the ground. Allow enough length for setting into the ground, or cut off the supports and join them to crosswise feet (Fig. 10-30E). As with the braces, keep the tops of the supports clear of sliding hands.

Materials List for Outdoor Slide

4 posts	3×110×3
2 tops	3×18×3
1 platform support	3× 24×3
3 platform supports	3× 24×2
2 rails	3×18×2
1 platform	24×24×1
7 rungs	1× 24 round rod
2 slide sides	5×130×1
5 slide stiffeners	2×19×1
1 slide	19×125×⅜ plywood
2 braces	3×65×1
2 slide supports	6×28×1
2 feet (optional)	3×72×3
2 feet (optional)	6×36×1
6 gussets (optional)	9×9×½ plywood
2 braces	3×42×1

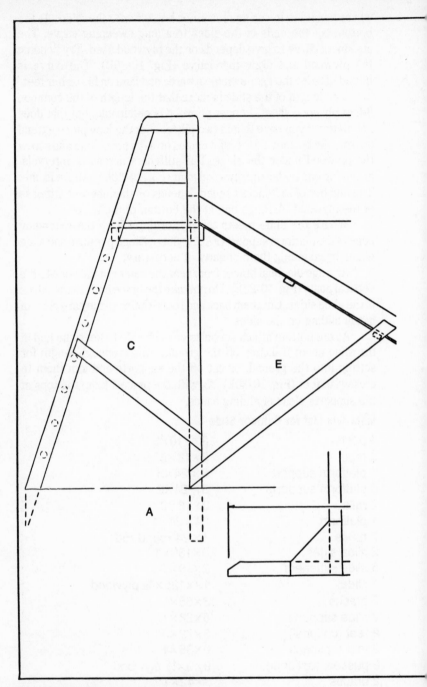

Fig. 10-28. Sizes of an outdoor slide.

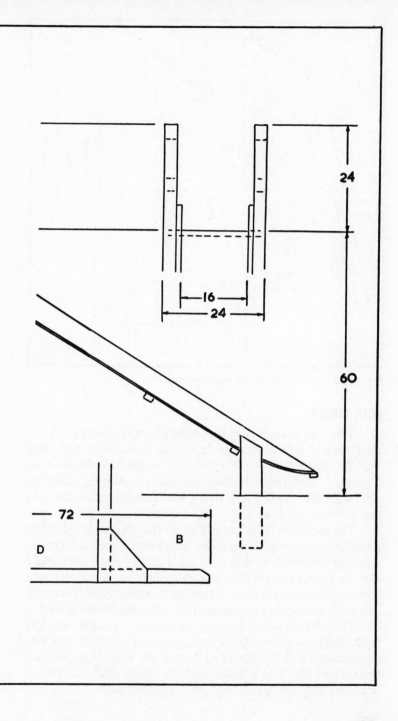

Fig. 10-29. Tower details for an outdoor slide.

POLE TENNIS

This is an outdoor game where two players try to hit a ball on a cord around a pole in opposite directions. A point is scored every time the opponent misses. The pole is in two parts, so the game can be easily transported in the trunk of a small car. Although the game can be played with ordinary strung tennis rackets, plywood ones will stand up better to fairly rough treatment.

The two parts of the pole (Fig. 10-31A) can be dowel rod or pieces of brush handle. If you round them from square stock, choose a springy hardwood like hickory or ash. Point the lower end slightly (Fig. 10-31B), but leave some thickness there or the end will soon splinter. Dome the top of the bottom section slightly, so it does not spread if a hammer has to be used to drive the pole into the ground.

The joint is a piece of metal tube about 5 inches long which is held to the top section with a screw. It slips over the lower part, and slots engage with the metal peg through the wood (Fig. 10-31C). Drill across the tube and saw into the holes, then file true. A 3/16-inch peg and ½-inch long slots are good sizes.

298

At the top the pivot for the cord must rotate easily. Ideally, a ball race can be let into a wooden disc, but it should be satisfactory for wood to turn on a screw (Fig. 10-31D). If you do not have a lathe to turn the button, it does not matter if it does not finish truly round when whittled by hand. Cut a deep groove so the knotted cord cannot slip off. When assembling, smear the moving parts with candle fat or another lubricant.

The ball should be solid rubber, and the cord should be a soft synthetic type like nylon. A *bodkin* is useful for pulling the cord through the ball. Put a small washer under the knotted end. The

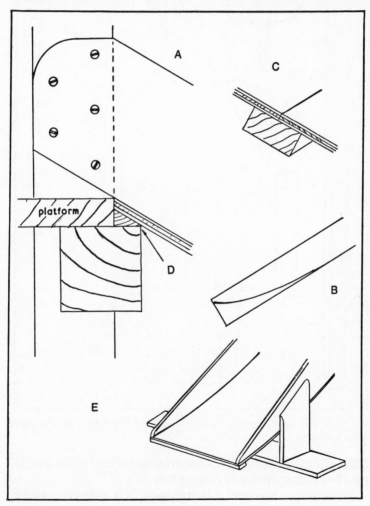

Fig. 10-30. Assembly details for the slide.

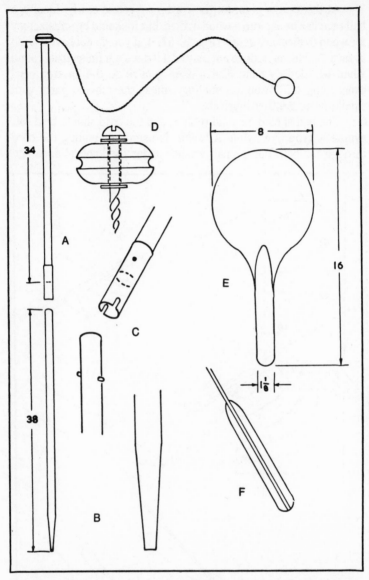

Fig. 10-31. Pole tennis is played by two people who hit the ball in opposite ways around the pole.

finished cord length should be enough for the ball to clear the ground by a few inches when it is hanging free.

Cut the two bats from ¼-inch plywood. It is at the point where the handle blends into the blade that a bat might break. To reduce this risk, curve long sweeps into the parallel handle. Let the thickening pieces continue into the blade (Fig. 10-31E). Round the edges of the blade. A handle about 1⅛ inches in diameter will suit a child's hands. Thicken the handle with strips each side of the plywood (Fig. 10-31F). Thoroughly round it in section and at the end.

The hitting surfaces of the bats should be left plain. Other equipment parts can be painted.

Materials List for Pole Tennis

2 poles	1× 38 round rod
1 button	1× 2×1
2 bats	8×16×¼ plywood
4 bat handles	1¼× 2×½

Index

302

Edited by Robert Ostrander